REVELATION

Brazos Theological Commentary on the Bible

REVELATION

JOSEPH L. MANGINA

BrazosPress

a division of Baker Publishing Group
Grand Rapids, Michigan

© 2010 by Joseph L. Mangina

Published by Brazos Press
a division of Baker Publishing Group
P.O. Box 6287, Grand Rapids, MI 49516-6287
www.brazospress.com

Printed in the United States of America

Library of Congress Cataloging-in-Publication Data
Mangina, Joseph L., 1957–
    Revelation / Joseph L. Mangina.
      p.   cm. — (Brazos theological commentary on the Bible)
    Includes bibliographical references and indexes.
    ISBN 978-1-58743-112-8 (cloth)
    1. Bible. N.T. Revelation—Commentaries. I. Title. II. Series.
  BS2825.53.M36 2010
  228'.077—dc22   2009038041

10   11   12   13   14   15   16   7   6   5   4   3   2   1

Dedicated to
Garrett Green
Stanley Hauerwas

CONTENTS

SERIES PREFACE

Near the beginning of his treatise against Gnostic interpretations of the Bible, *Against the Heresies*, Irenaeus observes that Scripture is like a great mosaic depicting a handsome king. It is as if we were owners of a villa in Gaul who had ordered a mosaic from Rome. It arrives, and the beautifully colored tiles need to be taken out of their packaging and put into proper order according to the plan of the artist. The difficulty, of course, is that Scripture provides us with the individual pieces, but the order and sequence of various elements are not obvious. The Bible does not come with instructions that would allow interpreters to simply place verses, episodes, images, and parables in order as a worker might follow a schematic drawing in assembling the pieces to depict the handsome king. The mosaic must be puzzled out. This is precisely the work of scriptural interpretation.

Origen has his own image to express the difficulty of working out the proper approach to reading the Bible. When preparing to offer a commentary on the Psalms he tells of a tradition handed down to him by his Hebrew teacher:

> The Hebrew said that the whole divinely inspired Scripture may be likened, because of its obscurity, to many locked rooms in our house. By each room is placed a key, but not the one that corresponds to it, so that the keys are scattered about beside the rooms, none of them matching the room by which it is placed. It is a difficult task to find the keys and match them to the rooms that they can open. We therefore know the Scriptures that are obscure only by taking the points of departure for understanding them from another place because they have their interpretive principle scattered among them.[1]

---

1. Fragment from the preface to *Commentary on Psalms 1–25*, preserved in the *Philokalia*, trans. Joseph W. Trigg (London: Routledge, 1998), 70–71.

As is the case for Irenaeus, scriptural interpretation is not purely local. The key in Genesis may best fit the door of Isaiah, which in turn opens up the meaning of Matthew. The mosaic must be put together with an eye toward the overall plan.

Irenaeus, Origen, and the great cloud of premodern biblical interpreters assumed that puzzling out the mosaic of Scripture must be a communal project. The Bible is vast, heterogeneous, full of confusing passages and obscure words, and difficult to understand. Only a fool would imagine that he or she could work out solutions alone. The way forward must rely upon a tradition of reading that Irenaeus reports has been passed on as the rule or canon of truth that functions as a confession of faith. "Anyone," he says, "who keeps unchangeable in himself the rule of truth received through baptism will recognize the names and sayings and parables of the scriptures."[2] Modern scholars debate the content of the rule on which Irenaeus relies and commends, not the least because the terms and formulations Irenaeus himself uses shift and slide. Nonetheless, Irenaeus assumes that there is a body of apostolic doctrine sustained by a tradition of teaching in the church. This doctrine provides the clarifying principles that guide exegetical judgment toward a coherent overall reading of Scripture as a unified witness. Doctrine, then, is the schematic drawing that will allow the reader to organize the vast heterogeneity of the words, images, and stories of the Bible into a readable, coherent whole. It is the rule that guides us toward the proper matching of keys to doors.

If self-consciousness about the role of history in shaping human consciousness makes modern historical-critical study critical, then what makes modern study of the Bible modern is the consensus that classical Christian doctrine distorts interpretive understanding. Benjamin Jowett, the influential nineteenth-century English classical scholar, is representative. In his programmatic essay "On the Interpretation of Scripture," he exhorts the biblical reader to disengage from doctrine and break its hold over the interpretive imagination. "The simple words of that book," writes Jowett of the modern reader, "he tries to preserve absolutely pure from the refinements or distinctions of later times." The modern interpreter wishes to "clear away the remains of dogmas, systems, controversies, which are encrusted upon" the words of Scripture. The disciplines of close philological analysis "would enable us to separate the elements of doctrine and tradition with which the meaning of Scripture is encumbered in our own day."[3] The lens of understanding must be wiped clear of the hazy and distorting film of doctrine.

Postmodernity, in turn, has encouraged us to criticize the critics. Jowett imagined that when he wiped away doctrine he would encounter the biblical text in its purity and uncover what he called "the original spirit and intention of the authors."[4] We are not now so sanguine, and the postmodern mind thinks

2. *Against the Heretics* 9.4.
3. Benjamin Jowett, "On the Interpretation of Scripture," in *Essays and Reviews* (London: Parker, 1860), 338–39.
4. Ibid., 340.

interpretive frameworks inevitable. Nonetheless, we tend to remain modern in at least one sense. We read Athanasius and think him stage-managing the diversity of Scripture to support his positions against the Arians. We read Bernard of Clairvaux and assume that his monastic ideals structure his reading of the Song of Songs. In the wake of the Reformation, we can see how the doctrinal divisions of the time shaped biblical interpretation. Luther famously described the Epistle of James as a "strawy letter," for, as he said, "it has nothing of the nature of the Gospel about it."[5] In these and many other instances, often written in the heat of ecclesiastical controversy or out of the passion of ascetic commitment, we tend to think Jowett correct: doctrine is a distorting film on the lens of understanding.

However, is what we commonly think actually the case? Are readers naturally perceptive? Do we have an unblemished, reliable aptitude for the divine? Have we no need for disciplines of vision? Do our attention and judgment need to be trained, especially as we seek to read Scripture as the living word of God? According to Augustine, we all struggle to journey toward God, who is our rest and peace. Yet our vision is darkened and the fetters of worldly habit corrupt our judgment. We need training and instruction in order to cleanse our minds so that we might find our way toward God.[6] To this end, "the whole temporal dispensation was made by divine Providence for our salvation."[7] The covenant with Israel, the coming of Christ, the gathering of the nations into the church—all these things are gathered up into the rule of faith, and they guide the vision and form of the soul toward the end of fellowship with God. In Augustine's view, the reading of Scripture both contributes to and benefits from this divine pedagogy. With countless variations in both exegetical conclusions and theological frameworks, the same pedagogy of a doctrinally ruled reading of Scripture characterizes the broad sweep of the Christian tradition from Gregory the Great through Bernard and Bonaventure, continuing across Reformation differences in both John Calvin and Cornelius Lapide, Patrick Henry and Bishop Bossuet, and on to more recent figures such as Karl Barth and Hans Urs von Balthasar.

Is doctrine, then, not a moldering scrim of antique prejudice obscuring the Bible, but instead a clarifying agent, an enduring tradition of theological judgments that amplifies the living voice of Scripture? And what of the scholarly dispassion advocated by Jowett? Is a noncommitted reading, an interpretation unprejudiced, the way toward objectivity, or does it simply invite the languid intellectual apathy that stands aside to make room for the false truism and easy answers of the age?

This series of biblical commentaries was born out of the conviction that dogma clarifies rather than obscures. The Brazos Theological Commentary on the Bible advances upon the assumption that the Nicene tradition, in all its diversity and

5. *Luther's Works*, vol. 35, ed. E. Theodore Bachmann (Philadelphia: Fortress, 1959), 362.
6. *On Christian Doctrine* 1.10.
7. *On Christian Doctrine* 1.35.

controversy, provides the proper basis for the interpretation of the Bible as Christian Scripture. God the Father Almighty, who sends his only begotten Son to die for us and for our salvation and who raises the crucified Son in the power of the Holy Spirit so that the baptized may be joined in one body—faith in *this* God with *this* vocation of love for the world is the lens through which to view the heterogeneity and particularity of the biblical texts. Doctrine, then, is not a moldering scrim of antique prejudice obscuring the meaning of the Bible. It is a crucial aspect of the divine pedagogy, a clarifying agent for our minds fogged by self-deceptions, a challenge to our languid intellectual apathy that will too often rest in false truisms and the easy spiritual nostrums of the present age rather than search more deeply and widely for the dispersed keys to the many doors of Scripture.

For this reason, the commentators in this series have not been chosen because of their historical or philological expertise. In the main, they are not biblical scholars in the conventional, modern sense of the term. Instead, the commentators were chosen because of their knowledge of and expertise in using the Christian doctrinal tradition. They are qualified by virtue of the doctrinal formation of their mental habits, for it is the conceit of this series of biblical commentaries that theological training in the Nicene tradition prepares one for biblical interpretation, and thus it is to theologians and not biblical scholars that we have turned. "War is too important," it has been said, "to leave to the generals."

We do hope, however, that readers do not draw the wrong impression. The Nicene tradition does not provide a set formula for the solution of exegetical problems. The great tradition of Christian doctrine was not transcribed, bound in folio, and issued in an official, critical edition. We have the Niceno-Constantinopolitan Creed, used for centuries in many traditions of Christian worship. We have ancient baptismal affirmations of faith. The Chalcedonian definition and the creeds and canons of other church councils have their places in official church documents. Yet the rule of faith cannot be limited to a specific set of words, sentences, and creeds. It is instead a pervasive habit of thought, the animating culture of the church in its intellectual aspect. As Augustine observed, commenting on Jeremiah 31:33, "The creed is learned by listening; it is written, not on stone tablets nor on any material, but on the heart."[8] This is why Irenaeus is able to appeal to the rule of faith more than a century before the first ecumenical council, and this is why we need not itemize the contents of the Nicene tradition in order to appeal to its potency and role in the work of interpretation.

Because doctrine is intrinsically fluid on the margins and most powerful as a habit of mind rather than a list of propositions, this commentary series cannot settle difficult questions of method and content at the outset. The editors of the series impose no particular method of doctrinal interpretation. We cannot say in advance how doctrine helps the Christian reader assemble the mosaic of Scripture. We have no clear answer to the question of whether exegesis guided by

---

8. *Sermon* 212.2.

doctrine is antithetical to or compatible with the now-old modern methods of historical-critical inquiry. Truth—historical, mathematical, or doctrinal—knows no contradiction. But method is a discipline of vision and judgment, and we cannot know in advance what aspects of historical-critical inquiry are functions of modernism that shape the soul to be at odds with Christian discipline. Still further, the editors do not hold the commentators to any particular hermeneutical theory that specifies how to define the plain sense of Scripture—or the role this plain sense should play in interpretation. Here the commentary series is tentative and exploratory.

Can we proceed in any other way? European and North American intellectual culture has been de-Christianized. The effect has not been a cessation of Christian activity. Theological work continues. Sermons are preached. Biblical scholars turn out monographs. Church leaders have meetings. But each dimension of a formerly unified Christian practice now tends to function independently. It is as if a weakened army had been fragmented, and various corps had retreated to isolated fortresses in order to survive. Theology has lost its competence in exegesis. Scripture scholars function with minimal theological training. Each decade finds new theories of preaching to cover the nakedness of seminary training that provides theology without exegesis and exegesis without theology.

Not the least of the causes of the fragmentation of Christian intellectual practice has been the divisions of the church. Since the Reformation, the role of the rule of faith in interpretation has been obscured by polemics and counterpolemics about *sola scriptura* and the necessity of a magisterial teaching authority. The Brazos Theological Commentary on the Bible series is deliberately ecumenical in scope, because the editors are convinced that early church fathers were correct: church doctrine does not compete with Scripture in a limited economy of epistemic authority. We wish to encourage unashamedly dogmatic interpretation of Scripture, confident that the concrete consequences of such a reading will cast far more light on the great divisive questions of the Reformation than either reengaging in old theological polemics or chasing the fantasy of a pure exegesis that will somehow adjudicate between competing theological positions. You shall know the truth of doctrine by its interpretive fruits, and therefore in hopes of contributing to the unity of the church, we have deliberately chosen a wide range of theologians whose commitment to doctrine will allow readers to see real interpretive consequences rather than the shadowboxing of theological concepts.

Brazos Theological Commentary on the Bible has no dog in the current translation fights, and we endorse a textual ecumenism that parallels our diversity of ecclesial backgrounds. We do not impose the thankfully modest inclusive-language agenda of the New Revised Standard Version, nor do we insist upon the glories of the Authorized Version, nor do we require our commentators to create a new translation. In our communal worship, in our private devotions, in our theological scholarship, we use a range of scriptural translations. Precisely as Scripture—a living, functioning text in the present life of faith—the Bible is not semantically fixed. Only a modernist, literalist hermeneutic could imagine that this modest fluidity is a liability. Philological precision and stability is a consequence of, not a basis for, exegesis. Judgments about the meaning of a text fix its literal sense, not the other way around. As a result, readers should expect an eclectic use of biblical translations, both across the different volumes of the series and within individual commentaries.

We cannot speak for contemporary biblical scholars, but as theologians we know that we have long been trained to defend our fortresses of theological concepts and formulations. And we have forgotten the skills of interpretation. Like stroke victims, we must rehabilitate our exegetical imaginations, and there are likely to be different strategies of recovery. Readers should expect this reconstructive—not reactionary—series to provide them with experiments in postcritical doctrinal interpretation, not commentaries written according to the settled principles of a well-functioning tradition. Some commentators will follow classical typological and allegorical readings from the premodern tradition; others will draw on contemporary historical study. Some will comment verse by verse; others will highlight passages, even single words that trigger theological analysis of Scripture. No reading strategies are proscribed, no interpretive methods foresworn. The central premise in this commentary series is that doctrine provides structure and cogency to scriptural interpretation. We trust in this premise with the hope that the Nicene tradition can guide us, however imperfectly, diversely, and haltingly, toward a reading of Scripture in which the right keys open the right doors.

R. R. Reno

AUTHOR'S PREFACE

I have learned so much from so many people over the years that I have largely forgotten what I learned from whom. Thanks are due first of all to Blanche and Robert Jenson, who made the Center of Theological Inquiry in Princeton such a conducive place for writing and research during my two stays there in 2002 and 2005. It was there that the project was first conceived, if in a somewhat different form from which it now sees the light of day. I am also grateful to CTI colleagues Gary Anderson, Brian Daley, Rifaat Ebied, Richard Hays, Arne Rasmusson, James Reimer, Robin Darling Young, and Darlene Weaver, for the opportunity of testing out ideas that were still in a very raw state. Fellow members of the Duodecim Society, including J. Louis Martyn, Beverly Gaventa, and Douglas Harink, further stimulated my thinking on matters apocalyptic. Other friends who cheered this book on in its early stages include Reinhard Hütter, Kendall Soulen, and Ross Wagner.

Thanks go out to my fellow faculty members as well as the staff at Wycliffe College, who have offered their support in countless ways. I am grateful to be able to teach in this true "school of the Lord's service." It was Krista Dowdeswell who first brought to my attention Elizabeth Rundle Charles's 1892 remarkable devotional commentary. Another doctoral student, the Rev. David Tiessen, came up with the apt phrase "apocalyptic haggadah" for describing Revelation, growing out of his own research into Jewish and Christian interpretive practices. My friend and former student Leah Canning has been a steady source of ideas and encouragement. Her fine Master's thesis on the role of the church in Revelation helped me to frame that topic much more clearly. My other students have generously tolerated having a professor who always seemed to have one foot planted "on the island called Patmos."

I cannot say enough good things about the Rev. Fleming Rutledge, whom my family and I had the privilege of welcoming to Toronto in the memorable fall of 2008. Her bracing, grace-filled sermons are a model of what it might mean to preach the gospel in an apocalyptic (and deeply Pauline) idiom. I have especially fond memories of a long evening we spent talking theology with Wycliffe students at a local pub. As the book neared completion, Mari Jørstad furnished invaluable assistance as a proofreader, style editor, and theological critic. Not only is her English better than my Norwegian, it is very likely better than my English. The commentary is greatly improved as a result of her efforts. I am grateful to Michael Root and Rusty Reno for their careful reading of the manuscript and for their constructive criticisms. Small World Coffee in Princeton and Crema Coffee Company in Toronto provided hospitable settings for my early-morning writing habits, the first near the beginning, the second near the end of this project.

Elisa Mangina has been more than patient throughout the long gestation of this book. I am grateful not only for her loving care of our two children, but for her exemplary dedication to her own craft as a musician: "Praise [the LORD] with the timbrel and dance: praise him with stringed instruments and organs" (Ps. 150:4 KJV). Frances and Nicholas Mangina fearlessly shared their father with the monsters of Revelation over several years. Finally, I thank St. Martin-in-the-Fields Anglican Church and St. James Anglican Cathedral, both in Toronto, for inviting me to lead adult study series on the Apocalypse. The enthusiastic response of these groups encouraged me to think this work might find a wider audience.

I am delighted to dedicate this book to two friends and mentors, both of whom have helped me toward a deeper understanding of the Christian faith: Garrett Green and Stanley Hauerwas. Their generosity, good counsel, and good cheer (in the sense of Bonhoeffer's *hilaritas*) have meant a great deal to me over the years. Each exemplifies the honorable vocation of "ecclesial theologian." May this commentary, too, serve to shed some light on what the Spirit says to the churches.

ABBREVIATIONS

General

→	indicates a cross-reference to commentary on a Revelation passage
ANF	The Ante-Nicene Fathers (repr. Grand Rapids: Eerdmans, 1957)
ESV	English Standard Version
KJV	King James Version (Authorized Version)
NA²⁷	*Novum Testamentum Graece*, edited by [E. Nestle and E. Nestle], B. Aland, K. Aland, J. Karavidopoulos, C. M. Martini, and B. M. Metzger, 27th revised edition (Stuttgart: Deutsche Bibelgesellschaft, 1993)
NRSV	New Revised Standard Version
RSV	Revised Standard Version

Biblical

Acts	Acts		Esth.	Esther
Amos	Amos		Exod.	Exodus
1 Chr.	1 Chronicles		Ezek.	Ezekiel
2 Chr.	2 Chronicles		Ezra	Ezra
Col.	Colossians		Gal.	Galatians
1 Cor.	1 Corinthians		Gen.	Genesis
2 Cor.	2 Corinthians		Hab.	Habakkuk
Dan.	Daniel		Hag.	Haggai
Deut.	Deuteronomy		Heb.	Hebrews
Eccl.	Ecclesiastes		Hos.	Hosea
Eph.	Ephesians		Isa.	Isaiah

Jas.	James		Neh.	Nehemiah
Jer.	Jeremiah		Num.	Numbers
Job	Job		Obad.	Obadiah
Joel	Joel		1 Pet.	1 Peter
John	John		2 Pet.	2 Peter
1 John	1 John		Phil.	Philippians
2 John	2 John		Phlm.	Philemon
3 John	3 John		Prov.	Proverbs
Jonah	Jonah		Ps.	Psalms
Josh.	Joshua		Rev.	Revelation
Jude	Jude		Rom.	Romans
Judg.	Judges		Ruth	Ruth
1 Kgs.	1 Kings		1 Sam.	1 Samuel
2 Kgs.	2 Kings		2 Sam.	2 Samuel
Lam.	Lamentations		Song	Song of Songs
Lev.	Leviticus		1 Thess.	1 Thessalonians
Luke	Luke		2 Thess.	2 Thessalonians
Mal.	Malachi		1 Tim.	1 Timothy
Mark	Mark		2 Tim.	2 Timothy
Matt.	Matthew		Titus	Titus
Mic.	Micah		Zech.	Zechariah
Nah.	Nahum		Zeph.	Zephaniah

INTRODUCTION

If contemporary Christians think about Revelation at all, they are likely to think of it as among the more peculiar, not to say bizarre, books in the canon of scripture. Revelation's numbers and symbols are famously hard to decipher, its images violent, its picture of God oddly disturbing. The book has a deserved reputation for being a happy hunting ground for people with pet theories about contemporary politics and precise timetables concerning the end. We hardly know what to do with a work at once so powerful yet so disquieting. Many traditionally minded Catholics and Protestants therefore tend to shy away from Revelation. The strategy of avoidance is perhaps best exemplified by John Calvin, who wrote commentaries on every New Testament book except this one.

As will be true for many people, my own first encounters with the Apocalypse (the work's other name) took place in the context of Christian worship. "Holy, holy, holy, Lord God of hosts, the whole earth is full of thy glory," we sang at Holy Communion; this is the song sung by seraphim in Isa. 6 and by heavenly creatures in Rev. 4. Likewise, Charles Wesley's great Advent hymn "Lo, he comes with clouds descending" powerfully evoked the coming of Christ in judgment. Notice how the following lines play on but a single verse from Revelation (1:7):

> Lo! He comes with clouds descending,
> Once for favored sinners slain;
> Thousand thousand saints attending,
> Swell the triumph of His train:
> Hallelujah! Hallelujah! Hallelujah!
> God appears on earth to reign.
>
> Every eye shall now behold Him
> Robed in dreadful majesty;
> Those who set at naught and sold Him,

Pierced and nailed Him to the tree,
Deeply wailing, deeply wailing, deeply wailing,
Shall the true Messiah see.

Yea, Amen! let all adore Thee,
High on Thine eternal throne;
Savior, take the power and glory,
Claim the kingdom for Thine own;
O come quickly! O come quickly! O come quickly!
Everlasting God, come down![1]

In Philipp Nicolai's "Wake, awake, for night is flying," the "twelve great pearls" in the final verse are the gates of the new Jerusalem (21:2), while the hymn's bridal imagery likewise draws on Revelation. In the haunting American folk hymn "Wondrous Love," Revelation's image of Christ as the Lamb (Rev. 5) becomes the occasion for a profound meditation on the atonement:

To God and to the Lamb I will sing, I will sing,
To God and to the Lamb I will sing.
To God and to the Lamb, who is the great I am,
While millions join the theme, I will sing, I will sing,
While millions join the theme, I will sing.

In singing such hymns, in participating in such liturgy, Christians are formed by the Apocalypse without realizing that it *is* the Apocalypse. The book has been among the great shapers of the Christian imagination across the centuries, reflected not only in music but in art, novels, poetry, and film. Truly Revelation is not just a set of words on a page, but a collection of pictures in our heads and sounds ringing in our ears.

Yet for all that, Revelation remains a suspect book in many quarters. One indication of this is its virtual absence from our lectionaries; the readings are often limited to such high points as the heavenly worship in Rev. 4–5 and the descent of the new Jerusalem in Rev. 21. Even that great climax gets bowdlerized, however: the Revised Common Lectionary leaves out the references to those who will burn in the lake of fire (21:8, 27). This is an example of how we frequently edit Revelation to produce "a more acceptable book" (Kovacs and Rowland 2004: 222). Ironically, the letters to the seven churches in Rev. 2–3 are almost never heard in our churches. But the problem goes beyond simply a lack of exposure. It is unfortunate that in the minds of many people, Revelation is associated exclusively with debates over end-time scenarios, often associated

1. In *Common Praise*, the hymnbook of the Anglican Church of Canada (Toronto: Anglican Book Centre, 1998), the final line is "Hallelujah! Come, Lord, come," a direct quotation of the closing lines of Revelation. The hymn has a complicated textual history; Wesley's version is partly indebted to an earlier hymn by John Cennick.

with particular political agendas and judgments. Too often, such readings reflect worldly interests that have little to do with the upbuilding of the church. In this climate, it is no surprise that Roman Catholics, mainline Protestants, and even many evangelicals wish to distance themselves from the book as being simply more trouble than it is worth.

One of Revelation's more insightful readers in the modern era was English novelist D. H. Lawrence, whose *Apocalypse* was published after his death. Lawrence was no Christian, certainly. His interpretation is often tendentious and unfair. Yet he understood better than most the peculiar power of the Apocalypse. In his view, the book proved the case for Christianity as being essentially a religion of the weak and powerless, whose pent-up rage finds expression in the fantasy of a world where *they* will be on top:

> If you listen to the Salvation Army you will hear that they are going to be very grand. Very grand indeed, once they get to heaven. *Then* they'll show you what's what. *Then* you'll be put in your place, you superior person, you Babylon: down in hell and in brimstone.
>
> This is entirely the tone of Revelation. What we realise when we have read the precious book a few times is that John the Divine had, on the face of it, a grandiose scheme for wiping out and annihilating everybody who wasn't of the elect, the chosen people, in short, and of climbing up himself right on to the throne of God. With nonconformity, the chapel people took over to themselves the Jewish idea of the chosen people. They were "it," the elect, or the "saved." And they took over the Jewish idea of ultimate triumph and reign of the chosen people. . . . It is doctrine you can hear any night from the Salvation Army or in any Bethel or Pentecost Chapel. If it is not Jesus, it is John. If it is not Gospel, it is Revelation. It is popular religion, as distinct from thoughtful religion.[2]

This is only a small sample of Lawrence's vitriol. At the same time, he sees much that is true about Revelation. He understands its appeal to the poor and despised, to "chapel" as opposed to "church." He grasps its profound Jewishness. He sees that it is all about the overturning of the accepted order of things, a great upheaval in which not one stone is left standing atop another. Above all, Lawrence sees the religious and moral passion that underlies the Apocalypse, that it is not a bare text but bears witness to a radical reshaping of human life in light of a very particular conception of God.[3] A Christian reading of Revelation cannot afford to be less passionate than was Lawrence's, nor can it afford to be less attentive than he was to the work's language, imagery, ideas, and transformative power.

At one level, writing a commentary on any book is a tribute to the conviction that the work in question is worth spending time with, that it challenges us to

2. D. H. Lawrence, *Apocalypse and the Writings on Revelation* (Cambridge: Cambridge University Press, 1980), 63 (emphasis original).
3. Lawrence also gets some things wrong, of course, such as his conviction that Revelation is largely an expression of lower-class *ressentiment*.

see and to live differently, that it rightly demands something of us. "When I am named 'Biblicist,'" wrote the young Karl Barth, defending himself against his critics, "all that can rightly be proved against me is that I am prejudiced in supposing the Bible to be a good book, and that I hold it to be profitable for men to take its conceptions at least as seriously as they take their own."[4] Central to what is involved in that is submitting ourselves to the discipline of the work, letting it speak to us in all its strangeness, perhaps freeing it from the burden of prejudice and overfamiliarity. We know, or think we know, what the book of Revelation is all about. It is about the end of history, or the cult of the emperor in the late first-century Roman world, or the resentment of the lower classes toward their social superiors (so Lawrence). But is it really about any of these things? Does not each of them betray a certain desire to render the book more manageable, less strange, finally less dangerous for us? In my own reading I try to take seriously the idea that the Apocalypse is actually about the God of the gospel, the God who is the Father, the Son, and the Holy Spirit, and that just so it seeks to transform our lives in unpredictable and uncomfortable ways. Like Jacob at Peniel, we can only walk away wounded from an encounter with this God. Discerning just how Revelation facilitates such an encounter will be the burden of the pages that follow.

This commentary traces the movement of Revelation in sequence, from John's self-introduction in the opening lines to the climactic vision of the new Jerusalem. In most cases I devote a chapter of the commentary to a given chapter of Revelation, but it seemed wise to treat Rev. 2–3 and Rev. 8–9 together. I do hope that readers will make their way through the commentary from beginning to end. The visions of John form a remarkable organic unity, and how we respond to images in the later portions may well depend on the way in which earlier episodes have affected us. Can we really taste the promise of the heavenly city, say, if we have not felt the chastening word of Christ to his churches or been exposed to the horror that is Babylon?

The commentator's task is to attend to the work at hand, but commentary is not autobiography. But perhaps a word about myself at the beginning will help in setting this distraction aside. I was raised in the northeastern United States but have lived in Canada over the past decade and claim citizenship in both countries. I teach at an Anglican seminary situated on the campus of a major research university. As a theologian, the particular lens I bring to reading Revelation is the desire to clarify what the Christian community confesses concerning God and to uncover the practical implications involved in living the Christian life—in short, doctrine and ethics. Like most contributors to the Brazos Theological Commentary on the Bible, I am not a professional biblical scholar, although I am tremendously grateful for what I have learned from New Testament scholars concerning the book of Revelation. I have kept a few

---

4. Karl Barth, *The Epistle to the Romans*, trans. Edwyn C. Hoskyns (London: Oxford University Press, 1933), 12.

works especially close at hand: the modern commentaries of Eugene Boring, G. B. Caird, Paul Minear, and Henry Swete (a neglected voice from the late nineteenth century); the indispensable studies on Revelation by Richard Bauckham; and among more recent works the fine narrative commentary by David Barr. I have learned from all these and more. But I have not seen it as my task to try to replicate their work. Whether this counts as a theological commentary I will let the reader judge, but it is certainly a theologian's commentary, and as a theologian I am grateful to have had such a prolonged exposure to the visions of the seer. I can only hope that the approach I have taken here will bear fruit for the life of the church.

"Church," of course, is one of those question-begging terms that cry out to be specified more clearly. To be specific: I write as an Anglican. Not only do I teach in a college where the training of priests is primary to our mission, but I am daily shaped by the experience of Anglican worship and prayer. Church for me means at the same time a particular local congregation, the worldwide Anglican communion, and the *una sancta catholica* of which it is but one part. At the same time, my college is part of an ecumenical consortium that also includes Roman Catholics, Presbyterians, and other Reformed denominations. In my classes I find all these traditions represented plus Pentecostals, Lutherans, Mennonites, Baptists, and many varieties of evangelicals. I have found that if pluralism at its worst can mean the banal celebration of difference as such, at its best it can spur us toward a serious quest for the unity of Christ's broken body, the church.

Wisdom dictates that any commentator should choose a particular form of the work being commented on and stick with it. My default text of Revelation is that of the English Standard Version, a successor to the Revised Standard Version and based on NA[27].[5] In addition, I have constantly consulted the Greek text and other English renderings of the Apocalypse.[6] I used to think that fidelity to the great tradition of English Bible translating that began with Tyndale, Wycliffe, and the King James Version and continues up through the ESV was a mere matter of literary style; surely theology ought not be beholden to such esthetic concerns? I now think that we receive the Bible as inheritors of a tradition, and that beyond a certain point the concern for translational purity leads us away from scripture to an abstract, disembodied, and a-ecclesial "text." While accuracy is certainly a virtue, it is also true that the Bible ought to sound like the Bible, that its cadences should bear some relation to the sweeping periods of biblical poetry and prose.[7]

5. The ESV has some liabilities with respect to inclusive language for humanity. I will correct for this where appropriate.

6. See especially the remarkable 1979 English version of Revelation by Richmond Lattimore, who came to the New Testament with the fresh eye of a classicist. Also worth consulting is Paul Minear's free, rhythmic yet faithful translation, appended to his 1968 commentary.

7. This is the very opposite of the advice often given for making scripture more accessible. "Dynamic equivalency" translations like the Revised English Bible or Eugene Peterson's *The Message* are

The medieval and Reformation-era translators inhabited a rhetorical culture similar to that of the early church. While there is nothing quite like hearing the Apocalypse in John's rough yet dazzling Greek, hearing it in the speech of the Elizabethan divines might be the next best thing.

On Apocalypses and Apocalyptic

The last book of the Bible has two names in English: Revelation (not Revelations) and the Apocalypse. The first term comes from the Latin, the second directly from the Greek. It is from the Greek name that we get our words "apocalypse," "apocalyptic," and "apocalypticism." These terms tend to be thrown about with abandon in both academic and popular discourse. They are important enough for grasping what Revelation is about that they deserve some preliminary treatment, although a fuller understanding will emerge only in the course of the commentary itself.

In the realms of journalism, entertainment, and popular culture, "apocalyptic" denotes a cataclysm of world-historical proportions. Thus an apocalyptic film is often a disaster movie about the end of civilization or even of life on this planet, whether on account of some cosmic catastrophe or of human beings' own self-destructive folly. Terrible events in the real world are also deemed to be apocalyptic. On the morning of September 12, 2001, a British tabloid used a single word to accompany its picture of the burning towers: "APOCALYPSE" (Kovacs and Rowland 2004: 1). Such language seems appropriate, not just because of the thousands who died, but because the event seemed to mark the end of the world as we had known it: in the world we *did* know, it was unimaginable that skyscrapers should be brought down by terrorists using airliners. Thus the common experience shared by so many on September 11: "This can't be happening." This combination of horror, excess, and the sense of an old order coming to an end and a new, more terrible one being born—this is what led us to call the event "apocalyptic." Reality, the sense of what is possible, was being redefined before our very eyes, as something radically new came into our field of vision—*apokalyptō* ("to reveal or disclose").

On the surface, the realm of "the apocalyptic" as seen in scripture might seem to have much in common with this popular usage. Here, too, human history reaches a kind of terminus. Here, too, people are awakened out of their

---

partly motivated by a desire not to sound overly pious or authoritarian, these being traits associated with "biblical" language. The problem with this approach is that it ignores the ways in which the forms of biblical speech are, if not absolutely identical with, nonetheless fitting vehicles for their content. This is why the Bible resists paraphrase. For a thoughtful application of this point to the doctrine of the inspiration of scripture, see David Yeago, "The Bible," in *Knowing the Triune God: The Work of the Spirit in the Practices of the Church*, ed. James J. Buckley and David S. Yeago (Grand Rapids: Eerdmans, 2001), 49–94.

complacency, as the world is shaken to its very foundations. Moreover, the Bible even employs a science-fiction-like idiom to describe events that exceed human capacities of expression. Thus we find in the various biblical apocalypses that the sun is darkened, the moon turns to blood, and the air is filled with locust-warriors who ravage the land; these cosmic events are signs of the approaching Day of the Lord, when YHWH comes to visit his people in judgment (e.g., Isa. 34:4; Joel 2). In the Gospels, Jesus makes these visions from the prophets his own as he seeks to describe the coming of the Danielic Son of Man, who sends his angels to gather the elect from the four corners of the earth (Mark 13; esp. 13:24–26).

But if we would hear this language rightly, we must grasp that for the early Christians the primary content of God's apocalypse is none other than this Son of Man himself. A properly *theological* understanding of apocalypse begins when we learn to use the term with a primary christological inflection. Douglas Harink makes the point with admirable precision:

> Most simply stated, "apocalypse" is shorthand for Jesus Christ. In the New Testa-
> ment, in particular for Paul, all apocalyptic reflection and hope comes to this,
> that God has acted critically, decisively, and finally for Israel, all the peoples of
> the earth, and the entire cosmos, in the life, death, resurrection, and coming
> again of Jesus, in such a way that God's purpose for Israel, all humanity, and all
> creation is critically, decisively, and finally disclosed and effected in the history
> of Jesus Christ.[8]

A central feature of New Testament apocalyptic, according to Harink, is that it lays primary stress on God's action in Christ rather than on human response. Harink characterizes this action in five ways: it is (1) a conflict with cosmic powers, preeminently the powers of sin and death, who have enslaved God's good creation; (2) invasive and decisive: humanity cannot save itself, but requires liberation by an agency beyond this world; (3) an act of judgment: in Jesus Christ both Israel and the nations encounter "the normative and critical measure of their faithfulness or faithlessness to God and so stand exposed in their deeds before the 'throne of God'"; (4) final: what happens in Jesus is unsurpassed and unsurpassable, *the* decisive event of salvation that requires no supplement; (5) cosmic and universal in scope. This last point is especially important, because it lifts the cross-resurrection event out of the realm of the mind, heart, or religious experience and into the

---

8. Douglas Harink, *Paul among the Postliberals: Pauline Theology beyond Christendom and Modernity* (Grand Rapids: Brazos, 2003), 68. Although Harink says "in particular for Paul," his description applies to much of the New Testament, especially writings like 1–2 Peter and the Gospels of Mark and of John. While John's Gospel may seem to lack the sense of a future-oriented eschatology required for apocalyptic, Christopher Rowland argues that apocalyptic is at least as much about "heaven opening" as about the historical coming of the end; cf. John 1:51; see *The Open Heaven: A Study of Apocalyptic in Judaism and Early Christianity* (New York: Crossroad, 1982).

realm of universal and cosmic history. What is at stake here is nothing less than the decisive clash between "the present evil age" and the age to come (cf. Gal. 1:4). In short, apocalyptic theology is a theology done "'without reserve,' that is, theology which leaves no reserve of space or time or concept or aspect of creation outside of or beyond or undetermined by the critical, decisive, and final action of God in Jesus Christ."[9]

Among the chief witnesses to this outlook in the New Testament is the Apocalypse, from which the very word "apocalyptic" derives. It displays all of the key features identified by Harink: the conflict between God and cosmic powers, unforgettably portrayed by John in the form of dragons, beasts, and monsters; an invasion of the fallen world by a Creator who is radically other than that world; an act of judgment: the language of the courtroom is pervasive in Revelation; a sense of the decisiveness and finality of God's action in Christ, such that there is no power, framework, or truth transcending it; the display of Jesus's cross and resurrection as an event of cosmic proportions, one that forces a massive rethinking of what we might formerly have thought of as the "real." As Harink points out, intrinsic to the grammar of apocalyptic theology is its making of totalizing claims, and the revelation of Jesus Christ to the seer is nothing if not a totalizing discourse. To be sure, this is precisely what makes the book so troubling in the minds of many. Much will depend on what the book actually claims to be totalizing.

It was Revelation that taught scholars to discern a family resemblance among a whole class of early Jewish and Christian writings, which we now call "apocalypses."[10] An apocalypse can be defined as "a form of literature with a narrative framework, in which a revelation or transcendent reality is given by an angel or otherworldly being to a human recipient. Usually the revelation unveils a supernatural world and points to salvation at the end of time."[11] The classic apocalypse in Israel's scriptures is Daniel, a work that John of Patmos knew intimately. The Latin Vulgate also includes a Jewish apocalypse, variously known as 2 Esdras or 4 Ezra, apparently written about the same time as Revelation. In addition there are myriad noncanonical apocalypses, both Jewish and Christian. But once modern scholars had identified the literary genre of apocalypse, it became obvious that this genre had been anticipated in the writings of the canonical prophets themselves. In addition to Daniel, apocalyptic motifs and images can be found in parts of Ezekiel,

9. Harink, *Paul among the Postliberals*, 68–69. I draw on Harink here, but much of his description is a distillation of J. Louis Martyn's groundbreaking work on Pauline apocalypticism, especially *Galatians*, Anchor Bible 33A (New York: Doubleday, 1997), 97–105. Harink borrows the phrase "without reserve" from Walter Lowe, "Prospects for a Postmodern Christian Theology: Apocalyptic without Reserve," *Modern Theology* 15 (1999): 17–24.

10. For a helpful introduction and overview to apocalyptic as a literary genre, see Raymond E. Brown, *An Introduction to the New Testament* (New York: Doubleday, 1997), 774–80.

11. Craig R. Koester, *Revelation and the End of All Things* (Grand Rapids: Eerdmans, 2001), 27.

Zechariah, Joel, and Isaiah, with Isa. 24–27 constituting a kind of apocalypse in miniature.

"Apocalypse" means a disclosure or revelation. Paradoxically, however, biblical revelation often stands in a certain tension with that which is hidden, mysterious, and obscure. It is this esoteric quality of apocalypses that makes them alternately so fascinating and so frustrating. The seer is shown the mysteries of heaven or God's secret plan for the future, but in signs and symbols that are hard to interpret. Instead of a clear word from the Lord, he is granted only ambiguous visions and troubling dreams—supernatural beings with flaming eyes, enormous statues destroyed by stones from heaven, horns making war on the saints. Even when the seer is granted the ultimate vision, the divine throne itself, he sees the latter supported by an entourage of fantastic animals and whirring wheels (e.g., Ezek. 1). It is indeed one of the more curious features of apocalypses that they employ so much zoological symbolism (e.g., Dan. 7; 10; 2 Esdras [4 Ezra] 11–12). One might almost say that the strangeness and dumbness of the animal, its opacity to the human gaze, serves as a sign of the unfathomable otherness and majesty of God. That which is below us sharpens our awareness of that which lies infinitely above.

It used to be argued that apocalyptic, with its otherworldliness and historical pessimism, represents but a degenerate form of prophecy.[12] Thus Martin Buber saw the prophets as hardy realists, the apocalypticists as heaven-struck idealists.[13] But this view precisely begs the question as to what constitutes realism. Apocalyptic theology might better be thought of as embodying a realism of a higher order. In the face of the challenge to human life and hope presented by the powers of this world, including the inexorable necessities of biology, entropy, and the rule of death—in Paul's words, creation's "bondage to decay"—apocalyptic sets forth an alternative causality, one that gives precedence to life and love.[14] This "spiritual causality" proclaims nothing less than the resurrection of the body, which from the perspective of natural causality is little more than food for worms. Historically speaking, it is surely no accident that apocalyptic begins to flourish at about the same time as Israel's resurrection hope.

But to discern such spiritual causality requires a form of vision that transcends our natural, this-worldly capacities for seeing. Apocalyptic insight requires wisdom; the seer is also a sage.[15] If Revelation is indeed a kind of wisdom book—and

---

12. The strong distinction between prophecy and apocalyptic has now been abandoned by scholars. Indeed, we shall see that Revelation is *both* an apocalypse *and* a prophecy.

13. Martin Buber, *Pointing the Way: Collected Essays*, trans. and ed. Maurice Friedman (London: Routledge & Kegan Paul, 1957), 203.

14. Travis Kroeker and Bruce Ward, *Remembering the End: Dostoevsky as Prophet to Modernity* (Boulder, CO: Westview, 2001), 25.

15. Gerhard von Rad derives apocalyptic from Israel's Wisdom traditions, noting that both are marked by displays of erudition and a concern for secret knowledge; for example, the wise man is an interpreter of dreams (Gen. 40; Dan. 2:48); see *Gesammelte Studien zum Alten Testament* (Munich: Kaiser, 1965), 306–8. Although von Rad probably presses this thesis too far, it is a telling insight.

13:18 and 17:9 would suggest that it is—then we should not expect that its riches will be unlocked by this or that theory of interpretation. The point of Israel's wisdom was always that *we ourselves* should become wise. Like wisdom, apocalyptic theology calls for transformation of the mind and heart combined with prudent action; we must seek not only wisdom but apocalyptic wisdom, the kind that sees deep into the spiritual causes of things:

> Yet among the mature we do impart wisdom, although it is not a wisdom of this age or of the rulers of this age, who are doomed to pass away. But we impart a secret and hidden wisdom of God, which God decreed before the ages for our glory. None of the rulers of this age understood this, for if they had, they would not have crucified the Lord of glory. But, as it is written,
>> What no eye has seen, nor ear heard,
>>> nor the heart of man imagined,
>> what God has prepared for those who love him—
> these things God has revealed to us through the Spirit. (1 Cor. 2:6–10)

Approaches to Interpretation

While we rightly think of the Apocalypse as a book about the future, the predominant approach to the book in the Middle Ages was to read it as an account of church history between the first and second comings of Christ.[16] The correlation between the sequence of visions and particular events and occurrences remained very loose, however. This widely influential approach to the book is indebted to St. Augustine, who saw all of history as an ongoing struggle between the city of God and the human city. In the later Middle Ages and into the Reformation, a new kind of reading took hold, in which the Apocalypse was seen as furnishing a detailed outline of history. This form of interpretation was pioneered by Joachim of Fiore writing in the twelfth century. Furious debates raged about the proper interpretation of the book's images and symbols. Not surprisingly, Franciscan friars enthusiastically identified the angel of the eternal gospel in Rev. 10 as St. Francis, while Lutherans insisted that this same angel could be only the one who had recovered the true, authentic gospel for the church—Martin Luther. The identity of the beast (666) in Rev. 13 was the object of even more intense speculation. Some very distinguished Christians engaged in this activity, including Dante, Jonathan Edwards, Charles Wesley, and Samuel Taylor Coleridge, along with a host of lesser figures.

16. The present commentary does not have the history of interpretation as its focus, although insights from earlier commentators will occasionally be cited. For an overview of historically influential readings, see Arthur William Wainwright's helpful *Mysterious Apocalypse: Interpreting the Book of Revelation* (Nashville: Abingdon, 1993). For a sense of how Revelation has shaped not only Christian theology but art, literature, and political thought, see Kovacs and Rowland 2004.

Judith Kovacs and Christopher Rowland aptly name this approach to reading the Apocalypse "decoding" interpretation. Its goal is to discern what the text *really* means behind the veil of its figures. They contrast it with "actualizing" interpretations that enact or perform Revelation "in relation to new circumstances, seeking to convey the spirit of the text rather than being preoccupied with the plethora of detail" (2004: 8). They suggest that any given reading of the book will fall somewhere between the poles of decoding and actualizing. Readings may also be plotted in accordance with whether the emphasis falls on the past, present, or future. For example, practitioners of historical criticism are by definition past-oriented readers (and are often passionate decoders besides, rivaling any fundamentalist in the attempt to pin down *the* meaning of the text). The Scofield Reference Bible used by dispensationalist Protestants offers a form of future-oriented exegesis. The pastor preaching from Revelation is a good example of a present-oriented reader, seeking to discern the challenge or comfort that the book presents for the life of the congregation.

What this tells us is that we must not be obsessed with hermeneutics. If this work is indeed holy scripture, a great gift of God to the church, then we need not worry about how to bridge the gap between the first century and the twenty-first; the Spirit is perfectly capable of overcoming any gap that may exist. It would be surprising if a book that names God as the one "who is and who was and who is to come" (1:4) did not have something to say about the past, present, and future alike. The question of time is secondary to the question of God. The same holds true for our obsession with codes. No doubt the Apocalypse has its share of puzzles, from the identity of Jezebel and the Nicolaitans, to the curious sequences of seven and of ten kings, to the mysterious number of the beast himself. No doubt we would like to know more about such matters. No doubt wrestling with them may sometimes help us to become better, more attentive readers. But no amount of hermeneutical prowess will save us if we do not approach the Apocalypse as a witness to *God's* action on behalf of his world, as the revelation of *Jesus Christ*, and as an instrument of the *Holy Spirit* in opening our minds and hearts to the things that God has done and is doing in our midst.

Prior to the questions we ask of Revelation, then, are the questions it asks of us. Prior to our ecclesial performance is the divine performance it sets forth in such a powerful, unforgettable way. And since Revelation comes to us as part of the larger, Spirit-authorized canon of holy scripture, it is important that we read it in light of the overall testimony of the apostles and prophets, rather than treating it as a rather bizarre special case. To read Revelation theologically is thus to uncover or display what might be called its "Christian coherence." The same word of God speaks here as is heard throughout the Bible. But *how* is this so? In what ways does Revelation embody the shared apostolic tradition of the early church, and in what ways does it inflect that tradition, perhaps showing us aspects of the gospel we might have overlooked or ignored?

Before the church can speak the word of God, it must listen for it. The very category of "scripture" implies that we must submit ourselves to this work, making ourselves vulnerable to it, letting it undermine our supposed certainties as it bears witness to the word of God. The task of this book, then, will be that of theological exposition, listening for the word in John's visions, hearing the book in the context of the entire canon, and letting ourselves be guided by the trinitarian faith of the church.

The Structure of Revelation

Does the Apocalypse have a basic organizing plan, an outline that joins the disparate visions into a unity?

The quest for the structure of Revelation is problematic, if for no other reason than that no two scholars can seem to agree on what it is: it is aptly said that there are almost as many outlines as there are interpreters.[17] One obvious possibility is to take the septenaries of seals, trumpets, and bowls as the basic organizing principle. The advantage of this proposal is that the sequences of seven are so clearly demarcated; the disadvantage is that after the pouring of the seventh bowl (17:1), this element seems to fade away. Although some scholars try to compensate for this by finding implied sevens beyond the ones named, this seems like special pleading. Another common proposal is to read Revelation as a chiasm, with twinned elements arranged around a central core (A-B-C-B´-A´). This idea is a bit more persuasive and has been adopted by some distinguished modern interpreters.[18] Chiastic structures ask to be read from the inside outward, with the key to the whole being found at the center. In favor of chiasm is that the middle chapters of Revelation contain some of the book's most vividly imagined scenes; moreover, many readers find a climax of sorts in the martyrdom of the two witnesses in Rev. 11 and a fresh beginning in the woman/dragon sequence in Rev. 12. There are also strong correspondences to be observed between the opening and the closing lines of the work, such as the pronouncement of blessings (1:3 and 22:7, 14), John's naming of himself (1:9 and 22:8), and the cry of "amen" (1:7 and 22:20).

Probably the most ancient structural proposal for reading the Apocalypse, however, is the idea that the book recapitulates itself, rehearsing the same basic set of events multiple times. This view goes all the way back to the second-century commentary by Bishop Victorinus of Pettau, who writes: "And although the same thing recurs in the phials [as in the trumpets], still it is not said as if it occurred twice, but because what is decreed by the Lord to happen shall be once for all.

17. Brown, *Introduction to the New Testament*, 796.
18. See Ellul 1977 and Elisabeth Schüssler Fiorenza, *Revelation: Vision of a Just World* (Minneapolis: Fortress, 1991).

... We must not regard the order of what is said, because frequently the Holy
Spirit, when He has traversed even to the end of the last times, returns again to
the same times, and fills up what He had *before* failed to say. Nor must we look
for order in the Apocalypse; but we must follow the meaning of those things
which are prophesied" (*Commentary on the Apocalypse* 7.2, quoted from ANF
7.352, emphasis original).

The recapitulation thesis does not mean that there is no forward progression
or movement in Revelation whatsoever. Rather, it means that the work should be
seen as a kind of spiral, with each vision retracing the same circle around time's
arrow. In each successive vision the same apocalyptic reality is shown forth. With
each tracing of the spiral, the eschatological urgency becomes ever greater. We
can thus see Revelation as a kind of "apocalyptic haggadah," a rehearsal, a narrative, a memory of an event in the past that is somehow *not* past, but our present
reality, and that toward which all of history is headed. Time is not annulled,
but transformed. The Spirit traverses even to the end of time, but then returns,
bringing the end itself with him. The one who stands at both the beginning and
the end is Jesus Christ.

In his narrative commentary on the Apocalypse, New Testament scholar David
Barr suggests a structuring of the book that in effect breathes new life into the
recapitulation thesis. Unlike Victorinus and other recapitulators, Barr does not
see the sequences of seven as being central. Rather, rightly taking Jesus Christ to be
the key to the book—"the Apocalypse is in its most basic sense a retelling of this
story of Jesus in a new way and with new images" (1998: 3)—Barr divides Revelation into three grand stories, each set in a different place and each corresponding
to a different book or scroll.

The first story is set on the island called Patmos, a thoroughly familiar and
this-worldly location. This is the "letter scroll." It describes the appearance
of the risen Christ to John and his dictating of letters to seven churches in
Asia Minor (Rev. 1–3). The second story is set in heaven and tells what John
sees when he is lifted up from earth to behold God's throne and the worship
that unfolds around it. Barr calls this book, which also includes the Lamb's
opening of the seven seals and the judgment that follows, the "worship scroll"
(4:1–11:18). While the third story is once again set on earth, it represents an
even greater departure from the world of our everyday experience. It relates a
cosmic battle between the Messiah, depicted as a warrior-king, and the forces
of evil. Compared with books 1–2, this part of Revelation has a distinctly
mythological[19] feel to it, being filled with dragons, monsters, demons, a cosmic
mother, and a world-conquering whore. Noting the affinity of this material to

19. The word "mythological" is a comment on literary convention, not on the truth or falsity
of the subject matter. If myths are simply stories about the gods, then Rev. 12–22 certainly has a
"mythic" ring to it.

warfare traditions in both the Israelite and pagan worlds, Barr calls this book the "war scroll" (11:19–22:21).[20]

Barr does not offer this analysis for theological purposes, but the theological interpreter can find much here that is useful. The threefold division has the advantage of locating the major breaks at obvious points. All commentators notice a break between the letters to the seven churches and the heavenly ascent at 4:1; many find a shift in tone and imagery at 12:1. For the theologian, however, the most persuasive thing about Barr's reading is the way it organizes the entire Apocalypse around successive images of Jesus Christ: the revealer in Rev. 1–3, the Lamb in Rev. 4–11, the messianic warrior in Rev. 12–22. Barr does not note, however, the way in which these three images correspond perfectly to what theologians call the "threefold office" of Christ: eschatological prophet, priest, and king. That the seer anticipated these dogmatics categories should not surprise us. Like other early Christian readers of Israel's scriptures, John cannot help but see Jesus as a prophet like Moses, as the high priest who has entered once for all into the heavenly sanctuary, and as the Messiah-King who is the true son and heir of David. This is another reminder that Revelation is unintelligible apart from the Old Testament.

In what follows I adopt the basic plan just described, modifying it only to the extent of adding to Barr's three stories a fourth: the concluding pages of the book, where the image of warrior gradually yields to that of Christ as the bridegroom. This is an image that Revelation likewise shares with the rest of the New Testament. If we then take into account the book's greeting and conclusion, which form a bracket around the whole, we arrive at the following rough outline:

1. prologue (1:1–3)
2. Jesus appears to John on Patmos, with messages for the seven churches (1:4–3:22)
3. the slaughtered Lamb remakes creation and judges history (4:1–11:19)[21]
4. the Messiah-King conquers the powers and brings down Babylon (12:1–20:15)
5. the church is invited to the marriage supper of the Lamb (21:1–22:7)
6. epilogue (22:8–21)[22]

20. Nineteenth-century Anglican commentator Elizabeth Rundle Charles was also sensitive to the military character of this part of Revelation, calling it "the book of battles." See her *The Book of Unveiling: Studies in the Revelation of S. John the Divine* (London: SPCK, 1892).

21. I call this part of the book "The Making and *Remaking* of the World," reflecting the confluence of creation and judgment themes in Rev. 4–11. The phrase is borrowed from Elaine Scarry's profound philosophical reflection on pain; *The Body in Pain: The Making and Unmaking of the World* (New York: Oxford University Press, 1985).

22. Other arrangements are, of course, possible. Minear 1968 organizes the book around the theme of "victory": announcement of promise of victory (Rev. 1–3), the Lamb as victor (4:1–8:1), prophets and the faithful as victors (8:2–15:4), victory over Babylon and the devil (15:5–22:21). By

Dating and Authorship

The book of Revelation was written in a particular place and time by a particular author.[23] The place we know: the island of Patmos, off the coast of Asia Minor (present-day Turkey). The time is less certain, although most scholars nowadays date the book in the mid-90s AD. As to the author, Christian tradition has long maintained that this John was the apostle, the son of Zebedee, also thought to have written the Fourth Gospel. In Eastern Christianity this apostle, evangelist, and seer is called "St. John the Divine" (that is, the Theologian), a title he shares among the church fathers only with St. Gregory Nazianzus. The supposition is that the apostle wrote Revelation in his extreme old age while imprisoned on Patmos.

The seer himself, however, does not identify himself as an apostle. All he tells us about himself is that he is named John (1:1, 4, 9; 22:8), that he is a Christian prophet (1:3; 22:6, 9), and that the risen Lord appeared to him, commanding him to "write." He tells us nothing about himself that is unrelated to his mission. With remarkable self-effacement he identifies himself simply as a "slave" of Jesus Christ (1:1) and as "brother" and companion in affliction to the churches (1:9).

Regardless of who the seer was, what is the situation his work addresses? The classic answer is that he wrote in the time of Emperor Domitian (ruled AD 81–96), whose demand that he be worshiped as a god led to an official state policy of persecuting Christians, who saw such worship as idolatry. This dating of Revelation has very ancient support: thus Irenaeus tells us that the Apocalypse was written "near the end of Domitian's reign" (*Against Heresies* 5.30.3). Ever since the nineteenth century there has been a strong dissenting view, holding that John wrote against the background of the turbulent 60s and 70s, in the days when Nero persecuted the church and Jerusalem was destroyed by Roman armies. David Aune, who explored this question perhaps more thoroughly than any other scholar, splits the difference, arguing that John wrote a "first edition" of Revelation around 70 and then edited his own work to reflect the new situation of the 90s. More important than this redaction theory is Aune's belief that John's roots are in Palestine: "The otherwise unknown author of Revelation . . . was probably a Palestinian Jew who

---

contrast, Boring 1989 focuses on the theme of "city": "God Speaks to the Church in the City" (Rev. 1–3), "God Judges the 'Great City'" (Rev. 4–18), and "God Redeems the 'Holy City'" (Rev. 19–22). Ellul reads the book as a chiasm, with two outer sections devoted to the church and the new creation, two inner sections on history and the judgment of the powers, and a "keystone" (8:1–14:5) organized around the incarnation of Christ (1977: 50).

23. The scholarly vogue about a hundred years ago was to divide Revelation among multiple sources, authors, or editors. The height of the mania for source criticism is reflected in R. H. Charles, *A Critical and Exegetical Commentary on the Revelation of St. John*, International Critical Commentary (Edinburgh: Clark, 1920). That day is past; today almost all scholars see Revelation as the work of a single hand.

had emigrated to the Roman province of Asia, perhaps in connection with the first Jewish revolt in A.D. 66–70" (1997: lvi).[24] If this theory is true—and it is only a theory—then John had lived through a time of intense crisis for the *ekklēsia*.[25]

Historical questions like these are endlessly fascinating. They help to remind us that the Apocalypse is not a timeless writing, but one rooted in the specificities of time, history, and human experience. Yet if we would read along the grain of Revelation itself, then we must confess that the book's concern is not with the circumstances of its own composition but with the sovereign, life-giving action of God. What is of urgent concern to the seer is not what the Romans or even the Christians are doing, but what God is doing. In a word, the Apocalypse demands to be read apocalyptically, with an eye to the victory of God and the Lamb over a world beset by the power of death.

24. In the nineteenth century the early dating was argued by a group of distinguished Anglican scholars associated with Cambridge, including Bishops Westcott and Lightfoot and F. J. A. Hort; see Fenton J. A. Hort, *The Apocalypse of St. John I–III: The Greek Text, with Introduction, Commentary, and Additional Notes* (London: Macmillan, 1908), ix–xliv. This view has recently been defended by Margaret Barker, who vigorously argues that the author of the Apocalypse was a Jewish temple priest and follower of Jesus who fled Jerusalem in the aftermath of the Roman invasion; *The Revelation of Jesus Christ: Which God Gave to Him to Show to His Servants What Must Soon Take Place (Revelation 1.1)* (Edinburgh: Clark, 2000). The temple background would certainly help to account for the book's extraordinary worship imagery.

25. Whether the atmosphere of crisis persisted into the 90s is an open question. While some scholars today hold the traditional view of a persecution taking place under Domitian, others find no evidence for this; see Leonard Thompson, *The Book of Revelation: Apocalypse and Empire* (New York: Oxford University Press, 1990). For a judicious balancing of the evidence see Brown, *Introduction to the New Testament*, 805–9.

PART I

✛ JESUS ON PATMOS ✛

REVELATION 1

SEEING VOICES

Then the Spirit lifted me up, and I heard behind me the voice of a great earthquake: "Blessed be the glory of the LORD from its place!" It was the sound of the wings of the living creatures as they touched one another, and the sound of the wheels beside them, and the sound of a great earthquake.

—Ezekiel 3:12–13

The book of Revelation opens with the Greek word for revelation, *apokalypsis*, suggesting a disclosure or unveiling—like pulling back a curtain or lifting a lid. The metaphor seems overwhelmingly visual. And indeed Revelation is a book of visions or showings, intended "to show [*deixai*] to his servants the things that must soon take place."

But the Apocalypse is equally a book of auditions. Trumpets sound, thunderclaps boom, angels cry out—almost always "with a loud voice." The absence of sound can be equally important. Silence in heaven marks a period of expectant waiting for fresh revelation (8:1), and the death of Babylon will later be denoted by the sound of silence—musicians, singers, the voices of the bridegroom and the bride all strangely quieted (18:22–23). But for the most part Revelation is a very loud book, situating us in the midst of an extraordinarily aural universe. This sets it in tension with the dominant traditions of Western thought, which have a long history of privileging the eye over the ear. From Plato onward, sight has been understood as the most powerful and reliable among the senses, the faculty that permits us to control the world in godlike fashion. But perhaps vision is not quite as sovereign as we like to think. *Ein Bild hielt uns gefangen*, wrote Wittgenstein; "a picture held us captive."[1] We must allow for the possibility that the Apocalypse subverts our confidence in our capacity to dominate the world by making representations of it.

So instead of reading the book in the usual way, perhaps we should begin by hearing it. Let us engage in a brief thought experiment.

1:1 We are in a city in Asia Minor in the late first century. We are part of a small group of people who have gathered on the Lord's Day to hear the word of scripture, pray, sing hymns, perhaps receive messages from those designated as prophets, and commune together in the Lord's Supper. This is the *ekklēsia*, the assembly of God's people. On this particular Sunday a courier has arrived with a letter from a prophet who cannot be present with us, a certain John who is, shall we say, detained on the island of Patmos. The courier—let us call him the "lector"—begs leave of the gathered assembly to read the letter aloud. Permission for this is granted by the community's elders. The lector opens the huge papyrus scroll and begins to read: "The *apokalypsis* of Jesus Christ, which God gave him to show to his servants the things that must soon take place."

The reading takes a fairly long time by twenty-first-century standards (in English it takes about an hour to read Revelation through from beginning to end), though in a highly oral and rhetorical culture it might not have seemed so strange; Protestants in the age of John Donne were accustomed to hearing sermons for hours at a time. Like all revelation, *the* Revelation is mediated. We are hearing a human voice, an embodied event. John may have received his visions in the imposed isolation of Patmos, but his words resound in the very public, visible, and material setting of the church. The lector is reading and interpreting marks on a scroll. This is very much an oral performance taking place in the church. The Coptic Orthodox Church preserves a memory of these origins in its practice of reading the entire Apocalypse on the vigil night preceding "Bright Saturday," as Holy Saturday is known in the West.[2] It is the only time the work is read in church.

But if Revelation has this oral/aural character, who is the speaker? Answering this question is not as straightforward as it might seem. In a remarkable essay on the voices we hear in this book, Eugene Boring suggests that we understand all the words from beginning to end as enclosed by three sets of quotation marks. The outermost set denotes the lector's voice, what he or she actually reads aloud to those present. Inside these is found a second set of marks denoting what is written on the scroll—unless the lector ad libs these will be the exact same words,

1. Ludwig Wittgenstein, *Philosophical Investigations: The English Text of the Third Edition* (Oxford: Blackwell, 1958), #115.
2. See the article "Coptic Worship" in *The New Westminster Dictionary of Liturgy and Worship*, ed. Paul Bradshaw (Louisville: Westminster John Knox, 2002), 135. Thanks to Dr. Rifaat Ebied of the University of Sydney for calling this fact to my attention.

though as Boring points out the first set will always be an interpretation of the second set, a particular performance of it with variations in tone, accent, pauses and the like. Finally, a third set of quotation marks, again bracketing the entire book, designates John as its human author.[3] Not just the lector's voice, nor the words on the page, but John's act of witness—this is what we hear when we hear the Apocalypse.

The simple act of reading aloud in church is a practice that should not be scorned. The public reading of scripture has been a particular emphasis in the Anglican tradition. While Anglicans highly value preaching, they also share the conviction that scripture has a voice of its own even prior to its exposition in the sermon. There is, one might say, a certain sacramentality that inheres in the scriptural word itself. I once heard a sermon by Oliver O'Donovan in which he said that "many a church has thrived under the ministry of its readers that would have starved to death under the ministry of its preachers."[4] The phrase *viva vox evangelii* ("the living voice of the gospel") is usually applied to the act of preaching, and yet it already applies to the public reading and hearing of the word of God.

And indeed, this is the extraordinary claim that Revelation makes: when we encounter the voice of the lector, or of the written work, or even of John himself, what we are really hearing is God's own voice. It is in the very nature of the Apocalypse that it *breaks open* any merely this-worldly occasion by a word that comes from above. Indeed, the opening lines of the book suggest a great chain of revelation reaching from heaven to earth:

God → Christ → angel → John → God's slaves

We are the slaves.[5] This in itself is already good news, insofar as it implies that we are not the slaves of the demonic powers and their earthly collaborators. To be a slave of God is to be a member of the *ekklēsia*, in the front lines of a resistance movement called to hold out until the ages fully turn. Happily the church does not have to engage in this service on its own. Positioned at the beachhead, it is in constant communication with headquarters, where its Messiah-general prepares for his advent at the front lines. Or to alter the metaphor, the church exists at the bottom of a ladder reaching from heaven to earth, up and down which there is a constant procession of angels bearing tidings between two realms. The ladder, of course, is Christ: "Truly, truly, I say to you, you will see heaven opened, and

---

3. M. Eugene Boring, "The Voice of Jesus in the Apocalypse of John," *Novum Testamentum* 34 (1992): 335–36.

4. Oliver O'Donovan, sermon preached at St. Margaret's Anglican Church, Winnipeg, Manitoba, April 20, 2008. I am quoting from memory.

5. The Greek is *douloi*. ESV has "servants," glossing this in a footnote as "bondservants." But this still seems euphemistic; the word means "slaves." See NRSV margin.

the angels of God ascending and descending on the Son of Man" (John 1:51; cf. Gen. 28:12).

1:2 We are now at a point where we can fully appreciate the opening words of the book: *Apokalypsis Iēsou Christou* ("the revelation of Jesus Christ"). Is this a subjective or an objective genitive? That is, is this the revelation that belongs to Jesus Christ, the one that he owns and enacts, or is this the revelation pertaining to Jesus Christ, the revelation that speaks about him? The answer is that it is both. Jesus is both the subject and the object of the apocalypse, both the revealer and the revealed. Like any prophet of Israel, John can describe his utterance as "the word of God" (1:2). Yet this word, in turn, cannot be divorced from "the testimony of Jesus," his *martyria*. This is the first time we encounter this pregnant term. For John the *martyria* of Jesus refers not only or even primarily to his spoken word, but to his life and death as an embodied act of testimony, a witness sealed in blood. John bears witness to Jesus, who bears witness to God, who acts in the world through the "apocalypsing" of his Son—the revelation of Jesus Christ.

A mediatory role is played by the angel in the chain of revelation. Like the epistle to the Hebrews, Revelation keeps angels in their place: any temptation to angel-worship is firmly excluded (19:10; 22:8; cf. Heb. 1:4–14). And yet this is very much a book of angels and other heavenly beings. As the church hears the book read, it cannot help but be drawn into a world of angelic voices, speaking, singing, crying out, bearing their own peculiar witness to the Creator. Does the Apocalypse then draw us upward into a purely religious sphere, in which the rough edges of the present age are smoothed over or forgotten? The next words disabuse us of this notion: "Blessed is the one who reads aloud the words of this prophecy, and blessed are those who hear, and who keep what is written in it, for the time is near" (1:3).

1:3 This utterance comes like a bolt from the blue and raises once again the question about the identity of the speaker. Even if the book as a whole is in some sense the speech of John, many particular voices intrude, some of them clearly identified (angels, elders, martyrs, the Spirit) but others that remain hard to pin down. It is tempting to assign the blessing to Jesus. The word *makarios* used here is the same word that appears in the Beatitudes in the Gospels of Matthew and Luke. The corresponding blessing at the end of the book (Rev. 22:7) is definitely the voice of Christ. But while this is strongly implied in 1:3 it is by no means certain. In cases like this the "reader hears a voice, but it is difficult to picture, on canvas or even in one's mind's eye, where such voices are located."[6] The elusive character of the voice perhaps points to the freedom of the risen Lord, who shares his bodily presence with us in the power of the Spirit. Here is an early signal not to try to conform Revelation to the expectations of this-worldly time, space, or language.

6. Boring, "Voice of Jesus in the Apocalypse of John," 341–42.

This beatitude is the first of seven spoken in Revelation, a number that can hardly be accidental: seven is John's number for completion or fulfillment.[7] A blessing is a performative utterance, a speech act that effects the very thing it describes: "I promise you," "I thank you," "I acquit you," "I now pronounce you husband and wife"—all are explicit instances of language in its performative use.[8] So the blessing spoken here brings the blessedness of God and of Christ right into the midst of the assembly. The blessing of God is his grace. But since God's grace, though free, is never cheap, as Bonhoeffer reminded us, the blessing also imposes constraint or obligation on the hearer: "Blessed is the one who reads aloud the words of this prophecy, and blessed are those who hear, *and who keep what is written in it*, for the time is near." There is no mistaking the urgency of this saying. If the apocalyptic opening of heaven serves to expand our world, the nearness of the end serves to contract it; we have less time than we thought. Just as in the Beatitudes spoken by Jesus to the poor, the meek, the peacemakers, and those who mourn, the blessings in Revelation bring the eschatological blessing of God into human life. The possibility of noncompliance is not even entertained. Transforming our reality, Christ's blessing cannot help but transform the way we live.

1:4–7 Revelation is both a book of apocalyptic visions and a work of prophecy, but it is also a third thing: a letter. Indeed, substitute the name "Paul" for "John" at 1:4 and the opening words could easily be mistaken for the greeting of a Pauline epistle:

> John to the seven churches that are in Asia:
> Grace to you and peace.

A letter is a means of personal communication. John names himself (only in the opening and the closing lines of Revelation) and offers a brief description of the addressees, namely seven Christian assemblies in the province of Asia. In Rev. 2–3 these will be specified in much greater detail. Before turning to matters of substance, however, it is important that John identify himself, state his motives, and establish the common concern that binds him in fellowship with the churches. The words "grace . . . and peace" begin this process.[9] Grace and peace! These are words we do not often associate with the Apocalypse. Many would say that there is more divine wrath than divine mercy here, more violence and

---

7. It is sometimes said that seven in Revelation is the number of perfection. In some cases this may be true, as with the seven stars and the seven spirits of God. But there are also seven last plagues and seven heads of the dragon. Not all completions are perfections. Seven plagues means the full range of plagues, just as seven heads means the enormity of evil, evil in excess. John revels in numerology; I will identify other symbolic numbers as they are introduced.

8. I say "explicit instances," because all speech has a performative aspect, as J. L. Austin makes clear near the end of his famous lectures on the subject; *How to Do Things with Words* (Cambridge, MA: Harvard University Press, 1960).

9. The word *charis* ("grace") is a Christian modification of the word *chaire* ("greetings") used in the salutation of Greek letters. *Eirēnē* ("peace") is a rendering of Hebrew *shalom*.

bloodshed than peace. Nevertheless, I think we need to take John at his word. Even if the usage is a borrowing from the conventions of early Christian letter-writing, it says something important. John does not write with hostile intentions toward the churches. He is but an ambassador of the one who is the source of all grace and peace and who—in another performative utterance—bestows these gifts upon the listener.[10] Grace and peace are the very content of this apocalyptic irruption into our world.

This ultimate sender of the letter is now named. In other New Testament letters, such as Paul's, the formula "grace and peace" would be followed by "from God our Father and the Lord Jesus Christ." These expected words do not appear, however. Instead, John offers greetings:

> from him who is and who was and who is to come,
> and from the seven spirits who are before his throne,
> and from Jesus Christ
>   the faithful[11] witness,
>   the firstborn of the dead,
>   and the ruler of kings on earth. (1:4–5)

A moment ago we were hearing a letter being read aloud, John offering greetings to the churches. We now learn that John is only penultimately the source of this communication. The real source of the letter is God. Even this turns out to be more complicated than we might think, for alongside God we also hear of Jesus and of the mysterious "seven spirits." Each of these three elements, in turn, is internally complex. The Father is named with reference to his relation to present, past, and future; Jesus is called witness, firstborn, and ruler of kings; and the spirits are seven rather than simply one. John has not simply expanded the Pauline greeting, he has deepened and enriched it in puzzling ways.

The first thing we notice is a proliferation of threes. Beyond the ones just cited, the ascription of Christ shifts into a doxology (1:5b) that yields three further sets of three:

> him who loves us
> has freed us from our sins by his blood
> has made us a kingdom

10. The wish of grace recurs at the very end of the letter (22:21), setting a bracket around virtually the entire work. Grace is not, to be sure, a key item in John's theological vocabulary; in this he differs from Paul and even from the author of the Fourth Gospel, who employs "grace" four times in his prologue.

11. The word *pistos* connotes "fidelity, loyalty, trustworthiness" and is related to the word *pistis* ("faith"). Lattimore 1979: 253 translates this phrase as "Jesus Christ, the witness who is to be believed"; Minear 1968: 301 has "Jesus the Messiah, who loyally confirmed God's work."

> he is coming with the clouds
> every eye will see him
> all tribes of the earth will wail on account of him

All this is rhetorically powerful. The number three is a universal element in myth and folklore. In fairly tales there are always three sons, three trials, three rings of power. But there is more than simply folklore going on here. As the doxological language and the liturgical "amen" (1:6–7) suggest, we find ourselves in the atmosphere of early Christian worship, an eschatological atmosphere permeated by a longing for Christ's future coming. At the heart of Christian worship is the God who is one, but one by being three—the Father, the Son, and the Holy Spirit. Worship is the primordial home of the Christian confession of God as Trinity. As Robert Jenson remarks, the "habit of trinitarian naming is universal through the life of the church. How far back it goes we cannot make out.... It appears to have been an immediate reflex of believers' experience of God. It is in liturgy, when we do not talk about God but to and for him, that we need and use his name."[12]

In mathematics, a fractal is a geometric figure, any part of which displays the same figure or statistical pattern as the whole. Familiar examples would be a jagged coastline or the crystalline structure of a snowflake. Fractal geometry offers a useful analogy for what is going on in our passage. Given that God is the Trinity and that the Trinity is unity, the trinitarian pattern is found *within* each of his three hypostases. To take the easiest case first, John's repeated, threefold ascriptions of Christ point to Jesus's belonging with the Trinity, to his life and death being the revelation of just *this* God and no other. This is so whether we speak of his person (1:5a), his activity (1:5b–6), or his future coming (1:7).

The Spirit, likewise, is none other than the Spirit of the Lord who appears throughout the Old Testament. That is why he is described as standing "before his throne." But why seven spirits? The origins of this phrase can be found in Zech. 4, an obscure passage that John seems to have found endlessly stimulating.[13] Wakened from sleep by the angel of YHWH, Zechariah is shown a lampstand with seven lamps and flanked by two olive trees. Asked by the angel what these are, he confesses his ignorance. The angel then instructs him: "This is the word of the LORD to Zerubbabel: Not by might, nor by power, but by my Spirit, says the LORD of hosts" (Zech. 4:6).

In Zechariah's understanding, Zerubbabel is a messianic figure who, along with Joshua the high priest, will help to complete the restored temple. The ideal king and the ideal priest—these are the "two olive trees" (imagery that appears again

---

12. Robert W. Jenson, *The Triune Identity: God according to the Gospel* (Philadelphia: Fortress, 1982), 10.

13. Zech. 4 "seems to have been the key Old Testament passage for John's understanding of the role of the Spirit in the divine activity in the world" (Bauckham 1993b: 110). Bauckham's whole discussion of the Spirit in Revelation is instructive, especially his treatment of the role played by Zech. 4.

in the story of the two witnesses in Rev. 11). Yet the restoration will be accomplished not by the power of any human being, but by the Spirit of God himself! As for the seven lampstands, the prophet is told: "These seven are the eyes of the LORD, which range through the whole earth" (Zech. 4:10). The messianism of this passage, the emphasis on the Spirit, even the number seven—all of these will later be applied to the Spirit-filled Messiah Jesus: "I saw a Lamb standing . . . with seven horns and with seven eyes, which are the seven spirits of God sent out into all the earth" (Rev. 5:6).

I can add one further tantalizing piece to this puzzle. In a famous prophecy in the book of Isaiah, we are told that a future king, the "shoot of Jesse," will be endowed by God's Spirit with a set of extraordinary gifts. In the Septuagint version of the passage, seven such gifts are named: wisdom, understanding, counsel, might, knowledge, piety, and fear of the Lord (Isa. 11:2–3). Here John would have found further confirmation of the Spirit's sevenfold character. The Spirit is the seven eyes of God, the seven burning lamps, the seven gifts poured out on Messiah whose rule extends over all the earth. Seven in Revelation is the number of completeness or plentitude. The sevenfoldness of the Spirit binds his identity to God and to Christ and symbolizes both the diversity of his gifts and their unrestricted scope.

The first of the three formulas, the one "who is and who was and who is to come," is in some ways the most mysterious.[14] Clearly this is a designation for God, *theos*, the first person of the Trinity. This is the one described as the Father of Jesus Christ both in Revelation (already in 1:6; see also 2:27; 3:5, 21; 14:1) and throughout the New Testament witness. John addresses his hearers bearing the grace and peace of this God. But why speak of God in just this way?

When Jenson writes that "it is in liturgy, when we do not talk about God but to and for him, that we need and use his name," he is underscoring the importance of the divine *identity*. The word "god" by itself does not say very much. There are many candidates for the ultimate reality that shapes human destiny: Baal, Shiva, the Free Market, Progress, the Holy Trinity. As Paul acknowledges with disarming honesty, "there are many gods and many lords" (1 Cor. 8:5 ESV slightly modified).[15]

14. Rev. 1:4 has a grammatical peculiarity. The formula "is, was, is to come" should technically be in the genitive case, given that it follows the preposition *apo* ("from"). But it is not; instead, the phrase is in the nominative. John writes not "from *him* who is" but rather "from *he* who is." Some commentators find this theologically significant: God, it is said, is always the subject, never simply object in relation to human beings. Even in relation to us, he remains mysteriously and irreducibly himself. The idea is interesting, the exegetical thread from which it is hung slender indeed. John's odd usage may simply reflect that he was more at home writing in Hebrew or Aramaic than he was in Greek. The Hebraic "feel" to Revelation's language contributes greatly to its jarring, unearthly beauty.

15. Modern Bible translations (RSV, New International Version, ESV) typically add scare quotes around Paul's words for rival divinities in this passage. But such embarrassment is uncalled for. In pragmatic and religious terms, the other gods and lords are all too real—as Paul well understood. I owe this point to Garrett Green, "Thinking about the Religions with Karl Barth," paper read at the Karl Barth Conference in Princeton, June 2, 2009.

One of the most important tasks that scripture performs for the church is to distinguish the one true God from the idols of the nations (1 Thess. 1:9).

In the Old Testament, the most decisive passage in this regard is the one where God reveals his actual proper name, YHWH (in most English Bible translations "the LORD"), when he speaks to Moses from the burning bush. In the Septuagint version, God "exegetes" his name with the saying "I am the one who is" (*egō eimi ho ōn*) (Exod. 3:14). In both Jewish and Christian tradition, "He Who Is" became one of the most central designations for the God of the Bible.[16] In an important study of Rev. 1:4, Sean McDonough shows how ancient Jewish writers extended the reach of this assertion into both the past and the future. The God who *is*, the rabbis argued, also *was* and *will be*. It is very possible that in so doing, they were seeking to answer similar claims on the part of Greek religion. Thus the oracle at Dodona in northwestern Greece exultantly proclaimed, "Zeus was, Zeus is, Zeus shall be. O mighty Zeus!" (*Zeus ēn, Zeus esti, Zeus essestai, ō megale Zeu*), while a famous inscription at Eleusis declared that Aion (Eternity) "is of such a nature that he is and was and will be, not having beginning, middle, or end, who does not partake of change, who produces the absolutely eternal divine nature."[17]

For the rabbis, the claims made by these pagan deities were simply false. YHWH alone is the Lord God, the Creator, the one who masters time and is never mastered by it. Nor were the rabbis saying anything different from what was already implicit in Israel's scriptures. "Thus says the LORD, the King of Israel and his Redeemer, the LORD of hosts: 'I am the first and I am the last; besides me there is no god. Who is like me? Let him proclaim it. . . . Let them declare what is to come, and what will happen'" (Isa. 44:6–7). "All flesh is grass, and all its beauty is like the flower of the field. The grass withers, the flower fades when the breath of the LORD blows on it; surely the people are grass. The grass withers, the flower fades, but the word of our God will stand forever" (40:6–8).

In the pagan and rabbinic threefold formulas for deity, the phrase ends as we might expect: God is praised as the one who is, was, and *will be*. But the Apocalypse deviates from that pattern: here God is, and was, and *is coming*. Elsewhere in Revelation, the phrase *ho erchomenos* ("he who is coming") is clearly used with reference to Jesus (1:7; 3:11; 16:15; 22:7). The foreshadowing of that christological

---

16. See, e.g., Thomas Aquinas, *Summa theologiae* 1.13.11. Thomas privileges the name "he who is" because it underscores God's character as "being itself," the source of all particular *beings*. But note also his little-known qualification: "But as regards the object intended by the name, this name *God* is more proper, as it is imposed to signify the divine nature; *and still more proper is the Tetragrammaton*, imposed to signify the substance of God itself, incommunicable and, if one may so speak, singular" (1.13.11 §1, emphasis added). Though it could easily be missed, Aquinas realizes that the name YHWH best bespeaks God's singularity, his mysterious, hypostatic "someone-ness."

17. Sean M. McDonough, *YHWH at Patmos: Rev. 1:4 in Its Hellenistic and Early Jewish Setting* (Tübingen: Mohr, 1999), 49, 52. It is extremely suggestive that the Eleusis inscription appears on a monument dedicated to "the power of Rome and the continuance of the mysteries." The gods of the nations claim to be the guarantors of a specific civic order. Rome and its modern equivalents always claim to be "the eternal city."

title tells us something important about God as such. In that the Father is fully present in the Son, and the Son in the Father, we must say that the Father, too, is coming toward the world as its judge and Savior. Whoever we are, whatever the particularities of our stories or situations, this eschatological judge is on the way to meet us. This is surely good news. God is not only the origin of the world but also its future.

The triple formula serves, then, as an initial clue to the identity of the God who speaks in Revelation. He is none other than YHWH the God of Israel, the one who is *also* the Holy Blessed Trinity, the Father, the Son, and the Holy Spirit, he who spoke out of the burning bush and from the cross.[18]

One final puzzle remains: why does John name the three persons in the order Father, Spirit, Son, instead of the more familiar Father, Son, Spirit? At one level this ordering reflects the requirements of rhetoric: the christological member of the triad is the one on which John will soon elaborate, therefore it has to come last. But there may also be something deeper at work. Naming the Spirit first underscores Jesus's character as Spirit-conceived and Spirit-anointed Messiah (Luke 1:35; 3:22).[19] If in a certain sense the Spirit exists for the sake of Christ, in another sense Christ exists for the sake of the Spirit, who makes the community of his followers participants in his *apokalypsis*.

Yet it is not the Spirit whom Christians praise in their worship; it is Christ, who is named in the language of doxological utterance: "To him who loves us and has freed[20] us from our sins by his blood and made us a kingdom, priests to his God and Father" (1:5b–6). With this threefold "us," the voice of the worshiping assembly is heard for the first time. The language is precise: the speakers confess that they have been delivered from the bondage of sin, constituted as a polity or form of common life, and summoned to a priestly existence. Freed slaves, they share in his rule and serve him in his kingdom. And all this as a result of their being loved by Jesus Christ, whose glory (*doxa*) they proclaim and whose royal authority (*kratos*) they now acknowledge. This is the way one talks about a king or emperor, which makes the use of the word "loves" all the more jarring. Jesus Christ loves us; that is what makes us who we are.

Let the people say, "Amen!" (1:6). The congregation's "amen" is their solemn "yes" to what has just been proclaimed. They are no mere passive spectators of Christ's love for them. Indeed the "amen" might be said to "rob [the churches] of

18. R. Kendall Soulen, "The Name of the Holy Trinity: A Triune Name," *Theology Today* 59 (July 2002): 244–61.

19. In his historical mission, Jesus is certainly endowed with the Spirit, as Luke's Gospel in particular emphasizes. For a compelling argument that the Father *eternally* begets the Son by the Spirit, see Thomas G. Weinandy, *The Father's Spirit of Sonship: Reconceiving the Trinity* (Edinburgh: Clark, 1995).

20. Some manuscripts have "washed" (*lousanti*) here, a reading reflected in both the Vulgate and KJV; but "freed" (*lysanti*) is much better supported.

the lethal luxury of considering themselves observers."[21] Their response to God's action is by no means redundant, but an essential outworking of the *apokalypsis* in time and history. This whole section breathes with the language and spirit of the liturgy. One scholar suggests that 1:1–8 be read as a liturgical dialogue, with lines alternating between the lector and the worshiping congregation.[22]

1:8 The climax of this sequence occurs when, for the first time in Revelation, we hear the voice of God himself, speaking through the mouth of the prophet: "'I am the Alpha and the Omega,' says the Lord God, 'who is and who was and who is to come, the Almighty.'" This act of divine *self*-naming brings God dangerously close. Worship is dangerous—and always one step removed from blasphemy. In presuming to speak for God, we easily forget that it is not our task to make an absent God present. As the Creator, God *is* present, closer to creatures than they are to themselves. God is even more intensely present in the person of his Son, whose glory we have just affirmed. The phrase "Alpha and Omega" echoes the "is, was, is to come" at 1:4, but gives a slightly different twist to that formula. Here the emphasis falls not so much on God's transcendence over time as on his perfect life and fullness, exceeding creation even as he embraces it, the way the letters Alpha and Omega bracket the Greek alphabet. It is also possible that these letters suggest the divine name. It is frequently pointed out that a common Greek abbreviation for the name was IΩA, which might have suggested the idea of using Alpha and Omega, A and Ω, as a cipher for the Tetragrammaton.[23] The ancients were fond of finding mysterious meanings in letters and numbers. That is why the decoding approach to Revelation cannot be completely discounted, even if we should avoid making a fetish out of it.

The introduction to the Apocalypse has so far fallen into two main parts. The first part declares the apocalypsing of God in Jesus Christ, describes the chain of revelation moving from God to Christ to the angel to John, and concludes with a blessing on the hearers (1:1–3). The second part begins with John's epistolary greeting at 1:4, which announces grace and peace coming from God, the seven spirits, and Jesus Christ and concludes with an elaborate doxology and a self-declaration on the part of God himself (1:4–8).

1:9–10 We enter a third part of the introduction. Unlike the first two, this one is circumscribed by a definite time and space: the time, "the Lord's day"; the space, "the island called Patmos." It is striking that immediately after the solemn self-testimony on the part of God—"I am the Alpha and the Omega"—we hear a parallel act of testimony spoken by John: "I, John, your brother." It is as if God's

21. J. Louis Martyn, *Galatians*, Anchor Bible 33A (New York: Doubleday, 1997), 106.

22. Ugo Vanni, "Liturgical Dialogue as a Literary Form in the Book of Revelation," *New Testament Studies* 37 (1991): 348–72.

23. McDonough, *YHWH at Patmos*, 91–93, 116–22, 219–20; Bauckham 1993b: 27–28. Austin Farrer offers an extraordinary, if highly speculative discussion of IΩA and its relation to the divine name in *A Rebirth of Images: The Making of St. John's Apocalypse* (Westminster: Dacre, 1949), chap. 10.

"I," sovereignly declaring itself in the world, fashions a parable of itself in John's subjectivity. God's omnipotence is such that it does not quash human capacities but liberates them. Yet note how little John's "I" is marked by self-assertion or ego! This is no general issuing orders and directives from a safe distance, but simply a fellow soldier in Jesus Christ, one who has himself served on the front lines of the battle. He stands in complete solidarity with his listeners: like them, he has suffered apocalyptic tribulation (*thlipsis*, a key term in the vocabulary of Revelation) and the patient endurance of suffering for Jesus's sake (*hypomonē*).

John tells his readers that he is on Patmos "on account of the word of God and the testimony of Jesus" (1:9). This circumstance adequately explains his absence from them—not the actions of the Romans, not some business that has detained him, but simply the word of God and the demands of testimony.[24] These are a prophet's reasons. This is not to deny that the Roman or local authorities may have served as unwitting instruments of God's design. It is possible, even very likely, that John's activities as a Christian leader got him into trouble and that it was found expedient that he should be removed from the scene. *Apostolus Iohannes . . . in insulam relegatur*, writes Tertullian; "the apostle John was deported to an island" (*Prescription against Heretics* 36).[25] Nevertheless, from John's own perspective it is God who has set him on Patmos. He has been exiled not so much by any human agency as by the will and intention of God.

Certainly, divine agency is the source of the visions that follow. John writes that he "was in the Spirit on the Lord's day," the day of the resurrection, the day when Christians typically gathered to share the Lord's Supper (1 Cor. 11:20; cf. Ignatius, *Magnesians* 9). Here is another link between John and his audience, who would probably have been hearing the letter on a Lord's day of their own. Even the fact of being "in the Spirit" does not set him apart from them completely. All Christians are possessors of the Spirit, who is poured into the hearts of believers at baptism and who can be said to indwell the body of the church and of each of its members (Gal. 4:6; 1 Cor. 3:16; 6:19). The early church lived and moved in an atmosphere stirred by the Spirit. Nevertheless, the Spirit of prophecy is a specific charism that not all receive. To be "in the Spirit" in this sense is to be rendered ecstatic, transported outside oneself, in such a way that it is the Spirit and not the ego or consciousness that comes to expression (which is not to say that the self simply disappears; John can still say "I, John"; cf. Acts 22:17). Doubtless there are psychological, cultural, and social dimensions at work here; prophecy is among other things a particular mode of human experience. But John has no interest in this side of the matter. It is the word of God and the testimony of Jesus alone

---

24. The phrase "testimony of Jesus" has in principle the same ambiguity as "revelation of Jesus Christ" in 1:1. The genitive can be taken as subjective or as objective. Here, however, it is primarily John's activity of witness that is meant. John's *martyria* shows forth the *martyria* of his Lord.

25. According to Tertullian, this happened only after John had first been boiled in oil, a torture to which the saint miraculously proved to be immune!

that concern him. These are the things he has been called on to suffer, to know, and to speak.

1:11 These things suffered and known begin with the hearing of a voice (1:10). As noted earlier, the Apocalypse is a profoundly acoustical work, full of sounds and voices (a single Greek word covers both: *phōnē*), tongues human and angelic, even natural phenomena such as thunder, waterfalls, and the wings of insects. Above all, it is a book of divine voices. The voice that John now hears has the force of a trumpet blast—perhaps an allusion to the trumpet that sounded when Israel encountered the Lord at Sinai (Exod. 19:16)—and commands him to write what he sees on a scroll and send it to the seven churches, which are here named individually for the first time. Because the voice emanates from somewhere behind him, he must turn around to see who the speaker is. Some literalness in translation is required at this point. John does not write, "I turned to see the one who was speaking to me," as some translations put it,[26] but rather, "I turned to see the *voice* that was speaking to me" (*epestrepsa blepein tēn phōnēn hētis elalei met' emou*; 1:12).

Surely this is more than just an instance of John's faltering command of Greek syntax. The being he turns to see is, to be sure, visible, indeed radiant, and the description of "one like a son of man" that follows is mainly a feast for the eyes. But at the outset John offers a subtle yet important clue to the identity of this figure: he is an embodied voice, a visible word, divine speech rendered in human flesh so as to be seen, heard, and even touched (cf. 1:17). Like other such striking passages in Revelation, this one has a precedent in pre-Christian Judaism: James Charlesworth argues that Jews in this period not only spoke of God's voice as a distinct "person," or hypostasis, but understood the voice as capable of being seen, not unlike the divine glory or *shekinah*.[27] John, then, is not just waxing metaphorical when he speaks of seeing the voice of God. He is telling us that he actually saw it.

1:12–16 While John never states in so many words that the voice visible is Jesus, the meaning is clear. To name him directly would have undercut the drama of the scene. It would also subvert a major purpose of the vision: that of rendering Christ strange to us, bringing the reader/hearer into his awesome presence, and forcing us to confront the unparalleled claim he makes on our lives. Every aspect of the vision in 1:12–16 serves to underscore the glory of Christ. Some of the features (hair white as wool, feet like bronze, eyes like a flame of fire) are drawn from pictures of supernatural beings found in the book of Daniel (Dan. 7; 10). Others (the sharp two-edged sword, voice like the sound of many waters) reflect the language of the great postexilic prophets (Ezek. 1:24; 43:2; Isa. 49:2; cf. Heb. 4:12). The face shining like the sun suggests the transfiguration of

26. So NRSV and New Jerusalem Bible, both of which smooth out the syntax so that the point is lost. The more literal rendering is preserved in KJV, RSV, and ESV.

27. J. H. Charlesworth, "The Jewish Roots of Christology: The Discovery of the Hypostatic Voice," *Scottish Journal of Theology* 39 (1986): 19–41. Psalm 29 draws a close connection between the majestic voice of God, which "breaks the cedars of Lebanon" and "flashes forth flames of fire," and the divine glory or *kabod*. This entire psalm might be read as a kind of hymn to the divine voice.

Christ (2 Pet. 1:16–18; 2 Cor. 4:6). G. B. Caird says that to isolate individual images from this whole and interpret them separately would be to "unweave the rainbow" (1984: 25). This is surely right: the vision is not reducible to a set of propositions, but is meant to be seen; it has the force of what might be called a verbal icon. Sight and speech converge, as John's language reproduces a visionary experience of the divine voice. The blurring of sensory modes adds to the reader's sense of disorientation.

Yet perhaps there is an even more fundamental kind of blurring going on here. The figure who appears to John—is he human or divine? Clearly he is human, anthropomorphic, "one like a son of man" (1:13). But he is also divine: some of the features are drawn from the vision of God as the Ancient of Days in Dan. 7:9–10. To confuse matters still further, there is something undeniably angelic about the figure, for other details reflect the supernatural but clearly nondivine being described in Dan. 10:4–6. While the Christ of the Apocalypse is clearly no angel, being the appropriate object of worship where angels are not (cf. Rev. 19:10; 22:9), it is nonetheless fitting that his *appearance* should be angel-like. Biblical angels stand guard at doors to transcendence. They tend to appear at places where earth and heaven meet. Does John see an angel? Does he see the Lord Jesus, whom early Christians also identified as the Spirit (2 Cor. 3:17)? Does he perhaps see God himself, the divine voice made visible? It is not clear that these are even alternatives.[28] The apocalypsing of Jesus Christ to which John bears witness is an act of God, energized by the Spirit and mediated throughout by angelic messengers. The pneumatic-angelic quality of Christ's appearing is suggested by one of the earliest Christian confessions: "He was manifested in the flesh, vindicated by the Spirit, seen by angels" (1 Tim. 3:16).

But if a divine, pneumatic, and angelic happening, then surely an ecclesial happening as well. Jesus is not only the bearer of the sharp two-edged sword; he stands among the seven golden lampstands and holds the seven stars—symbols, he tells John, for the seven churches and their seven angels (1:20). Like the seven spirits of God, the image of the lampstands comes from Zech. 4. Christ walks among the churches. Even as one who is "coming soon" he is already present among them. The presence of Christ among his people is not, to be sure, a guarantee of their obedience, much less a human bargaining chip: in Rev. 2:5 we will see that Christ is perfectly capable of removing a church's lampstand, but for now, the image is one of comfort and affirmation.

28. Boring, "Voice of Jesus in the Apocalypse of John," 351, writes: "If a Christian prophet had used a formula like 'Thus says the Lord,' who would have understood 'the Lord' to be? Since God/Christ/Spirit collapse into an experienced unity, no one of these is an alternative answer that excludes the others. There is a kind of 'Trinitarianism' here, but it is of a phenomenological and experiential kind, not a matter of theological reflection." Boring goes on to point out that while the mediating angel is part of the overall "gestalt" of Revelation, we should resist seeing him as a "fourth" alongside God, Christ, and the Spirit. The angel is medium, not message.

In the long tradition of artistic depictions of Revelation, one of the more common subjects is that of Christ surrounded by the lampstands—for example, the second woodcut in Albrecht Dürer's famous *Apocalypse* series. In contrast to Hieronymos Bosch, Dürer sets the seer in the clouds, where he kneels before Christ, enthroned upon the rainbow. The Lord is surrounded by the seven lamps, which circle him like planets. He holds the seven sparkling stars in his right hand and an open book in his left. A quite literal sword proceeds from the mouth of Christ.[29] The figure is one of complete majesty. It could not be clearer that the churches are dependent on Christ, not Christ upon them.

As for the seven stars, this is a good example of explanations in Revelation being more puzzling than the things they purport to explain. What does Christ mean when he says that the stars are "the angels of the seven churches"? Both ancient and modern commentators sometimes interpreted the angels as bishops or at least ecclesiastics; sixteenth-century Reformer Heinrich Bullinger called them "messengers, ministers, and pastors" (Kovacs and Rowland 2004: 53). But this seems a fairly earthbound reading of the image. Surely the proper move is to connect the seven angels with the seven spirits of God (1:4). Just as the Spirit was distributed among the apostles at Pentecost like tongues of fire (Acts 2:3) and bestows a diversity of gifts upon the church (1 Cor. 12:4–11), so Revelation depicts the Spirit as essentially pluriform. Each church receives the Spirit in its own way, in accordance with its peculiar angel, character, or *genius loci*.[30] This is an ecclesiological point of some importance. Because the church is a creaturely reality, located in time, history, and culture, there is a proper sense in which different churches receive the gospel differently. This points to the catholicity of the church, its embrace of genuine, Spirit-created particularity within a common love and devotion to Jesus Christ. Churches are neither all the same (integralism) nor merely different (pluralism), but joined in a communion that is one, holy, catholic, and apostolic.

1:17–20 John responds to the heavenly figure by falling down at his feet "as though dead"—literally, "like a dead man." It is a pattern acted out many times in the Bible: to meet God is to die (Deut. 4:33; 5:23–27; cf. Luke 5:8). Fragile, corrupt human flesh is no match for the holiness, glory, and majesty of the living God. To encounter God as such is to have one's world shattered. This is an undeniable

29. Dürer might be faulted for his absurdly literal representation of this sword, the hilt of which seems attached directly to Christ' lips. Alternately, he might be praised for retrieving the strangeness and wildness of the image of the "harp two-edged sword," thus reasserting the sovereignty of Christ as the Word of God. To treat the metaphor as mere trope would only weaken it. See my comments on the image of the Lamb, p. 88.

30. In Roman literature, this phrase refers to the "spirit of the place," the god who watches over it. A parallel may perhaps be found in New Testament passages that seem to assume the existence of guardian angels. When Peter miraculously escapes from prison in Acts 12, the frightened community at first think that they are seeing his "angel." In Matt. 18:10, Jesus speaks of the angels of "these little ones" who stand in God's presence in heaven. If individuals are typified by their angels, why not churches?

aspect of the biblical witness, but so is its counterpart, that what God wills for the creature is life and peace. And so Christ's next words to John are "Fear not!" Christ is a servant not of death, but of life; indeed, he *is* life itself: "I am the first and the last, the living one. I died, and behold I am alive forevermore, and I have the keys of Death and Hades" (Rev. 1:17–18).

The words "the first and the last" echo God's own self-designation as "Alpha and Omega" (1:8). Jesus is life because he participates in the perfection, creativity, and overflowing generosity of God. But when this divine life enters history it takes on the character of a conflict, contending with and overcoming the power of death. It is important to grasp, writes Bruce Marshall, that the words "dead" and "lives" in this verse "have their usual meanings; the astonishment lies in conjoining them in this sequence—in saying that there is a temporal point at which 'lives' may rightly be applied to this person which follows the point at which 'is dead' may rightly be applied to him."[31] No wonder Christ holds the keys of death and hades! His resurrection from the dead clearly shows that he is Lord over death, life, angels, rulers, and all other heavenly and earthly powers (cf. Rom. 8:37–39).

In his famous work on Dostoevsky, Mikhail Bakhtin argues that the Russian novelist was a master of polyphony, creating characters whose voices are genuinely "other" to each other and who therefore convey something of the drama of human, historical existence. Dostoevsky's people do not play out a preordained script. They discover who they are and what choices confront them only through event, encounter, and dialogue. They are creatures of history, drawn out of their self-enclosure by the voices of others.[32]

Bakhtin's notion of polyphony may serve as a parable of the divine voice that meets us in the Apocalypse. Contrary to what we might expect, that voice does not present us with a divine *fait accompli* to which earthly reality must simply conform. It encounters us as a person, Jesus the Son of Man, whose voice, coming as it were from behind us, forces us to turn around, to listen to what he has to say, to hear his voice along with those of the almighty Father and the Spirit of prophecy. There is but one God, and one Word of God, and yet precisely as his *trinitarian* Word it refuses to be conscripted into the way we would narrate our own and the world's story. The origins of the church reside in an act of profound listening.

31. Bruce D. Marshall, *Trinity and Truth* (Cambridge: Cambridge University Press, 2000), 128.

32. Mikhail Bakhtin, *Problems of Dostoevsky's Poetics*, ed. and trans. Caryl Emerson (Minneapolis: University of Minnesota Press, 1984), 5–47.

REVELATION 2–3

THE CHURCHES OF ASIA

And when this letter has been read among you, have it also read in the church of the Laodiceans; and see that you also read the letter from Laodicea.

—Colossians 4:16

When the loyal citizen of Pergamus looked up at his Acropolis, he saw above him, and unquestioningly accepted, the temple of Augustus and Roma. But the seer of the Apocalypse could tell the Church of Pergamus: "I know where thou dwellest, where the seat of Satan is" (Apoc. 2:13). He saw more than the citizen.

—Heinrich Schlier, *Principalities and Powers in the New Testament*

While the opening vision in Rev. 1 is impressive enough, it is clear that it is really only a preamble to what follows, a commissioning scene in which Christ appears to John and commands him to write. The opening words of the book promise a revelation from Jesus Christ. What follows—the letters to the seven churches—is that revelation. The letters are not, as might be thought, a mere set of practical instructions, or even a "theology of the church," to be followed by the truly apocalyptic visions beginning in Rev. 4. No, we now find ourselves *in media res*. While the letters to the churches do not exhaust the revelation of Jesus, there is, nevertheless, a sense in which the whole event is organically contained in this one part. By the end of these messages the Christians of Asia Minor know everything they need to know in order to become victors. There is much more still to come, of course; and yet there is no going beyond these messages. They show the Lord's own presence in the midst of the *ekklēsia*.

We are still on Patmos, and the discourse of Jesus in Rev. 2–3 is continuous with his speech to John in the opening vision. He is dictating the letters to John—Bosch depicts the seer with pen in hand, ready to write—who records them on the scroll, presumably in the great uncial characters typical of Greek manuscripts of the day (ΑΠΟΚΑΛΥΨΙΣ ΙΗΣΟΥ ΧΡΙΣΤΟΥ). By contrast with the heavenly ascent starting in 4:1 this is still a relatively this-worldly setting, defined by the horizontal coordinates of Asia Minor and its coastal islands. Patmos, Ephesus, Smyrna, Pergamum, Thyatira, Sardis, Philadelphia, Laodicea—these are not fictional but real places, locatable on any map of the ancient Mediterranean world.

That John should have written a letter to these communities was nothing extraordinary, given the common practice of sharing and exchanging letters in the early church. A letter may have been explicitly written as a circular letter, or an author may have asked that his letter to a given community be passed along to others, as Col. 4:16 indicates. The literary peculiarity of the Apocalypse is that it contains seven specific messages for individual communities, each of which would have been heard by all the others (Bauckham 1993b: 12–17). Revelation thus combines the pointedness and personal character of, say, 1 Corinthians or Galatians with the catholic reach of Paul's letters to the Romans or the Ephesians. It is local and universal at the same time. Just as, in a city like Toronto, "the church" encompasses everything from St. Michael's Cathedral to the poorest storefront assembly, so the churches of Asia share much in common culturally and geographically, while yet being very different from each other. It does not take much experience of church life to know that congregations have their own unique histories, dynamics, and communal spirits ("angels" again). This will not have been any different in the first century.

The word "church" is an analogous term that may be applied on at least three different levels of ecclesial reality: (1) the local assembly of believers gathered around the word of God and the sacrament, (2) the universal church consisting of all the baptized, at a given time or across time, and (3) hovering between these, such regional groupings as may promote the church's unity and mission in particular areas. The Apocalypse speaks to all three of these levels.

That John is concerned with universality can be seen in his writing to precisely seven churches, seven being the number of fullness or completion. This point was recognized early on by commentators, for example, Victorinus writing in the late second century:

> Those seven stars are the seven churches, which he names in his addresses by name, and calls them to whom he wrote epistles. Not that they are themselves the only, or even the principal churches; but what he says to one, he says to all. For they are in no respect different, that on that ground any one should prefer them to the larger number of similar small ones. In the whole world Paul taught that all the churches are arranged by sevens, that they are called seven, and that the Catholic Church is one. And first of all, indeed, that he himself also might maintain the type of seven churches, he did not exceed that number. But he wrote to the Romans, to

the Corinthians, to the Galatians, to the Ephesians, to the Thessalonians, to the Philippians, to the Colossians; afterwards he wrote to individual persons, so as not to exceed the number of seven churches. (*Commentary on the Apocalypse* 1.16, quoted from ANF 7.345)

Besides being significant in itself, it may also be important that seven is the sum of four plus three, numbers that have their own mystical meanings in the Apocalypse. In John's numerology three is the number of God, while four is the number of creation. These come together in Jesus Christ, who unites God and creation in himself, and whose mission to all the nations of the earth is provisionally displayed in the *ekklēsia*.

At the level of the regional church, it is significant that Revelation is addressed first of all to "the seven churches that are in Asia" (1:4), a designation that precedes their being named individually (1:11). For all their differences, the churches share a life in common. They are located "in Asia," a region to the east of the Aegean Sea once ruled by the Seleucid kings but, by the time of John's writing, a Roman province for over a century. We can visualize this by imagining the circular route the lector would have followed in delivering John's letter. As commentators often note, the seven cities named form a rough circuit, beginning with the port city of Ephesus, proceeding upward along the coast to Smyrna and Pergamum, and then heading inland to Thyatira, Sardis, Philadelphia, and Laodicea. But this circle is more than simply a question of geography or Roman postal roads. While the assembly in each city may previously have been tempted to go it alone, seeing itself as a self-sufficient path to salvation or doorway into the sacred mysteries, such an identity is no longer an option. Even if the churches previously had little in common, the fact of their being addressed together by Christ renders them mutually accountable, giving each an interest in the lives of the others. Just what this means concretely can be discovered only as they engage the tasks to which all and each are summoned. Only Ephesus and Pergamum were threatened by the Nicolaitan teaching, only Thyatira had to deal with Jezebel, but these problems are the other churches' problems too. What he says to one, he says to all.

Finally we come to the individual assemblies, the *ekklēsiai* as such. The formula at the head of each letter identifies the churches by the cities in which they are located: "in Philadelphia," "in Laodicea," and so forth; a similar formula is employed by Paul (cf. 1 Cor. 1:2; Phil. 1:1).[1] The church is merely "in" these places. It is not qualified by them adjectivally. Strictly speaking there can be no "American

1. In 1961 the New Delhi Assembly of the World Council of Churches declared: "We believe that the unity which is both God's will and his gift to his Church is being made visible as *all in each place* who are baptized into Jesus Christ and confess him as Lord and Saviour are brought by the Holy Spirit into one fully committed fellowship"; "The New Delhi Report: The Third Assembly of the World Council of Churches, 1961" (London: SCM, 1962), 121 (emphasis added). Of course, concepts like "local" and "each place" are themselves ecumenically contested: does "local" mean the individual congregation or the diocese under its bishop?

church" or "Canadian church," any more than there could be a church composed of "German Christians" in the 1930s. There is only the Christian community as it is gathered in these particular geographical and cultural settings. "The Resurrection has proved its power: there are Christians—even in Rome."[2] But before there were Christians in Rome, there were Christians in Ephesus and the cities of Asia Minor. Now they, too, are being caught up in the *apokalypsis* of God in Jesus Christ.

There are seven particular letters, differing from each other in terms of content, length, and especially the tone that Christ adopts in addressing each church. Some churches are blamed, others are praised, while still others seem to be a mix of good and bad. Bauckham reminds us that these differences should serve as a caution against making sweeping generalizations about the Apocalypse, like the common notion that it functions mainly as consolation for persecuted Christians (1993b: 15). The problem with at least some churches is not that they are suffering tribulation but that they are *not* suffering it. I again cite Victorinus, who shrewdly notes that the book's addressees include not only "those who dwell in cruel places among persecutors, [so] that they should continue faithful," but also "those that are at ease in the Church . . . those who are negligent, and Christians only in name" (*Commentary on the Apocalypse* 1.16, quoted from ANF 7.346). Being the church of God is never just one thing. While it is the same Lord who apocalypses himself into each church's reality, he does so as the Lord of *this* community in *this* place and under *this* set of historical circumstances.

Contrary to some overly theorized accounts of the church in modern Protestantism, the church is not an occasional, purely eventlike reality—though no doubt the Spirit's activity *within* the church must be thought of as "eventful." It lives in a specific matrix of history, culture, and tradition. As such it requires institutional structure so that the gospel may be passed along intact and believers formed from one generation to the next. This is the grain of truth in the idea, mentioned in the previous chapter, that the "angels" of the seven churches are in fact their leaders, those charged with responsibility for the communities' well-being. There is such a thing as apostolic succession in teaching, a fact that Revelation itself seems to acknowledge (cf. 21:14).

But while this form of ecclesial continuity is necessary, it is not sufficient. Taken in isolation, it will lead to a one-sidedly christological picture of the church's life, in the form of either hyperinstitutionalism (in its Roman Catholic form) or hyperdoctrinalism (in its classic Protestant form)—developments that will call forth in turn a one-sidedly charismatic reaction (revivalism, spiritualism, and the individualism that marks so much of modern Christianity). Robert Jenson writes: "If Christ and the Spirit are not experienced in the *mutuality* of their ecclesially

2. Karl Barth, *The Epistle to the Romans*, trans. Edwyn C. Hoskyns (Oxford: Oxford University Press, 1933), 32.

founding roles, neither will the church's institutions and her charismatic reality be seen in their proper congruence."[3]

"To the *angel* of the church in Ephesus write." No doubt the churches have their bishops, or at least their presbyters/elders; elders will play a major role in the heavenly worship described in Rev. 4–5. Yet the identity of each church is also a function of the one Spirit. The seven angels of the churches clearly correspond to the seven spirits of God. On the one hand, to say that each church has its own angel is to say that each has its own unique character, its "spirit," that which makes it just *this* community and no other. Jenson again: "A community's spirit is the liveliness that blows through it, the freedom in which it is more than the sum of its parts because each member moves in the liberating impetus from all the others."[4] On the other hand, such communal spirit is not self-generating or self-sustaining. It derives from the Spirit of God, who according to Revelation is himself pluriform, creating difference in ways that make our self-conscious efforts at pluralism seem clumsy and forced by comparison.

The historical character of the church always renders its identity problematic, in large part because its members are always trying to turn it into something else: mystery cult, nationalist ideology, self-help group, political action committee. This renders necessary the existence of such continuity-enabling structures as the scriptural canon and the teaching office in its various forms. The pastoral office, the episcopacy, the peculiar ministry exercised by the bishop of Rome—are all aspects of such structures, which Christians believe are not simply bits and pieces of human improvisation but divine gifts. But by themselves, they do not constitute the church's identity. The church's ontology is angelic in the sense that it is a creaturely reality (angels are creatures) who yet moves in a heavenly milieu, a community whose atmosphere is permeated by the seven spirits of God. The church is what it is by virtue of the Father's gift, the Son's word of address, and the Spirit's enlivening power.

The seven letters all follow a common pattern. All include a naming of the addressee ("to the angel of the church at ____ write") followed by a specific designation of Jesus, in most cases drawn from the opening vision of the Son of Man. Then comes the body of the letter, praising the church for its faithfulness or admonishing it for its shortcomings. Then comes an admonishment to "hear what the Spirit says to the churches," followed by a promise made to "the one who conquers." The only variation is that in the last four letters the final two items are reversed, so that the promise precedes the call to heed the Spirit. John has a habit of dividing his sevens into groups of four and three; this is the first of several examples (Barr 1998: 42). The common pattern underscores the unity of the seven churches, at the same time making it easier to detect the differences

3. Robert W. Jenson, *Systematic Theology* (New York: Oxford University Press, 1999), 2.181.
4. Ibid., 181.

between them. Moreover, the strict use of a common form serves to underscore the solemnity of these messages. These are letters, but they are not *only* letters. David Aune argues that from a form-critical perspective the closest analogy is the imperial decree—an appropriate analog, given that the one who speaks is the one who "holds the seven stars in his right hand," an image of cosmic rule.[5] Christ speaks these messages into the churches not only that they may be heard but so that they may be obeyed.

So far, I have tried to provide a synoptic overview of the letters. But now it is time to hear the letters the way they would have been heard in the assembly— serially, as a word addressed to each of the churches in turn and to all of them together. There is a terrible intimacy about these communications, the impact of which must not be blunted or domesticated by overanalysis. What, then, is the Spirit saying to the churches?

2:1–7 In the letter to Ephesus, Christ identifies himself as the one "who holds the seven stars" and "who walks among the seven golden lampstands." This is in some ways the simplest and the most basic such identification. Jesus is the Lord of the church. He is in it, with it, moving among it; the participle *peripatōn* ("walking") suggests that he is not simply seated in place (as in Dürer's woodcut) but actively circulating among the communities. His first words to the Ephesian church are "I know your works." The words "I know" (*oida*) are a constant refrain in the letters. Jesus knows these communities, in the deep biblical sense of "know"; indeed he knows them far better than they know themselves. Thus we hear in John's Gospel that Jesus "needed no one to testify about any person, for he himself knew what was in that person" (John 2:25, my translation). No doubt what makes the letters disturbing is that they are exercises in truth-telling by the true witness, who brings the hidden things of the churches into the clear light of day.

But what Christ knows are the *works* of this church. In the Apocalypse, works matter. This church has labored on Christ's behalf, and it has suffered much at the hands of a group falsely calling itself "apostles." The impression conveyed by this letter is of a community that has both worked hard and been beaten down, as implied by the repeated use of words for suffering—enduring (twice), bearing (twice), testing—but despite all this, they "have not grown weary." Both in its actions and in its suffering the church is a community of works; it hastens toward the end, even as it patiently waits for it. The church in Ephesus is in this sense a model church.

There is a striking concentration of "love" vocabulary in the letters to the seven churches. Christ's love for the church, first mentioned in the opening doxology (1:5), is referred to again in the last two messages (to Philadelphia [3:9] and Laodicea [3:19]). In both of the latter two instances, the word appears on the lips of Christ himself. Within this rough bracket we find two references to the church's

5. David Aune, "The Form and Function of the Proclamations to the Seven Churches (Revelation 2–3)," *New Testament Studies* 36 (1990): 182–204.

love for Christ, once in our present passage and then again at 2:19.[6] The theme of love—like "grace" and "peace," terms not often associated with Revelation—is in fact determinative for understanding the seven letters, as indeed the book as a whole. Christ loves the *ekklēsia* (Eph. 5:25), as God loved and loves Israel. He yearns to have that love returned. While love is not opposed to works—indeed, Rev. 2:4–5 suggests that love will express itself precisely in active form—those works will be pleasing to God only to the extent that they are offered up as acts of devotion, gestures of love to the one who loves us. Our orthodoxy will not save us, our traditions will not save us, our soup kitchens and our social programs will not save us; what will save the church is Christ, whose self-giving cannot but call forth a similar response on the part of his people. Evidently the church in Ephesus once manifested this love, but its passion has cooled, with the inevitable result that it has begun to turn away from Christ toward other concerns. This is why it is urgent that they repent, turning back to "the love you had at first."

The alternative to such repentance is stark: Christ threatens to remove this church's lampstand from its place. The church itself, to be sure, will continue; it is just that this particular human community will no longer be a part of it. It will merge back into the general social milieu of which it is a part and will no longer deserve the name *ekklēsia*. This fate is, so to say, analytic: the church's calling is to be a shining lamp in the world, the light of Christ, and if it no longer loves him how can it fulfill this mission? His removing of the church's lamp will only set a divine seal on an event that has already occurred. Thankfully things have not yet reached this point. This church's lamp, like its love, has not gone out entirely. If it had, the church would hardly be opposed to "the works of the Nicolaitans" (2:6), a group whose teachings are lost in the mists of ancient history; our only source of knowledge about them is what we find in Revelation.[7] Whatever their error may have been, the salient thing here is that love for Christ entails the denial of all false teaching and practice. The yes of the gospel sometimes requires us to say no.[8]

What can the Ephesian Christians expect if they rekindle their love? Nothing less than life itself. Christ promises those who conquer the right "to eat of the tree of life, which is in the paradise of God," an obvious allusion to Gen. 2–3. We will not hear of this tree again until the very end of Revelation (22:2, 14, 19). Here we learn that the way to it involves being a conqueror, a victor, a term that as yet remains vague and undefined; we will not really understand what it means until

6. A note on semantics: John's primary verb for love is *agapaō* (1:5; 2:4, 19; 3:9; 12:11; 20:9). In two instances he employs *phileō* (3:19; 22:15). There is no apparent difference in meaning between the two verbs, as indicated by both being used to describe Christ's love for the church (3:9, 19).

7. It is possible that the name is purely symbolic. It means "conqueror of people," and it is possible that John intends it as an analog to the Hebrew name "Balaam," meaning "Lord of the people," in 2:14 (see Caird 1984: 31; Barr 1998: 50). Balaam's sin was cultural syncretism; is the implication that this is true of the Nicolaitans as well?

8. An entire theological textbook has been organized around this point. See Christopher Morse, *Not Every Spirit: A Dogmatics of Christian Disbelief* (New York: Trinity, 1994).

we have read the entire book. For now all we know is that the tree of life is the gift of the Lord of life, who holds us in his hand like the seven stars.

2:8–11 The word to Smyrna is the shortest of the letters, disproportionate to the city itself, which was among the great seaports of the Mediterranean world. And yet it says a great deal in a few lines. The message opens with Christ introducing himself as the one "who died and came to life," and it closes with the promise of the crown of life. While the theme of life connects it with the letter to Ephesus, the circumstances described seem to be very different. Here the threat to the church's existence is not the cooling of love toward Christ, but external forces—the Jewish community on the one hand, Satan on the other—and the first is depicted as an agent of the second: "a synagogue of Satan." At first reading this might seem like an especially vicious example of Christian supersessionism, in which the (literally) demonized Jews are replaced by the "true" synagogue, the church.

This flat reading of the text is to be resisted, however. In the last half of the first century, the familiar power-relations of Christians and Jews were exactly reversed: Jews were the established, accepted group within the Roman Empire, while Christians—at first just another Jewish sect—had only lately arrived on the scene. Moreover, in this context being a "Jew" is considered *desirable*. The rivalry between the synagogue and the Jewish-Gentile church is a contest over who gets to bear the name "Jew," along with the even more fundamental name "Israel." Synagogue and church alike are still in the process of emerging out of the disastrous destruction of Jerusalem by the Romans. Each was still trying to figure out what it meant to be God's people in this new situation. The synagogue's answer to the destruction of the temple was devotion to Torah. The church's answer was adherence to Jesus Christ. Both traditions were "portable" in that they did not require a single, fixed site of religious observance.

But in the meantime, the communities were locked in conflict; and in this conflict the synagogue had the advantage, because Judaism was an established cult with certain rights acknowledged by the empire, whereas this was not so with Christianity. In this situation, one can easily imagine that in a conflict between the Christians and the civic authorities the Jews might have sided with the representatives of the *polis*. Seeing the followers of Jesus as a heretical sect, the Jews likely felt little obligation to come to their aid. The situation in Smyrna was rapidly deteriorating; John foresees a time in the near future when some members of the church will be thrown into prison "for ten days."[9] Who else could be the agent behind such evil, if not Satan himself? And if the local Jews were aiding and abetting the church's enemies, were they not "a synagogue of Satan"?

This, at least, is one possible reading of the background of the letter to Smyrna. The Jews criticized as the devil's agents are not Jews in general, and certainly not Jews living today, but particular Jews living in Smyrna at the time John writes.

9. Bauckham 1993a: 263n35 wryly remarks: "Anyone who doubts that all the time-periods in Revelation are symbolic should consider 2:10 and 17:12."

This is hardly a developed theology of supersessionism. Indeed, by the standards of passages like Matt. 27:25 and Acts 7:51–53 it is even rather mild.

Far more interesting is the way this letter imagines a "good church." A good church is one that has not lost its first love. But at least for the Christians in Smyrna, the proving of this love takes place as they are willing to be "poor" for Christ's sake. The good church is the poor church, the suffering church, the church that, far from being in control of its life and fate, experiences apocalyptic tribulation (*thlipsis*). These are Revelation's "marks of the church." They put us in mind of the Sermon on the Mount: "Blessed are you who are poor. . . . Blessed are you who weep. . . . Blessed are you when people hate you . . . and revile you" (Luke 6:20–22). But to be poor in *this* sense is to be rich in the eyes of God (Rev. 2:9).

For this reason, the community in Smyrna should not fear what they are about to suffer. If there is a troubling aspect to this letter it may well be the little word *hina* ("in order that") in 2:10: "The devil is about to throw some of you into prison, *that* you may be tested." We must be careful not to spin whole theories about God as the cause of evil out of this one verse. Rather, Christ here seeks to affirm God's providential care for his people in the midst of, in spite of, and even through the actions of those arrayed against them. The powers cannot help but serve God's sanctifying of his church—admittedly a hard saying, especially for those on the receiving end of such "sanctification."[10]

Like the letter to the church in Ephesus, this one, too, is marked by the radical opposition between death and life. There, what was promised to the victor was the tree of life. Here, the prize is the crown of life, which will be bestowed upon whoever is "faithful unto death"; the adjective *pistos* forges a link between Christ's faithfulness (1:5) and that of the Christian (2:10). Faithfulness unto physical death will deliver one from the terror of the second death, the spiritual condition that Vernard Eller denotes as "second-order DEATH" (1974: 57).

2:12–17 The tone of the letter to the church at Pergamum is signaled from the outset, when Christ identifies himself as the one "who has the sharp two-edged sword." This letter is truly a wartime communication, a summons to do battle with enemies both without and within. Pergamum was a beautiful city, built on a steep mountain and with a palace and fortifications on its acropolis. It was home to the cult of Asklepios, the god of healing, and even had a sanatorium or spa devoted to him. On the heights of the acropolis one could see magnificent temples honoring Athena and Zeus,[11] and from AD 29 onward there was also a shrine dedicated to Emperor Augustus. One imagines Pergamum as being a

10. That the suffering of God's people should be, at the same time, their sanctification may be taken as a core conviction of the New Testament. See, e.g., Rom. 5:1–5; 1 Pet. 1:3–9; 4:12.

11. The altar to Zeus has long been identified with the magnificent altar excavated by German archeologists in the nineteenth century and later reconstructed in Berlin's Pergamon Museum. I have a happy memory of seeing this altar while living in Berlin in the early 1980s. Although the identification is not certain, the scale and grandeur of this altar provides a sense of the solidity and power of the religious world in which the first-century Christian community found itself.

city of extraordinary presence, combining political importance with cultural and religious power.

But Christ says to his *ekklēsia* in Pergamum: "I know where you dwell, where Satan's throne is" (2:13). The Christian community in Pergamum is not to be in awe of this splendid city. They know the truth about it: it is where "Satan's throne" is. This is not an arbitrary judgment. It is not based on John's hatred of Roman culture, the way radical Muslims are sometimes said to hate "our way of life." It is based on real evidence. For what the Christians in Smyrna only fear—harassment, imprisonment, death—has already happened in Pergamum: "Yet you hold fast my name, and you did not deny my faith even in the days of Antipas my faithful witness, who was killed among you, where Satan dwells."

Again we encounter the theme of death, but this time it is an actual death, of a certain Antipas, a Christian martyr known only from this passage. "Even" in the days of Antipas (meaning, when things were worse than they are now), the church in Pergamum did not waver in its confession of the faith. Moreover, the crisis is not yet past. The system that sent Antipas to his death is still firmly in place: this is perhaps why John lays such emphasis on the word "dwells" (*katoikei*) in 2:13—to denote both the dwelling of Christians and the dwelling of Satan. The persecution that killed Antipas was no accident. Satan "dwells" in Pergamum, he inhabits its leaders, structures, and institutions. Those who have killed Christians once will kill again if it suits their interests.

Like the church in Smyrna, then, this is very much a good church, but it is not perfect. While it has passed the big test, it is failing in what might at first seem to be a much smaller test: the question of food sacrificed to idols. One group argues that participation in the pagan meat market is nothing to get worked up about. Perhaps they base their arguments on Paul's teaching that, since the pagan gods are not really real, they are doing nothing wrong when they engage in such practices (1 Cor. 8–9; Rom. 14). John identifies this party with the figure of Balaam, who in Jewish tradition had become the type of the faithless prophet who practiced divination for his own gain (Num. 22:21–35; Josh. 13:22; 24:9; Neh. 13:2; 2 Pet. 2:15; Jude 11).

It is one thing to resist the temptation to apostasy in the midst of crisis, when the battle lines are clearly drawn and when taking a heroic stand may even win praise and admiration. It is another thing to resist when life is comfortable and when things are going well. The challenge faced by the church in Pergamum seems to have been of the latter sort. Satan dwelt in Pergamum as part of a permanent, subtle, and highly ramified system of power; his corrupting influence poisoned the air and fouled the water; the city and all its institutions were "Satan's throne." In this situation, it was necessary to cultivate those habits that would allow the church to continue resisting over the long haul. Concretely, this means avoiding meat sacrificed to idols. A comparison with Paul is instructive: while Paul may have sympathized with the "strong" party in Corinth, he urged this group to let their behavior be dictated by the "weak," whose consciences forbade them from participating in the pagan sacrifices. While Paul's attitude is often contrasted with the more severe policy advocated in the Apocalypse, I am not at all sure that Paul would have disapproved of what John commands his hearers, especially since it is not John doing the commanding, but Jesus Christ!

The apparently intense struggle over this issue in the early church recalls the teaching about the so-called *casus/status confessionis* ("case/situation of confession", i.e., confession of the true faith) at the time of the Reformation. According to this idea, practices that might at least be considered tolerable in particular situations, things *adiaphora* or indifferent, could in another situation make the difference between witnessing to the gospel and obscuring it in the here and now. Sixteenth-century examples include such matters as Catholic vestments and ceremonies: it was argued that while these did not in themselves compromise the Reformers' teaching on justification, holding on to them might trouble the consciences of weaker members of the community, who might not be capable of making such fine distinctions.

In the case of the church in Pergamum, it is not a question of discerning whether the practice of eating meat from the market constitutes an emergency requiring extraordinary measures. The emergency already exists. The scandal or stumbling block has already proved the undoing of some in the community (2:14). The situation is, we might say, so inherently unstable that to draw a less strict boundary between church and world would give a false picture of the situation. The matter is at any rate not to be left to the church's own theological or prudential judgment. It is Christ who holds the sharp two-edged sword, and he has already decided. For the foreseeable future, *everyone* in Pergamum is the "weak."

One of the simpler lessons to be drawn from this message is that the food one eats and the people one eats with really do matter. To eat is always to commune, whether with the meal or with one's table companion. But it may also mean to commune with the god (1 Cor. 10:21). Eating establishes an intimacy not unlike sex. This is why John can call eating meat sacrificed to idols a kind of "sexual immorality" (*porneuō*), even if there was nothing directly sexual about the practice itself. In our own day we use the phrase "sleeping with the enemy" to describe being co-opted or manipulated by one's adversary. That is how the Apocalypse wants its readers to regard the question of idol meat. It is that important.

The alternative to communion with the idol is communion with God and with Christ. The promise in this letter combines the image of food (the hidden manna) with that of a mysterious white stone, on which is written a name that "no one knows except the one who receives it." White in Revelation always signifies victory, while name signifies character, identity, the final reckoning that says of a person "this is who you are." But in this apocalyptic setting, identity is achieved by suffering in the name of Christ. The archetype of such identity is Antipas, "my faithful witness," who comes to bear the name that Jesus himself bears (cf.

1:5). It is fitting that he should be the only named disciple in the entire book of Revelation.[12]

2:18–29 The letter to the church in Thyatira is the longest of the seven letters.[13] Its christological frame highlights the question of power or rule: the flaming eyes and bronze feet of Christ identify him as a lordly figure, and at the end of the letter he promises the victors that they will rule the nations with a rod of iron. The same thing will later be said about the Messiah himself (12:5).

Once we look inside this frame, however, we see that the church in Thyatira is a divided people, with perhaps three major factions. One group follows the teachings of a certain female prophet,[14] who takes the more tolerant position in the controversy over meat sacrificed to idols. John calls her "Jezebel"—a not-so-subtle hint that she is an idolater like her namesake (1 Kgs. 16:29–34). A second group is composed of those who, while not Jezebel's disciples, are at least willing to put up with her (Rev. 2:20). A third group not only does not hold this teaching, but further refuses to practice "the deep things of Satan" (2:24).

This last phrase suggests that what is going on in Thyatira is more complex than just the debate over where to buy tonight's supper. It is a matter of knowledge, of the Spirit (Jezebel is a prophet like John), of having deep insight into the things not only of God but of Satan. The church is always tempted to imagine that it knows more than its Lord. Christianity so often seems flat and uninspired, a simple faith for simple people. The kind of "esoteric Christianity" that seeks to go beyond Jesus into the realm of spirit and gnosis will always be appealing to some—especially if this sophisticated theology is coupled with a tolerant ethics, which does not require that we distinguish ourselves overmuch from the life of the city.

3:1–6 The letter to the church at Sardis opens with a reminder of what the church truly is: it is the community held and sustained by Christ, the living one, who breathes the life-giving Spirit upon his people. As such it is a community whose very essence is defined by life. But if this is so, then the church at Sardis stands in complete contradiction to itself: "You have the reputation [literally, 'name'] of being alive, but you are dead" (3:1). Could there be a more savage indictment of a Christian church?

The church at Sardis *seems* alive. Everyone shows up on Sunday morning. Sermons are preached, the sacraments are celebrated, instruction is given. Perhaps there is even a charismatic group that loudly advertises its aliveness in the Spirit. Yet all this activity masks the essential fact that what seems like life is, in fact, a kind of death. Christ's evaluation of this church differs radically from the community's own self-evaluation: "I know the character of your works, you Christians of Sardis; but you, evidently, do not."

---

12. Assuming, of course, that "Jezebel" is not the real name of the woman in the letter to follow.

13. Lydia, Paul's first convert at Philippi, was from Thyatira (Acts 16:14–15). She is said to be a "worshiper of God," implying the existence of a Jewish community there.

14. The translation is precise: the feminine form of the Greek word for "prophet" is used here.

What is lacking in a church like Sardis is not the objective indicators of ecclesiality, such as the word, sacraments, doctrine, apostolic succession—all these may very well be in place. Especially since the Reformation, when the question "where is the true church?" has become more and more pressing, theologians have been inclined to come up with lists of the *nota ecclesiae*, the notes or marks that allow us to identify a given community as the church of Jesus Christ. This is not a vain exercise. In a given context I may precisely need to know whether a community proclaims the gospel and faithfully performs the sacraments, or whether it sets forth "another gospel." Moreover, such discernment will inevitably have a public, institutional dimension, whether with respect to teaching standards or to the bonds of life in covenant ("are they in communion with the bishop of Rome? with the see of Canterbury?" etc.).

There is no indication that false teaching is even an issue in Sardis, however. This community is not devoid of the means of grace. What is lacking is that it does not *use* these means. What it has "received and heard," it does not "keep" (3:3). In the absence of a lively communion with the Lord of life, the church is on the point of becoming dead. What exactly was going on in Sardis remains obscure, of course, and yet this obscurity is to our benefit. Rather than seeking to discern what was happening behind the text, this letter (like all the letters) invites present-day churches to ask themselves whether their impressive human appearance masks a radical deficiency "in the sight of my God" (3:2).

If the church in Sardis is not dead yet, this is at least partly the result of there being a small group within it, a remnant, that has not yet lost its passion. The question arises as to the status of this group. Jacques Ellul is surely right when he comments that "this remnant cannot endure for long by itself as such. It is not *itself* the church. It cannot survive if the church is not reconstituted. . . . A group faithful to the heart of the church does not survive indefinitely if the latter does not become truly the church" (1977: 136, emphasis original). Here is at once the promise and the danger of all renewal movements. Their existence is justified precisely to the extent that they live *pro ecclesia*, for the good of the entire church. To the extent that they seek a private salvation on their own terms, they will suffer the same fate as everyone else.

3:7–13 The church in Philadelphia forms a striking contrast to its immediate predecessor. As was the case with the church in Smyrna, Christ has nothing but good things to say about this community. He introduces himself to it as "the holy one, the true one, who has the key of David, who opens and no one will shut, who shuts and no one opens."[15] This is one of the few ascriptions of Christ in the letters not drawn from the opening vision. It gestures forward to the "open door" that John himself will pass through in 4:1, the door that joins earth to heaven and that leads into God's own presence. Christ alone can open this door, and for the Philadelphia church he does open it.

15. The image is taken from Isa. 22:22. These words form part of the famous "O Antiphons," a set of ascriptions to Christ traditionally employed in the Advent season.

Why? What makes this church especially worthy of his love? Simply its having "little power." It is striking that the two churches about which Jesus has nothing bad to say are both marked by the virtue of poverty (cf. 2:9). Poverty, the keeping of Christ's name, and the courageous confession of his word—these things belong together.[16] The powerful church has far too much to lose, humanly speaking; therefore it will shy away from the risks involved in bold confession. Again like the church in Smyrna, the Christians in Philadelphia have had their share of conflict with the local synagogue, as reflected in the promise that these "false Jews" will stand humiliated before the church when Christ comes (3:9). This is harsh language, but again it must be read with some care. Christ does not say "I will come and banish them to the hell of fire," but "I will make them come and bow down before your feet and they will learn that I have loved you."

But if Christ has loved the church called from among Jews and Gentiles, will he not love the synagogue also? Has the appellation "Jew" become so fixed so that it no longer applies to Israel after the flesh? Or does the Messiah, the one who alone possesses the key of David, not reserve the right to claim David's children as his own? Who is the church to say that this door may not be opened for others too? The point of the letter to Philadelphia is not Christ's hatred of the synagogue but his love for the *ekklēsia*. The church's love, in turn, is proved by its "patient endurance," which will help to preserve it amid the apocalyptic upheaval that is coming on the whole world and that is only hinted at by their sufferings up till now. "Save us from the time of trial, and deliver us from evil [*or* 'the evil one']"; here is Christ's promise that this prayer will be answered.

3:14–22 The letters conclude with the famous letter to the church at Laodicea. It is a harsh note to end on: this letter is as unremittingly negative as those to the churches in Smyrna and Philadelphia are positive. The Son of Man spares nothing as he excoriates this church: "I know your works: you are neither cold nor hot. Would that you were either cold or hot! So, because you are lukewarm, and neither hot nor cold, I will spit you out of my mouth. For you say, I am rich, I have prospered, and I need nothing, not realizing that you are wretched, pitiable, poor, blind, and naked" (3:15–17).

The reader's attention is naturally drawn to the image of "lukewarmness." Commentators regularly note that Laodicea was located near the hot springs of Hierapolis, whose waters cooled to tepid by the time they arrived in Laodicea—a point that at least shows John was capable of wit. Thankfully the metaphor does not stand on its own; the speaker unpacks it in the words he mockingly attributes to this church: "I am rich, I have prospered, and I need nothing." It is the smugly self-satisfied attitude of this church that disgusts Christ, making them so disgusting that he has no choice but to spit them out. A church filled with the Spirit necessarily

16. RSV, ESV, and NRSV have "you have but little power, *and yet* you have kept my word." The word "yet" is highly interpretive: while the word *kai* can have adversative force, there is no need to translate it that way. Here it means simply "and."

burns with the fire of love (Song 8:6–7). A church that is cold—perhaps close to death, like the assembly in Sardis—can be miraculously revived by the one who brings life to the dead. But the lukewarm church, the church that imagines that it has everything, neither needs nor expects anything of him. The pathos of this situation lies in the absolute dichotomy between reality and perception, so that the community that is the most "wretched, pitiable, poor, blind, and naked" is at the same time the one most impervious to help.[17]

There is no hope, then, for the Laodicean church. Unlike Sardis, there is not even a faithful remnant that might serve as a seed for regeneration. Yet it is wrong to say there is no hope, for this church is still the subject of address by the risen Lord: "And to the angel of the church in Laodicea write: 'The words of the Amen, the faithful and true witness, the beginning of God's creation'" (3:14).

The use of creation language is not accidental. The church at Laodicea needs to undergo a kind of re-creation, a movement from indifference to desire, from death into life. And this is possible, because the one speaking to it is himself alive with the reality and the possibility of God. Even the sin of lukewarmness is not the unforgivable sin against the Holy Spirit. Even a church dead in its sins may yet become a place of life and hope.

The pitiless letter to the Laodiceans concludes with an image that is among the most beautiful in all the letters: "Those whom I love, I reprove and discipline, so be zealous and repent. Behold, I stand at the door and knock. If anyone hears my voice and opens the door, I will come in to him and eat with him, and he with me" (3:19–20).

These words serve as a fitting conclusion to the letters to the churches as a whole. They capture two essential themes that emerge from a reading of this material: (1) the love between Christ and the church, as expressed by the image of communion, the guest who arrives at the door to receive hospitality, only to become the host of the meal within; and (2) the call for repentance, addressed to bodies who are in varying degrees unfit for precisely such fellowship. The tension expressed in "those whom I love, I reprove and discipline" accounts for much of the pathos that marks this strange, one-sided correspondence.

The church as the community that is loved by and that loves Jesus Christ—who would quarrel with that? Yet we all know that the notion of love is easily sentimentalized and trivialized. In the sense in which the Apocalypse uses the term, love for God or for Christ is something that must be tested and proved in the midst of struggle. Thus Christ praises those churches that have exhibited patient endurance on his behalf, and especially those churches that are poor, poverty being the condition of those who have little to lose and so can take risks on behalf of the kingdom. To the extent that the Apocalypse exhibits a form of "communion

---

17. The charge of blindness, along with the counsel to purchase eye salve (3:18), is consistent with the emphasis on truth and perception in this letter.

ecclesiology," it is a communion in poverty and in suffering for Christ's sake. The theme of apocalyptic patience thus rescues the notion of communion from the false abstraction to which it is often subject in theological discussion.

This is good news for us. Among other things, it means that the struggles in which the Anglican communion and other churches are currently embroiled are not, in themselves, signs that something is wrong with the church. The rending of communion may be wrong, the lack of charity and forgiveness is certainly wrong, but not the fact of conflict as such. The church's call is not to float above the turmoil of history in a kind of religious safe zone—perhaps it was the desire for such a safe zone that earned the epithet "lukewarm" for the church in Laodicea—but to seek to hear the word of him who bears the sharp two-edged sword. Perhaps John of Patmos and the prophetess Jezebel can never be reconciled in this life. The Thyatiran church must decide which one is truthfully speaking the word of Christ. But this act of discernment will occur within the space defined by "the tribulation and the kingdom and the patient endurance that are in Jesus" (1:9). It is in and through such testing that they will show whether they love him.

In her late-nineteenth-century study of Revelation, a work that is no less shrewd for being "edifying," Anglican writer Elizabeth Rundle Charles notes that all seven messages are addressed to the church corporately through its angel, while the rewards/promises are held out to the individual victor: "For these two, the corporate and the individual life, are interwoven throughout, in a way which might do much to adjust the true balance, now so much discussed, between 'socialism' and 'individualism.'"[18] In each case the church is the primary addressee. If the scroll of the Apocalypse is being read aloud in the liturgical assembly, *this particular assembly* is being asked to act in concert—to rekindle a lost love, to reject false teaching, to abstain from idolatry, and so forth. And what the Spirit says to one, he says to all: "Whoever has an ear, listen to what the Spirit says to the churches."

And what does the Spirit say? That the churches should repent. Of the seven churches, only Philadelphia and Smyrna are exempted from the call to repentance, which otherwise runs like a red thread throughout the letters (2:5, 16, 21–22; 3:3, 19). The unfaithful church must repent. It must desist from idolatry and return to the Lord. As John's references to Balaam and Jezebel suggest, the model here is Israel, whose continuation in the covenant is a matter of God's grace rather than of human entitlement. The Lord can remove a church's lampstand from its place, he can spit it out like so much tepid water.

But if the church can repent, does this mean the church can sin? Protestants generally have little difficulty affirming the fact of ecclesial sin, while Roman Catholics, pointing to the *una sancta* of the creed, are inclined to locate sin in the church's members rather than in the church itself—a dubious distinction, and one

18. Elizabeth Rundle Charles, *The Book of Unveiling: Studies in the Revelation of S. John the Divine* (London: SPCK, 1892), 54.

that would seem to find little support in Rev. 2–3.[19] We need not resolve the issue here, however. Whether we are confronted with sin *of* the church or merely *in* the church, all would agree that the church is a place where sin can be met only with resistance, where sin can never be treated as anything other than an abnormal, indeed impossible state of affairs.[20] Indeed, the ecclesial "we" is virtually defined as those who have been set free from the power of sin.

What the letters to the seven churches show us is not what is normal in the church, but what is typical. Churches lose their early zeal, they are led astray by false prophets, they struggle to define the relation between themselves and other communities or with their host culture. Or they do not struggle, giving up without a fight. The churches of Asia are truly a mixed lot, with two groups exemplifying heroic resistance (Smyrna, Philadelphia), two that are a record of utter failure (Sardis, Laodicea), and three that are predictably somewhere in between. No doubt this variation reflects something of the empirical range found in the actual churches of late-first-century Asia Minor. But more to the point, it is meant to provide a kind of mirror in which we may discern the truth about the churches we ourselves inhabit. Perhaps even more than repentance, the question of truth lies at the heart of the letters: "I know your works."

Elizabeth Rundle Charles notes that unlike the words of praise and blame, which are addressed by Christ to whole communities, the promises are made to "the one who conquers/overcomes." What conclusion should we draw from this? Surely not that Revelation views the church as dispensable, or that it pictures believers busily saving themselves in spite of a lost and hopeless church. Setting individual and community against each other in a zero-sum game is a characteristically modern error. On the contrary, the same Lord who is passionately concerned for the welfare of the churches also addresses the individual disciple, constituting her as a *martys*, a witness to Jesus Christ, and therefore as a conqueror. Part of what is so remarkable about the letters is that though they read like documents of struggle, there is nothing anxious or hesitant about them. Oddly, their very harshness seems to open up a wide space in which the church can live and move. They breathe an atmosphere of victory, of resurrection. And this victory is big enough to encompass the life of both the individual believer and the church as a whole. We might even say that the more faithful a church is, the more it will

---

19. The problem with some Catholic thinking on this question is, obviously, the bifurcation of the church between its sinful members and an ontological core whose holiness is divinely guaranteed. This is not just a theoretical issue. It is all too tempting to locate the hierarchy within the ontological core, thereby exempting it precisely from the need to repent. Conversely, the problem with the Protestant view is that it may lead to confessions of sin that are all too cheap and culturally driven. For a thorough, ecumenically sensitive treatment of the whole question of ecclesial repentance, see Jeremy M. Bergen, "The Emerging Practice of Ecclesial Repentance and the Nature and Mission of the Church" (PhD diss., St. Michael's College, University of Toronto, 2008).

20. Barth famously called sin an "impossible possibility." Sin is possible only in the sense that it happens. It is impossible in the sense that it is ontologically absurd, being by definition that-which-God-does-not-will.

tend to spawn "characters," with their own unmistakable witness to the God of Jesus Christ.

The resistance movement that is the church requires both solidarity in the common cause and the initiative of those who can act, and suffer, as genuine disciples of Jesus. There is no one who is not a candidate for such discipleship: "If anyone [*ean tis*] hears my voice and opens the door, I will come in to him and eat with him, and he with me. . . . Whoever has an ear, then hear what the Spirit says to the churches" (3:20, 22 ESV slightly modified).

PART II

THE MAKING
AND REMAKING
OF THE WORLD

REVELATION 4

THE EYES OF THE CHERUBIM

> I saw a throne set in the sky and a figure seated on the throne. The face of the Seated One was stern and impassive, the eyes wide and glaring over a terrestrial humankind that had reached the end of its story.... The face was illuminated by the tremendous beauty of a halo, containing a cross and bedecked with flowers, while around the throne and above the face of the Seated One I saw an emerald rainbow glittering. Before the throne, beneath the feet of the Seated One, a sea of crystal flowed, and around the Seated One, beside and above the throne, I saw four awful creatures— awful for me, as I looked at them, transported, but docile and dear for the Seated One, whose praises they sang without cease.
>
> —Umberto Eco, *The Name of the Rose*

The implied location for everything that has taken place in Revelation so far has been (1) the liturgical assembly, where the work is being read aloud and heard; (2) Patmos, where the risen Lord appeared to John and dictates the letters to the churches; and (3) the Asian cities, where the churches are living out their day-to-day struggles with the pagan world and with themselves. For all their oddity, these settings all have a thoroughly familiar and this-worldly feel to them. We know, or think we know, our way around here. We are on earth, the realm where human beings (or at least some human beings) are used to exercising power and being in control.

The next scene represents a startling shift, apparently ushering us into a different world altogether. Appropriately, the Spirit is the agent of the transition. A great boundary is crossed. Now the implied location is no longer earth, but heaven. Heaven is clearly the setting for the worship scene portrayed in Rev. 4–5, and while the location of subsequent events is less certain, heaven continues to be the source of energy and direction for the entire narrative arc covering Rev. 6–11. I call this part of Revelation "The Making and Remaking of the World," because it begins with a vision of God as the sovereign Creator and then describes God's act of delivering his world from hostile powers—an act so radical that it is nothing less than a re-creation of the cosmos itself. The agent of this great reversal is the slaughtered Lamb, by far the dominant figure throughout these chapters.

4:1–2 We begin, however, with God. In some ways, Revelation follows the classic script of Jewish and Christian apocalypses, narrating a visionary ascent into heaven in which the seer is permitted to see the divine throne: "After this [*meta tauta*] I looked, and behold, a door standing open in heaven! And the first voice, which I had heard speaking to me like a trumpet, said, 'Come up here, and I will show you what must take place after this [*meta tauta*].' At once I was in the Spirit, and behold, a throne stood in heaven, with one seated on the throne."

The phrase *meta tauta* (literally, "after these things") is used several times in Revelation to denote a transition between one vision and the next (7:1, 9; 15:5; 18:1, all with *eidon* ["I saw"]; 19:1 has "after this I heard"). If the first *meta tauta* in 4:1 indicates a sequence in the order of signs, of knowing—John's initial vision of the Son of Man is followed by his being rapt into heaven—the second occurrence, connected with "what must take place," suggests a sequence in reality. "After this," that is, in the future, the realm of that which has not yet happened from the perspective of John and his churches. Yet we must be careful not to reduce Revelation to a simple matter of chronology. Just as heavenly space cannot be confined to the spatial coordinates of either physics or human construction, so heavenly time is not the time of the calendar.[1] It is not that heaven is either atemporal or aspatial, but it is surely other than the cosmic order that is now in place. The disruption of the present age by the age to come is indicated by John's use of the apocalyptic word *dei*, the "must" in "what must take place after this." It is the same word used by Jesus to describe his necessary suffering, the destiny laid upon him by his Father (Mark 8:31; Luke 9:22).

And it is Jesus, "the first voice, which I heard speaking to me like a trumpet," who now commands John to pass through the open door in heaven. The letter to the church in Laodicea concluded with the promise that "if anyone hears my voice and opens the door, I will come in to him and eat with him" (3:20). Now John hears Jesus's voice, but the door opens of its own accord, and in the ecstasy of the Spirit he passes through it. This is truly a liminal passage, the crossing of a threshold from what can be humanly experienced and imagined to what lies beyond our ken. Unlike other apocalyptic writers, John offers no detailed travelogue of his passage to heaven. He treats the voyage itself as incidental: he is simply rapt by the Spirit, instantaneously, all "at once" (*eutheōs*; 4:2).

1. Travis Kroeker and Bruce Ward, *Remembering the End: Dostoevsky as Prophet to Modernity* (Boulder, CO: Westview, 2001), 100–101.

4:3–6 What John sees is extraordinary. Philosopher William Christian once defined religion as that which is taken to be "more important than everything else in the universe," so that all else in life gets organized around this center.[2] But for the faithful Jew, what is more important than everything in the world is, of course, no part of the world, but its Creator and ruler, the God who is the maker of all things. This is where John finds himself: before the throne, in God's immediate presence. The scene is marked by a tremendous dynamism, an energy that flows first of all centripetally: God, seated on the throne, occupies the center, while the other characters—the elders and the four living creatures—surround him, their gaze directed toward the brightness in their midst. But there is also centrifugal energy, as power flows from the throne out into the world: thus the flashes of lightning, the rumblings and peals of thunder, and most of all the seven Spirits of God, who are not static but are sent out into all the earth (5:6; cf. Zech. 4:10).

John was not the first prophet to behold the throne of YHWH. Isaiah's famous vision of God in the Jerusalem temple, "in the year that King Uzziah died," reminds us that the temple was understood as the ordinary site of God's presence, his earthly dwelling, his throne. And yet the temple itself was a kind of self-consuming artifact: the space where YHWH sat enthroned "between the cherubim" was significantly marked by an absence, an empty space. The temple could not contain God, even if it was the place where he could reliably be encountered. And so other visions of the divine throne make no direct reference to the temple or to Jerusalem (1 Kgs. 22:19; Dan. 7:9–10). Here John makes clear that not only is he not in Jerusalem, he has been rapt to a place that cannot be located by any earthly set of temporal or spatial coordinates: "a throne stood in heaven" (Rev. 4:2).

And yet heaven is, for all that, a "somewhere," a definite place, a bounded arena where the praise of God is focused and where the divine court can convene. That it cannot be located by means of Euclidean geometry or any other system of co-ordinates is no argument against its spatial character. There is space (God's space) beyond the capacities of unaided human reason, as Karl Barth writes:

> Heaven is a place: the place of God in view of which we have to say that God is not only transcendent in relation to the world but immanent and present within it. . . . As the place of God heaven is, of course, a place which is inconceivable to us. It cannot be compared with any other real or imaginary place. It is inaccessible. It cannot be explored or described or even indicated. All that can be affirmed concerning it is that it is a created place like earth itself . . . and that it is the place of God.[3]

Barth's comments offer shrewd insight into what might be called the biblical grammar of heaven. It would seem obvious that heaven is the site of God's tran-

---

2. William A. Christian, *Meaning and Truth in Religion* (Princeton: Princeton University Press, 1964), 60–61.
3. Karl Barth, *Church Dogmatics*, ed. G. W. Bromiley and T. F. Torrance (Edinburgh: Clark, 1960), 3/3.437.

scendence, insofar as heaven transcends or exceeds our fragile, finite earth. But since heaven is itself created, God's location *in* heaven has as much to do with his intimacy with creation as with his distance or otherness. In the witness of the Gospels, the salient thing about the kingdom of heaven is that it has *drawn near.* John can be lifted up to heaven in the Spirit, precisely by virtue of the convergence between heaven and earth that has taken place in the incarnation.

In light of John's apocalyptic journey, it might seem that Barth is wrong to say that heaven "cannot be explored or described or even indicated." The present episode is both powerfully imagined and vividly rendered. It is full of color, light, and movement. Along with the vision of the new Jerusalem at the very end of the book, it may be the closest thing we find in Revelation to a scene that is simply beautiful. Yet Barth's assertion is partially justified in the extraordinary restraint that John shows in his description. All he says about the figure on the throne, for example, is that he "was like stone of jasper and cornelian to see, and a rainbow in a circle around the throne, like emerald to see" (4:3 in Lattimore 1979: 259). John avoids anthropomorphism both through his use of mineral imagery and by the repetition of the word "like" (*hōs* or *homoios*), which underscores the apophatic character of all our language about God. We cannot see or know God directly. At best we can use the disciplines of analogy and metaphor to convey something of what God is "like." "Such was the appearance of the likeness of the glory of the LORD," writes Ezekiel of his vision by the river Chebar (Ezek. 1:28). Not the glory, not the likeness of the glory, but at best the *appearance* of the likeness of the glory is all that human language can hope to convey. This is not to say that we are consigned to absolute ignorance concerning God. While we may know only in part (1 Cor. 13:12), we do know something. Truthful speech about God must be possible, otherwise the church's witness is in vain. But truthfulness also requires an acknowledgment of the limits of our speech. "To do theology . . . is to be careful about one's words in the fear of God."[4]

The throne of God is surrounded by the rainbow, sign of the Noachic covenant and therefore of peace. Here is one of the things we can know for certain about God: he intends peace for his creatures. The tableau that unfolds before us is the well-ordered cosmos, creation as it ought to be; even the sea—in Israel's imagination the source of disorder and chaos—appears here as tamed, a smooth, glassy sea spreading out before the throne (4:6). After the flood comes the rainbow that seals the covenant. Nowhere is this rainbow more vividly depicted than in William Blake's watercolor *The Four and Twenty Elders Casting Their Crowns before the Divine Throne*, which art critic Morton Paley cites as a rare instance of "the apocalyptic beautiful" genre.[5] This is one answer to those who equate apocalyptic

---

4. John Howard Yoder, *The Royal Priesthood: Essays Ecclesiological and Ecumenical,* ed. Michael G. Cartwright (Grand Rapids: Eerdmans, 1994), 140.

5. Morton D. Paley, *The Apocalyptic Sublime* (New Haven: Yale University Press, 1986), 81. The "apocalyptic beautiful" is to be contrasted with the "apocalyptic sublime," the name Paley gives to an artistic style that arose in Europe in the late eighteenth and early nineteenth centuries,

only with themes of gloom, doom, and destruction. The apocalyptic imagination encompasses the harmony and unity of creation as it is fulfilled beyond the horrors of this age.[6] God created all things good in the beginning, and he will finish what he has begun.

4:4 Heaven is filled with life. If the glory of God defies description, we can at least discern something of that glory as it is displayed in his creatures. In the present vision two groups of beings fulfill this role, organized in concentric circles around the throne of God. The outer circle is constituted by the twenty-four elders, clothed in white robes and wearing golden crowns. Commentators argue about the identity of these elders—are they a species of heavenly courtiers, like the "sons of God" who wait upon the Lord in the book of Job? Is there some memory here of the twenty-four orders of priests mentioned in 1 Chr. 24:4–19? It is suggested that the number twenty-four refers to the hours of the day, marking the movement of sun and the stars across the heavenly dome, and so bears a relation to astronomy or astrology. Babylonian astrology knew twenty-four special stars (Swete 1908: 69). Given the cosmic, universal character of the heavenly liturgy as John describes it, this is not so outlandish an idea as might first appear. But the most convincing proposal comes from Victorinus, who identifies the elders as "the twenty-four fathers—twelve apostles and twelve patriarchs" (*Commentary on the Apocalypse* 4.7, quoted from ANF 7.348). Twelve in Revelation is the "ecclesial number," applicable to both Israel and the church (cf. 7:1–8; 12:1). The identification is confirmed by John's vision of the new Jerusalem, where the gates of the city are inscribed with the names of the twelve tribes, and the foundation walls bear the names of the twelve apostles of the Lamb (21:12, 14).

In heaven, the church—that is to say redeemed humanity—rules. It is remarkable that in a scene so dominated by *the* throne of God there should be other thrones, and that human beings should occupy them. This might, of course, seem to justify the worst fears of D. H. Lawrence: a marginalized, disenfranchised group hungering for the day when *we* are finally in the driver's seat. But to make this leap is to ignore what Revelation actually has to say about the use of power. For now, I simply note that while God is jealous he is not miserly. To be human is to be called to a vocation of right rule in the context of a shared common life—in a word, politics. The rainbow surrounding God's throne underscores this point in a subtle but powerful way. The same chapter in Genesis where the rainbow appears also sees the beginnings of human political existence, as God lays down the requirements of justice binding one human life to another and reasserts the command "be fruitful and multiply" (Gen. 9:5–7).

---

emphasizing feelings of awe, wonder, and dread in the face of apocalyptic upheaval. Significantly, the style arose in the wake of the French Revolution. Most of Blake's work on Revelation falls into the category of the "apocalyptic sublime."

6. The ultimately nondualistic character of Revelation is well argued by Leonard Thompson, *The Book of Revelation: Apocalypse and Empire* (New York: Oxford University Press, 1990).

4:6–8a If the outer circle of worshipers consists of the twenty-four elders, the inner circle, composing God's immediate entourage, consists of the four animals or living creatures (*zōa*). These are the cherubim, the strange beings who spread out their wings in the temple, whom Ezekiel saw by the river Chebar with their many-eyed wheels and whirring wings, supporting the throne-chariot of Yнwн (Ezek. 1:1). The ark of the covenant had two cherubim, while Ezekiel saw four, each one having the face of a lion, ox, man, and eagle. John likewise beholds four *zōa*, each, however, having only one of these faces. He is fascinated by their multiple eyes (Rev. 4:6b, 8). Other details of the animals are derived from Isaiah's seraphim: their six wings, and the *hagios, hagios, hagios* that they cry day and night before the throne (Isa. 6:1–7).

As the elders represent humanity, gathered by and gathered into the church, so the animals represent creation in a larger sense, the visible and invisible powers that surround us, the world in all its strangeness—though also in its familiarity and usefulness to human beings. An ancient rabbi wrote concerning Ezekiel's four-faced beings: "Man is exalted among creatures, the eagle among birds, the ox among domestic animals, the lion among wild beasts; all of them have received dominion. . . . Yet they are stationed below the chariot of the Holy One."[7] There is no sense of estrangement here between humanity and the rest of creation. We are not the only creatures on this earth ("*all* of them have received dominion"), but at the same time human beings clearly are assigned a special role ("man is exalted among creatures"); this view is consistent with the witness of both Testaments.

There is also an ancient tradition of identifying the animals with the four Gospels, going back to Irenaeus of Lyons. Arguing against those who, like Marcion, would deny the church's fourfold gospel, Irenaeus developed a typology in which each evangelist highlights a different aspect or dimension of Jesus Christ. Mark's is the lionlike gospel, showing forth Christ's "effectual working, . . . leadership, and royal power"; Luke is the sacrificial ox, depicting Zechariah offering sacrifices in the temple; Matthew is shown as a man because he is especially interested in Christ's human nature, beginning his gospel with a genealogy; while John is the eagle in his concern for the Spirit hovering on eagle's wings. Irenaeus concludes that "the living creatures are quadriform, and the Gospel is quadriform, as is also the course followed by the Lord" (*Against Heresies* 3.11.8, quoted from ANF 1.428–29; see Kovacs and Rowland 2004: 66). Irenaeus's interpretation is followed by Victorinus, the first Latin commentator on Revelation.

There is something undeniably attractive about this typology, although one might quibble with some of Irenaeus's specific characterizations. Matthew's genealogy, for example, traces Jesus's ancestry not to Adam but to Abraham, and to call Luke an especially "sacrificial" gospel would appear to be stretching a point. But what Irenaeus gets right is his viewing the four animals, and hence all of creation,

---

7. *Midrash Shemoth* R. 23, quoted from J. P. M. Sweet, *Revelation* (Philadelphia: Westminster, 1979), 120.

in light of Jesus Christ. The living creatures dimly hint at Jesus's identity as Messiah, Priest, Son of Man, and Spirit-bearer—all of which characterizations are to be found in Revelation itself. The first creation is oriented toward its fulfillment in the new creation; Genesis foreshadows Apocalypse.

4:8b–11 Typological or figural reading, however, is faithful only if the type retains a reality of its own and is not simply absorbed into its antetype. At the literal level of the narrative, surely the animals represent something like the astonishing vitality and diversity found in creation. They represent nature, just as the twenty-four elders represent the specifically human. One of the remarkable things about the heavenly worship in this chapter is the way nature takes the lead and the church follows.[8] The cherubim—we might even call them "powers" in the Pauline sense, except that these are powers who never rebelled—gaze at the throne with their many eyes, drinking in the reality of God whose glory can never be exhausted. They sing a version of the great hymn of the seraphim in Isa. 6:

> Holy, holy, holy is the LORD of hosts;
>   the whole earth is full of his glory! (Isa. 6:3)

This hymn formed the basis of both the Jewish liturgical blessing *Kadosh, Kadosh, Kadosh* and the Christian hymns *Sanctus* and *Trisagion*. In Revelation, however, the wording differs slightly:

> Holy, holy, holy, is the Lord God Almighty,
>   who was and is and is to come! (Rev. 4:8)

It is answered immediately by the cry of the twenty-four elders:

> Worthy are you, our Lord and God,
>   to receive glory and honor and power,
> for you created all things,
>   and by your will they existed and were created. (Rev. 4:11)

This is truly a cosmic liturgy, as nature and the church join together to praise the God who is the source of the life of both. God is glorified simply for being God. Where Isaiah has "the whole earth is full of his glory," Revelation substitutes the phrase "who was and is and is to come." Perhaps one might say that the hymn in Isaiah emphasizes God's spatial presence to creation, while the hymn in Revelation emphasizes his temporal presence. At any rate, the triadic formula seems at home, its three elements echoing the rhythm of the *hagios, hagios, hagios* in the preceding line.

The elders' act of self-prostration and of casting their crowns before the divine throne is their embodied "amen" to what the living creatures have just declared.

8. Barth, *Church Dogmatics*, 3/3.467.

We can see this action as a kind of parable of authentic human political author-ity (which includes authority in the church). The elders are not absolute kings, but servant-kings. By God's wisdom and sufferance they exercise a real, though limited, authority in their own sphere, yet they are eager to come down from their thrones in the presence of the one true King.

The hymn they sing magnifies God for his gift of creation, and the concluding lines give the reason for the elders' offering glory and honor and power, namely that "you created all things, and by your will they existed and were created." The two parts of the clause might simply seem to be saying the same thing, in the style of much Hebrew poetry; but in fact there is a subtle but important shift in meaning. To say that God is worthy of praise because he created all things is to say something important about *God*. That God should determine himself to be the Creator is itself a cause for gratitude, even apart from the results of that act of self-determination—the world.[9] On the other hand, because God *is* the Creator, there exists the cosmos in all its boundless energy, diversity, and fullness—an extraordinary mystery we can never fathom. The affirmation that creatures exist only "on account of [God's] will" hints at what later tradition would call the doctrine of creation *ex nihilo*, affirming God's unconstrained freedom in calling the world into being.

And having been created they "were." The order of the verbs in 4:11d is coun-terintuitive: we would expect to find "by your will they *were* created and so *are*," and indeed some textual variants try to smooth out the difficulties.[10] One explana-tion is that this is an instance of *hysteron-proteron*, a stylistic device in which what happens second is mentioned first.[11] Beyond being simply a quirk of John's Greek, the device has the function of highlighting the goal or outcome of an action. The telos of God's creative work is the reality of creatures, their being in time and space, their peculiar existence as *this* thing and not *that*. The gift of creation is a real gift, not only given but received, eventuating in a world of creatures that constitutes a genuine "other" for God. Up to this point in the book, the only voices we have heard have been divine voices. Now for the first time creaturely voices speak and sing. God himself remains mysteriously silent, but all around him swirls a lively, antiphonal, and polyphonic chorus of creatures.

This is a cosmic and eschatological liturgy, clearly, but does it reflect historical forms? It is very likely that the present vision incorporates aspects of the worship of both church and synagogue.[12] Both the *kadosh* and the prayer of thanksgiving

9. Neil B. McDonald, *Metaphysics and the God of Israel: Systematic Theology of the Old and New Testaments* (Grand Rapids: Baker Academic, 2006), 24–52.

10. One creative scribe fixed the problem by inserting "not": "By your will they were *not* and were created." This makes sense, but the more difficult reading has better support. See the apparatus in NA[27].

11. Other examples include 3:17; 5:2, 5; 10:4, 9; 19:13; see Aune 1997: 312.

12. Pierre Prigent, *Commentary on the Apocalypse of St. John* (Tübingen: Mohr, 2001), 233–35.

for creation were staples of Jewish worship. The latter made its way into Christian liturgy as the great thanksgiving of the Eucharist, as, eventually, did the *Sanctus*— by the fourth century in the Eastern church, somewhat later in the West.[13] The point, however, is not whether John drew on historical models, but that he employs real or imagined liturgical elements—burning torches, prostrations, hymns, antiphonal speech—to show his readers what heaven is like. This is the cosmos as well ordered, with God's dazzling form at the center and creatures doing their own thing in a kind of endless dance around him.[14] This is not yet the church's worship, but it is a worship that the church may aspire to and that its own liturgy may at times hint and gesture toward.

The thrust of this vision is powerfully affirmative; yet the affirmations have an edge to them. To confess that God alone is the Creator, that only he is worthy of our worship, entails the denial that anyone or anything else should occupy the heavenly throne. Indeed, the word "throne" offers a powerful clue: of the sixty-two occurrences of this word in the New Testament, forty-seven occur in Revelation. Revelation is interested in thrones because it is a book about power, divine and human, good and evil, historical and cosmic.[15] A common modern reaction to Rev. 4 might be to see it as a typical religious ceremony. But this assumes the existence of a discrete sphere of human life known as religion. In the ancient world the realms of the civic and the political freely mingled with devotion to the gods; religion as the uniquely *private* affair imagined by moderns scarcely existed. Thus when we see John describing a worship that is heavenly, we must not make the mistake of confusing "heavenly" with "otherworldly," that which simply floats free of earthly power relations. Quite the opposite is true: the throne in heaven has everything to do with earthly thrones: "Not only do the worship elements here derive from a tradition of God-as-ruler, but they contrast with elements in John's world that think of ruler-as-God" (Barr 1998: 63).

The intersection of worship and politics may extend even to the literary form of this vision. David Aune offers a form-critical analysis of Rev. 4–5 in which he argues that the heavenly worship should be read as a parody of ceremonies practiced in the Roman imperial court: for instance, the silent figure at the center, the courtiers prostrating themselves, the hymnic acclamation of the ruler as lord and god.[16] This is a very attractive idea, although, from the perspective of Revelation, Aune's argument gets it precisely backward: it is the Roman emperor cult that offers a grotesque parody of the true worship of God.

13. Josef A. Jungmann, *The Mass: An Historical, Theological, and Pastoral Survey* (Collegeville, MN: Liturgical Press, 1979), 202.

14. Perhaps the odd expression in 4:6b, literally "in the midst of the throne, and around the throne," implies that the animals are in motion, like the cherubim in Ezek. 1:12. Translators generally do not know what to do with this phrase.

15. In Paul's letter to the Colossians, "thrones" are one rank of heavenly power (Col. 1:16).

16. David E. Aune, *Prophesy in Early Christianity and the Ancient Mediterranean World* (Grand Rapids: Eerdmans, 1983).

The first commandment of the Decalogue, "You shall have no other gods before me," is never quoted in Revelation. Yet the argument can be made that it is the most important single passage in the Old Testament for understanding the book. The vision of "him who sits on the throne" is, one might say, a powerful display of the impossibility of idolatry. If all this is true, if reality is essentially defined by the eternal service of cherubim and elders around the Creator's throne, who would not wish to add their voice to the heavenly worship? Alas, this "impossible" has proved to be all too possible in the course of church and of world history! The human heart, the Reformers said, is a factory busy churning out idols—Caesar, the state, *das Volk*, ideologies of the left or the right, or in late modernity the inexorable logic of the free market, which reduces us to the level of consumers.

In light of this fundamental human dynamic, which Christians call "sin," there is comfort to be derived from the simple biblical conviction that "God reigns." Whatever we make of our lives, whatever fantasies we allow to shape our destinies, we cannot undo that God is God and that the idols of the nations are not—no more than are the idols of our own hearts. The "gospel" of Rev. 4 was already stated long ago by the psalmist:

> The LORD reigns; let the peoples tremble!
> He sits enthroned upon the cherubim; let the earth quake!
> The LORD is great in Zion;
> he is exalted over all the peoples.
> Let them praise your great and awesome name!
> Holy is he!
> The King in his might loves justice.
> You have established equity;
> you have executed justice
> and righteousness in Jacob. (Ps. 99:1–4)

Especially Caesar's victims can take comfort in the Lord, not Caesar, being king and in his both "loving justice" and "establishing equity." While the liturgy in Rev. 4 focuses on God's gift of and rule over creation, rather than on the execution of his righteousness, later on in the Apocalypse we hear hymns that praise God's judgments as both "righteous" and "true" (e.g., Rev. 15:3; 16:5, 7; 19:2). This profoundly Old Testament theme is as important for Revelation as it is for Paul.

From the perspective of the powers, then, the worship of the true God cannot help but be a profoundly subversive act. The church's confession and worship does not need to be translated into political terms, as if, once again, worship subsisted in some purely religious sphere unrelated to the blood, sweat, and tears of human existence. Rather, *leitourgia* is as such political; it is the priestly service that the church carries out "before the watching world."[17] This does not mean that the

---

17. John Howard Yoder, *Body Politics: Five Practices of the Christian Community before the Watching World* (Nashville: Discipleship Resources, 1992).

church always "gets it right," or indeed that we may not at times employ worship as a tactic for evading God's demands on us. The whole point of the scene in Rev. 4 is not that the church gets it right, but that *God* gets it right and that his truth and goodness are objectively acknowledged by his creation. "Your kingdom come, your will be done, on earth *as it is in heaven*": whatever evils may prevail on earth, God is gazed on by the teeming eyes of the cherubim. This knowledge allows the church to act with confidence and even a certain disdain for the shifting tides of worldly opinion.

This point was driven home to me in a story I once heard concerning Will Campbell, the Mississippi Baptist preacher, writer, and civil rights activist.[18] Speaking at a conference on the theme of Christianity and politics, Campbell was asked what he thought to be the most significant thing going on in Washington these days. His answer could not have been more blunt: "There is nothing significant going on in Washington these days." In saying this, Campbell lived up to his reputation as a theological gadfly. No matter how politically engaged, he is saying, the church must not allow "Washington"—a symbol not limited to a city on the Potomac—to set the terms for what is significant and what is not. When the church lets this happen, it abdicates its specific vocation and calling as a witness. Campbell's point is not, of course, that the church should be unconcerned with what the state is doing, only that its sense of priorities must be shaped by apocalyptic perception rather than by the powers of this world. "Washington" is simply not a reliable guide to what is most important in God's eyes.[19]

If we were to ask what purpose is served by the ceaseless service before the divine throne, what creation's worship of the Creator is good for, we would be asking the world's question. Pragmatically speaking worship is not "good for" anything, serving no end or purpose outside itself. At a deeper level, it is the most worthwhile thing that can possibly be imagined. If God is "the living and true" (1 Thess. 1:9), then to worship him is to participate in this life and this truth. Doxology is its own justification.

---

18. Many thanks to Beverly Roberts Gaventa for sharing this story with me.

19. Campbell's remark is reminiscent of Barth's scandalous advice to his fellow theologians upon Hitler's accession to power in 1933: they should carry on "as if nothing had happened." That is, they should continue to exercise their freedom as Christian theologians. Under the circumstances, this was itself a summons to resistance. See Eberhard Busch, *Karl Barth: His Life from Letters and Autobiographical Texts*, trans. John Bowden (London: SCM, 1976), 226.

REVELATION 5

THE SLAUGHTERED LAMB

The assumption made by the Book of Revelation is affirmed by the rest of the New Testament: the Son comes forth from the Father; and the Father, out of his love for the world, has given his Son to be slain, "for thou wast slain and by thy blood didst ransom men for God from every tribe and tongue and people and nation" (5:9). The Lamb is God's mode of involvement in, and commitment to, the world; the Lamb is both "worthy" and "able" not only to symbolize God's involvement but to *be* it.

—Hans Urs von Balthasar, *Theodrama IV*

5:1–4 The flow of action established in John's vision of the divine throne remains unbroken as we move to Rev. 5. The throne is still the focal point, but now John sees something in the hand of "him who was seated on the throne." This object is a *biblion*, a book-scroll. We stand at a critical point in the narrative, as indicated by the intervention of a "strong angel" who proclaims with a loud voice: "Who is worthy to open the scroll and break its seals?" (5:2).

The reason this declaration is so arresting is that the entire preceding vision had seemed to be that of a cosmos well ordered, caught up in an endless liturgy of praise to the thrice-holy God. But now the voices of elders and living creatures are silenced. A disturbing question has been raised. At one level this question is merely rhetorical: the angel is speaking on behalf of God, whose impressive silence from the previous scene is maintained, and the question is uttered merely to elicit the right answer. We are in the midst of a solemn ceremony, and in such ceremonies questions are typically raised as a way of impressing the gravity of the proceedings on all concerned. Examples from everyday life are: "Who gives this woman to be married to this man?" and "Are you ready to take the oath of office?"

But if the question is at one level rhetorical, at another level it probes deep into a wound at the heart of all things. This becomes apparent when the narrator comments, "No one in heaven or on earth or under the earth was able to open the scroll or to look into it" (5:3). On hearing this, John begins to weep. This is one of the handful of instances in Revelation where John takes center stage (cf. 1:9–20; 10:8–11; 22:8–9). Here he has a representative function: he typifies the reader, the church, and all humanity; he is "man." The question raised by the angel, we might say, is the human question. John's weeping reminds us of the tears of other biblical figures, such as Rachel, who "refuses to be comforted" for her lost children (Jer. 31:15; cf. Matt. 2:18); Jesus weeping over Jerusalem (Matt. 23:37–39) or at Lazarus's tomb (John 11:35); and Mary Magdalene weeping in the garden on Easter morning (John 20:11). "Blessed are those who mourn, for they shall be comforted" (Matt. 5:4). Tears are the natural human response in the face of death. Tears not only mark the loss sustained by the self as the beloved is torn from us, but can serve as a form of protest in a world where death so often has the upper hand. Christopher Morse says: "What Rachel does is refuse all false comfort and facile explanation. . . . [Her] refusal is honored in the Gospel as a faithful testimony."[1] We could press the point one step further and say that John's tears are his part in that travail and "groaning of creation" of which Paul writes in Rom. 8.

The reason for John's weeping is that a *book* is sealed. If the space in which we find ourselves is a throne room and if the figure seated on the throne is the king, then the book he holds in his hand must be a royal decree. A biblical analog might be the edict issued by Cyrus of Persia, in which he gave the Judean exiles permission to rebuild the temple (Ezra 1:1–4; 5:13). But since the ruler in this case is not just any king but *the* King, the Lord of hosts, then the content of the seven-sealed scroll can be nothing but the divine will. The scroll both symbolizes and embodies God's intention to execute justice "on earth as it is in heaven." It entails the setting right of all that is wrong in human history, the defeating of the demonic powers who seek to frustrate God's purpose, and the establishment of that city in which the horrors of all merely human cities will be overcome.

How will all this be accomplished? Until the scroll is opened, no one knows; as Paul puts it, this is precisely "the plan of the mystery hidden for ages in God who created all things" (Eph. 3:9). Nor is it simply the case that God wills for this plan to be revealed, but rather he wills that it be executed by a creature, and more particularly a human creature, for the divine covenant (the rainbow again!) is specifically with Noah and his descendants. Jacques Ellul writes that the scroll can only be

the book of that which man is called by his Father to be, to do, and to become (this is why it is held out to all men). . . . This man is both the heir of God and engaged

1. Christopher Morse, *Not Every Spirit: A Dogmatics of Christian Disbelief* (New York: Trinity, 1994), 10.

in a process by which he becomes himself, which is to say, a history. . . . It is the book of the secrets and of the meaning of human history, both accomplished, assured, but incomprehensible, illegible, which on the other hand is disclosed as a succession of time, which is in fact to fill all time. This book contains then the secret of the history of men, of humanity; but this secret is inevitably the disclosure of the profound forces of this history and, much more, of the action of God in the history of men. This is why there is mention of the throne (the place where God reigns and pronounces his decision) and why it is sealed by the Spirit (the plan of God for man is realized by the Spirit and it is that which gives meaning to all history). (1977: 145)

This is a powerful reading. If it has a weakness, it is that his concentration on generalities such as "man" and "history" causes Ellul to miss the Israel-specific character of the passage. In the Bible the human creature with whom God has dealings is not humanity in general, but Israel, the covenant people who are the representative of all peoples. The tears of Rachel, Mary, Jesus, and John himself are Jewish tears. The tears of Gentile mothers are not forgotten, but they are redeemed by being caught up in this uniquely messianic history. This lets us say something else important about the scroll: it is identical with the scroll that Daniel was told to seal up until the end, in that Old Testament apocalypse at once so Jewish in content, so Gentile in setting, and so eschatological in its concern with the end (Dan. 12:4).[2]

If the scroll remains locked under its seven seals, there is finally no redemption, no relief for history's victims, no salvation for the Jews, no hope for the Gentiles. The modern project since the Enlightenment has been driven by the conviction that human beings hold the scroll of destiny in their own hands and that the redemption of history's victims lies in the future perfection of humankind—a perfection that the victims themselves, alas, will never have the chance to enjoy. In the postmodern world we now inhabit, the departure from the Christian narrative has proceeded a decisive step further. It is not that the scroll remains unopened, a view we might perhaps associate with the tragic sense of life, or that we ourselves can open it, as in the Enlightenment project. *There is no scroll,* no grand metanarrative tying everything together and holding out the hope that the angel of death will be stayed by the hand of a just, merciful God. In such a world all that would remain is a kind of practical muddling through in the face of death,[3] or

2. This interpretation was held by two notable eighteenth-century commentators on Revelation: Charles Wesley and Sir Isaac Newton (Kovacs and Rowland 2004: 71).

3. The absence of a shared conviction concerning the purpose of human life in liberal societies means that, to a very great degree, all we share in common is our fear of death. This helps account for the widely lamented loneliness of modern and postmodern life, which the technology that allows us to instantly "connect" with others serves only to underscore. The fear of death is the theme of Kazuo Ishiguro's novel *Never Let Me Go* (New York: Knopf, 2005), which describes a dystopian England where human clones are bred for the sole purpose of harvesting their organs. The clones' meek acceptance of their fate is part of what makes the book so terrifying. At the same time, the

a resisting of death by invoking the power of love—"We must love one another or die," as W. H. Auden put it in his great poem "September 1, 1939." Yet in the absence of the God of Daniel and of Revelation it is deeply questionable whether our love can save us.[4]

5:5–6 John's tears, then, hold out the profoundly Jewish hope for a Messiah who will right wrongs, execute justice for the oppressed, and overcome the slaughterhouse that is human history. These tears are answered: "And one of the elders said to me: Weep no more. See, the lion from the tribe of Judah, the scion of David, has prevailed to open the book and the seven seals upon it" (5:5 in Lattimore 1979: 260).

When Jacob blesses his sons on his deathbed, he likens Judah to a lion; he is destined to rule (Gen. 49:8–10).[5] The lion of whom the elder speaks comes from Judah's tribe and is a descendant of David. Like David, he is a victorious warrior-king. This is the fully human yet divinely authorized agent who has prevailed (*enikēsen*, literally "conquered") so as to open the sealed scroll. The announcement builds up a tremendous expectation for the hearer. Naturally we expect a powerful, resplendent, and fear-inducing figure to step forth.

All that is implied by what John hears. This, however, is what he sees: "And I saw, in the space between the throne and the four animals and the elders, in their midst a Lamb standing, like one that has been slaughtered, with seven horns and seven eyes, which are the seven Spirits of God sent about to all the earth" (5:6 in Lattimore 1979: 260).

What John hears is a Lion, what he sees is a Lamb. What he hears is strength, what he sees is weakness. What he hears is a conqueror, what he sees is the quintessential victim—the Lamb. This Lamb is not just destined for sacrifice, moreover, but has actually been slaughtered (the participle *esphagmenon* is in the perfect tense, suggesting an act completed in the past). If what John hears is life, what he sees is death. And yet not so, because the Lamb is *standing*, so that the slaughter is the mark of his victory; he has passed through death and now stands somehow beyond it.

How we interpret the entire Apocalypse depends on how we interpret the scene that now lies before us. In effect, there are three options. (1) The scene could be viewed as Christ's assuming of a mask, so that his true lionlike character is hidden for a time in the form of lowliness. This suggests that at the second coming he will once

---

care they show for each other is a sign that their humanity has not been extinguished entirely. They are indeed far more human than the society whose needs they fulfill, a society that can imagine no other goal for life than its indefinite extension.

4. In later years, the Christian Auden would repudiate the line for its liberal sentimentalism. In later editions of his poetry, Auden emended it to read "We must love one another *and* die" (emphasis added), a rather more cynical-sounding assertion.

5. See also 2 Esdras (4 Ezra) 12:31–34, where the angel explains that the lion in the prophet's vision is "the Messiah whom the Most High has kept until the end of days, who will arise from the offspring of David" (NRSV). In this vision the lion is the enemy of the eagle, probably symbolizing Rome.

more become the lion and destroy his enemies. (2) It could be viewed in terms of an ontological kenosis, in which Christ, who as God's Son had actually been powerful, renounces his power in favor of love. This interpretation suggests a kind of Marcionism, according to which the vindictive God of the Old Testament is superceded by—or possibly discovers his true identity as—the New Testament God of love. (3) Or the scene is a kind of diptych, in which each of the two panels interprets the other, but where the priority belongs to the second panel. Christ really is and never ceases to be the Lion of the tribe of Judah. He is indeed a figure of power, but his power is realized precisely in the self-giving love he displays at the cross. In favor of this last view is the Apocalypse's consistent description of Christ as victor while at the same time using "lamb" as the dominant christological image; the word *arnion* appears twenty-nine times in Revelation, twenty-eight times in reference to Jesus Christ (at 13:11 it refers to the beast who mimics Christ's appearance).

This third possibility is the one we should follow. It is well stated by Vernard Eller: "The Lamb's very defenselessness *is* his lion-like strength; his suffering death *is* his victory; his *modus operandi* . . . always is that of the Lamb, but the consequences, the results, always are a victory that belongs to the character of the Lion" (1974: 80, emphasis original). The Lamb embodies the triumph of life; he is slaughtered, but stands and lives: "I died, and behold I am alive forevermore" (1:18).

Other indications that the Lamb is a powerful figure are the seven horns, symbols of strength, and his possession of seven eyes, the same seven spirits of God that burn before the throne. If one tries to picture all this literally, the results are grotesque, as in Albrecht Dürer's depiction of the Lamb in the woodcut from his *Revelation* series, showing horns and eyes sprouting in profusion from the Lamb's head, almost like a creature from science fiction. While it would be easy to criticize Dürer for being overly literal, perhaps he grasped precisely the point of the text. To the extent that the Lamb is a verbal icon, we cannot help trying to picture it; and the picture that emerges from John's description is strange and disturbing.[6] Whatever else this Lamb is, he is not *cute*. He is nothing less than "the Lamb of God, who takes away the sin of the world" (John 1:29, 36).[7] The very grotesqueness of the image invites us to eliminate every trace of sentimentalism from our Christology.[8]

6. It was perhaps understandable that the Eastern church proscribed the depiction of Christ as the Lamb, although as a Western Christian I would be sorry to lose some of the more moving portrayals of the *agnus dei*. For example, in Grünewald's famous *Crucifixion* in the Isenheim altarpiece, the living Lamb in the foreground helps us interpret the tortured figure on the cross as the victor.

7. The word used for "lamb" in John's Gospel is *amnos*, whereas Revelation employs *arnion*. Not too much should be made of this difference. In Septuagint Isa. 53:7, *probaton* and *amnos* are used interchangeably, as are *probaton* and *arnion* in Jesus's command to Peter in John 21. All these terms move within basically the same semantic range. The seer's use of *arnion* may have been influenced by Jeremiah's description of himself as "a gentle lamb led to the slaughter" (Jer. 11:19). Finally, while *arnion* is technically a diminutive, it was no longer heard as such in the Greek of the first century. Jesus is not a "little lamb."

8. I am indebted to Mari Jørstad for helping me see this point.

In the Old Testament, the lamb belongs to the realm of sacrifice. Is the Lamb in Revelation such a sacrificial animal? Scholars suggest at least three possible sources underlying John's image: (1) the Passover lamb, whose blood, sprinkled on the doorposts of the household, served as a sign that YHWH should spare the inhabitants within (Exod. 12:1–14); (2) the general practice of sacrifice in ancient Israel, especially the *hattat* sacrifice, in which the blood of the sacrificial animal served to restore the broken communion between worshiper and God;[9] (3) the Servant Song in Isa. 53, which likens the suffering servant of YHWH to "a lamb that is led to the slaughter . . . a sheep that before its shearers is silent" (53:7). In favor of the first view is Revelation's use of Passover imagery; in favor of the second view is its frequent emphasis on the blood of Christ and on priesthood; in favor of the third view are certain striking parallels between John's Lamb and Isaiah's Servant, whose deaths are said to be the cause of salvation for a great number (Rev. 5:9–10; 7:9–13; 14:1–5; cf. Isa. 53:12) and who are both finally vindicated by God (Isa. 53:10 and throughout Revelation).[10]

We have to choose among these alternatives. The figure of the Lamb is an intertextual image, located at a nodal point where many lines of scripture converge—divine deliverance from death, as in the Passover; the restoration of lost communion, as in the *hattat*; the death of the one as a gift to the many, as in the Servant Song. What all of these have in common, I argue, is that they help give expression to the work of Christ understood as a sacrifice. Here the communion or covenantal idea is central: the human partner in the covenant has failed in its obligations, has fallen into a state of cultic defilement or guilt, and needs to be brought back from death to life. When we view Christ's work from this perspective, the question of external forces or powers of evil hardly even arises: what is at stake is humanity's standing before God. It is important to underscore that the Apocalypse is concerned *also* with the principalities and powers. Like all apocalyptic theology in the New Testament, Revelation is shaped by what may be called a "three-actor drama" involving God, human beings, and the anti-God forces of sin and death.[11] The three-actor pattern is one in which God acts to deliver human beings *from* these forces; the operative soteriological metaphor is that of deliverance from bondage or defeating an enemy in warfare.

In the covenantal perspective, by contrast, what human beings need is not so much liberation as reconciliation or forgiveness. Here the primary agents in the drama are not three but two: God and his covenant partner. If the Christology of the three-actor drama is that of *Christus victor*, Jesus trampling down the powers of hell, the Christology of the covenantal view is that of the high priestly office.

9. Gary A. Anderson, "Sacrifice and Sacrificial Offerings (OT)," in *Anchor Bible Dictionary*, ed. David Noel Freedman (New York: Doubleday, 1992), 5.870–86.

10. José Comblin, *Le Christ dans l'Apocalypse* (Paris: Desclée, 1965), 31.

11. J. Louis Martyn, "Epilogue: An Essay in Pauline Meta-Ethics," in *Divine and Human Agency in Paul and His Cultural Environment*, ed. J. Barclay and Simon Gathercole (London: Clark, 2006), 177–78.

If in the three-actor drama Christ destroys the power of death, in the covenantal view he submits to death in order to make his atoning sacrifice, the priest who is at the same time the victim. In the first instance the emphasis falls upon the resurrection as the site of Christ's triumph; in the second the emphasis falls upon the cross as the place where his blood was shed, once for all.[12]

But in fact there are not two dramas or stories in the New Testament, but only one—the story of the Messiah who is both victorious Lion and self-offering Lamb. The sacrifice is the victory. This unity is made strikingly clear in the Gospel of John, which famously presents the moment of Christ's death as the moment of triumph (John 19:30). Although its atmosphere is in many ways quite different from that of the Fourth Gospel, Revelation, too, preserves the unity of these two moments. The images of Christ liberating or ransoming his people (1:5; 5:9), holding the keys of death and hell (1:18), and defeating the powers (19:11–21) coexist alongside sacrificial motifs such as temple, altar, and the Lamb himself (e.g., 6:9; 7:14).[13] Linking the two patterns is the image of blood flowing from the side of the Lamb even as it stains the robe of the Messiah-King (19:13). These two are one, just as Jesus Christ himself is one. His suffering and death as the great high priest[14] are the very basis for his rule as the royal man.

5:7 To return to the action: the Lamb steps forward and takes the sealed book from the hand of the enthroned God. This act must be read as completely continuous with the previous scene, in which God was worshiped as the Creator and ruler of all. The Lamb has received authority, not to rule in God's place or in God's stead—the exclusivity of the heavenly worship makes any such idea unthinkable—but to execute God's will in history. The cosmic liturgy in Rev. 4 celebrated God

---

12. The preceding analysis draws on Michael Root, "Dying He Lives: Biblical Image, Biblical Narrative, and the Redemptive Jesus," *Semeia* 30 (1985): 155–69.

13. In the history of Christian theology, the work of Christ understood as "reconciliation" or "satisfaction" is especially associated with St. Anselm's *Cur Deus Homo*. J. Denny Weaver's deep antipathy to Anselm and to substitutionary accounts more generally leads him to deny that there is anything Anselmic about the Lamb in Revelation. Indeed, he argues for the latter as a *Christus victor* alternative to Anselm, who Weaver believes is hopelessly committed to a picture of God as violent; J. Denny Weaver, *The Non-Violent Atonement* (Grand Rapids: Eerdmans, 2001). Without wanting to defend everything in Anselm (e.g., his tendency to treat the resurrection as an afterthought), I maintain the generally sacrificial and in this sense Anselmic character of the Lamb. Weaver's attempt to read this feature out of Revelation strikes me as rationalizing, moralizing, and strangely at odds with the Old Testament flavor of the work. For a spirited defense of Anselm from an Eastern Orthodox perspective, see the discussion in David Bentley Hart's *The Beauty of the Infinite: The Aesthetics of Christian Truth* (Grand Rapids: Eerdmans, 2003), 360–73.

14. Reading the Apocalypse side by side with Hebrews is a highly profitable exercise, and one that I highly recommend. Both works abound in temple imagery, although admittedly this is more florid in Hebrews. Both have an interest in angels, acknowledging their importance but demoting their status (Heb. 1:4–14; Rev. 19:10; 22:8–9). Both assume the tribulation of the church and summon its members to patient endurance (Heb. 10:33, 36; Rev. 1:9). Both envision God's future under the figure of a city (Heb. 13:14; Rev. 22). Perhaps one might say that the Hebrews account of Christ's sacrificial death is the condition of possibility for the Lamb's action in Revelation.

---

as Creator and the world as his creation. But in light of the terrible realities of history that have occasioned John's tears, the Lamb now steps onto the scene as the one who will make creation right again, enacting nothing less than the righteousness of God in human history. He alone is allowed to open the scroll and read the mysterious divine plan written in it. He alone has the authority to carry out that plan. What John sees here can rightly be seen as the Lamb's investiture in his office, as he receives public acknowledgment of the status to which his victory entitles him (Aune 1997: 336–38).[15]

So if we now ask "who rules the cosmos?" the correct answer can only be "the Lamb rules the cosmos," that is, "the crucified rules it." This spells the end of any rationalist or materialist conception in which creation is a closed system tending toward death, in which flesh corrupts and decays, and in which history consists in a never-ending struggle for dominance and power. In the world as we know it, it is empirically the case that lions win and lambs lose—and given these alternatives, who would not rather be a lion? But what the Apocalypse "apocalypses" to us is that the world is not so constituted by loss. As the Creator gives himself to his creatures out of overflowing fullness, so the Lamb gives himself to his people out of his victorious life, death, and resurrection—*and these two movements of grace are one*. It is the same God who pours himself out for the life of the world in creation, redemption, and consummation. In the contest between life and death, life—or rather the living one—wins.

What John sees happens in heaven. And yet we would misunderstand it if we failed to see that heaven here celebrates the Lamb's action on earth, his historical life and suffering. In apocalyptic thought, the strict boundary between heaven and earth is dissolved. This interpenetration of the two realms was well perceived by Christoph Blumhardt, who wrote amid the turmoil of the Great War:

> We are involved in two wars. The one on earth is earthly, waged with physical force; the one in Heaven is divine and brings in the end the victory of the Savior over the whole world.
>
> At any rate, something must burn in Heaven if earth is to become bright. Something is being prepared in Heaven and then comes to the earth as well so that we are joyful.
>
> That will be a rejoicing throughout the whole of creation! For it does not concern only people but also all the angels, who wait eagerly for God's will to be accomplished and revealed, especially on earth where sin and death rule. . . . Even Heaven has its unclear elements—it must become new.[16]

---

15. The closest intertextual connection is with Dan. 7:9–14, where the Son of Man is presented before the Ancient of Days to receive "dominion and glory and a kingdom" so that "all peoples, nations, and languages" might serve him. In light of this parallel, Aune notes that we should speak not of the Lamb's "enthronement," as some scholars argue in reliance on dubious Near Eastern parallels, but rather of his investiture in office.

16. Christoph Blumhardt, quoted in Karl Barth, *Action in Waiting* (Rifton, NY: Plough, 1969), 34–35. I am indebted to Michael D. O'Neil for drawing my attention to this passage.

5:8-10 The "something" that is "being prepared in heaven and then comes to the earth as well so that we are joyful" is the Lamb's victory. It is a source of joy not only for the church on earth, but even for the angels in heaven. Blumhardt's comments read like a gloss on the three hymns that conclude Rev. 5. In the first of these, the living creatures and the twenty-four elders prostrate themselves and sing a "new song," proclaiming the Lamb's worthiness to open and read the sealed scroll. What is remarkable about this song is that its primary focus is Christ's work of calling into existence a community, drawn "from every tribe and language and people and nation . . . a kingdom and priests to our God" (5:9–10). This is no merely transcendent or religious action. The whole world is being made new—and in its midst is a visible people bearing witness to its transformation! Here the churches of Asia Minor should be able to see themselves, or if they do not, then they need to let themselves be corrected by the voice of the Spirit.

5:11-12 Now the circle widens. The second song is sung by a chorus that has been silent and invisible up to this point, composed of "myriads of myriads and thousands and thousands" of angels. Their song again praises the Lamb, but in terms that directly echo the praise of God in 4:11: "Worthy is the Lamb who was slain, to receive power and wealth and wisdom and might and honor and glory and blessing!" (5:12). Richard Bauckham and others argue that the roots of Christology are to be found in the church's worship.[17] As the early Christians engaged in the practice of worshiping Jesus Christ, they gradually discovered that the logic of this practice entailed the conviction that Jesus is not other than God, assuming, of course, that Christians still wished to honor Israel's faith in God's utter singularity: "You shall have no other gods before me" and "Jesus is Lord!" The only way to square this circle is to acknowledge that God and the Lord Jesus are somehow one. This "somehow" already sets us on the road to Nicea.

5:13-14 The chorus of praise expands one last time, to encompass "every creature in heaven and on earth and under the earth and in the sea, and all that is in them" (5:13). Every creature! Is John being deliberately hyperbolic? Is he forgetting the (surely created) forces of evil and their human collaborators? And yet perhaps that is just the point. While the agents of evil are created, evil is not woven into the fabric of creation itself. That which ought to be—creation's praise of God—is ultimately grounded in what is. "Let us give thanks unto the Lord," says the minister in some of the oldest eucharistic liturgies of the church, to which the congregation replies: "It is meet and right so to do." Meet, right, proper, fitting, even cosmically inevitable—what could be more natural to the creatures of God than the praise of God?

If we had any lingering doubts about the high Christology of the Apocalypse, the climactic hymn in this scene should dispel them. The designation "him who sits on the throne," used frequently of God in Revelation, assigns a certain priority

17. Richard Bauckham, *God Crucified: Monotheism and Christology in the New Testament* (Grand Rapids: Eerdmans, 1998).

to the Father among the persons of the Trinity. But "the Lamb [is] in the midst of the throne," that is in God's direct presence (7:17; cf. 5:6). Toward the end of the book even this cautious formula is dropped, so that John can speak boldly of "the throne of God and of the Lamb" (22:1, 3). No wonder the early Christians soon developed the reputation of "singing hymns to Christ as to [a] god."[18]

The worship scenes described in Rev. 4–5 are critical for a proper interpretation of the work as a whole. Their primary function is to establish the identity of the acting subject, the God whose *apokalypsis* this is. This God is the Lord of Israel, of the nations, and of the entire cosmos; and this God is also the Lamb, the crucified and risen Jesus. There will be much that is dreadful and terrifying in the pages that follow, beginning already with the opening of the seven seals. We will hear these passages differently if we bear in mind that it is the Lamb who opens these seals, indeed, that he is the only one worthy to do so.

In the introduction, I argued for a rough division of the Apocalypse into three sections corresponding to the prophetic, the priestly, and the royal work of Jesus Christ. While this is certainly illuminating, it is also a bit too neat. The work of Christ the high priest, the focus of the current section (Rev. 4–11), already beckons forward to the kingly work that will be the primary focus of Rev. 12–22. "In the book of Revelation," George Hunsinger writes, "the Lamb is metaphorically displaced from a priestly to a royal context, standing at the throne of God (Rev. 5:13; 7:9–10; 22:1), and living at its very center (7:17). The blood of the Lamb proves itself to be stronger than all God's enemies and is the means through which they are finally conquered (12:11; 17:14). Here the blood of Christ conveys the basic Christian conviction that in reigning from the cross, the suffering love of God will triumph in its very weakness over all that is hostile to itself (cf. 1 Cor. 1:25)."[19]

This is surely right; and perhaps the point is driven home most powerfully in the form of a visual and spatial representation. In the city of Berlin there is a Roman Catholic church called Maria Regina Martyrum, "Mary Queen of Martyrs," built following World War II near the site of the Plötzensee prison, where political opponents of the Nazi regime were incarcerated and killed. It was the site of execution of members of Dietrich Bonhoeffer's family, among many others. The exterior of the church is forbidding: all reinforced concrete, and a bell tower that looks disconcertingly like the guard tower of a prison. To enter the church one descends a long, low series of steps, with walls on either side depicting the stations of the cross. It is a little hard to imagine Christian worship happening in such a space.

But when one enters the church itself, everything is transformed. The interior is a typical modern space, plain and unadorned. Wooden pews frame a central

---

18. As Pliny put it in his famous letter to Emperor Trajan: *carmenque Christo quasi Deo.*

19. George Hunsinger, *Disruptive Grace: Studies in the Theology of Karl Barth* (Grand Rapids: Eerdmans, 2000), 363.

aisle; at the front is a simple altar table surmounted by a cross. As the eye sweeps forward one catches sight of a vast mural covering the rear wall, displaying irregular splotches of black, yellow, green, and red, the splotches themselves suspended in space, vying with one another in mortal combat. These are the forces of light and of darkness as described in the Apocalypse. Floating just above the center point of the mural is a great eye, reminding us of the eyes of the cherubim and of the seven spirits. Surely this is the eye of God himself. Nothing escapes the sight of the one who pierces to the truth of things; no victim is forgotten, no victimizer immune from his wrath: "No creature is hidden from his sight, but all are naked and exposed to the eyes of him to whom we must give account" (Heb. 4:13).

God not only sees, but he acts and judges and saves. And so at the very center of the mural is the slaughtered Lamb, a tiny figure compared with the swirling shapes around him, and yet somehow the key to the whole. The worshiper's eye moves straight down from this center to the altar table, where the Lamb will become present again to feed his people in the gifts of bread and wine. He is embodied judgment and mercy for all human beings, the Servant whose life is poured out for "the many."[20] Maria Regina Martyrum is ultimately a hopeful and beautiful space, an affirmation of the Lamb's victory in the midst of a world beset by so much darkness. It speaks of God's "yes" that calls forth the "yes" of his creatures: "'To him who sits on the throne and to the Lamb be blessing and honor and glory and might forever and ever!' And the four living creatures said, 'Amen!' and the elders fell down and worshiped" (Rev. 5:13–14).

20. Since Plötzensee was devoted to specifically political prisoners, its victims included many non-Christians—for example, Communists and Social Democrats. The site is no longer a parish church, but serves as the chapel for a community of Carmelite sisters. I am not quite sure what to make of this, other than to say that perhaps it takes a special vocation to pray in a place like this.

REVELATION 6

THE WRATH OF THE LAMB

The verdict of the faithful God on the whole world, which is revealed in Jesus Christ, has this side, this dark side as well: it is also the revelation of God's wrath. . . . The death of Jesus Christ on the cross is the revelation of God's wrath from heaven.

—Karl Barth, *A Shorter Commentary on Romans*

The Lamb, the Lion of Judah, has conquered. Does this mean that, with his work completed, he can retire gracefully from the scene? Such an outcome would run entirely against the grain of early Christian confession. To say "the Lamb has conquered" is simply another way of affirming that "Jesus is Lord" or "Jesus reigns." The place of his rule is heaven, where he is seated "at the right hand of God the Father almighty"—not a spatial coordinate, but a reality at once cosmic and theopolitical in nature. Yet the events and affairs over which Christ rules are located on earth. Jesus Christ is the Lord of history. And so the central chapters of the Apocalypse, roughly Rev. 6–18, are devoted to the Lamb's actions that hasten the coming of God's kingdom on earth.

This is the section of the work that most people probably think of when they hear the words "Apocalypse" or "book of Revelation." Here we begin to encounter the famous septenaries: seven seals, seven trumpets, seven bowls. The septenaries serve less as an outline of the book than as a kind of dramatic technique, which John uses to build suspense and to draw his hearers into the story. They may also have served as a mnemonic device to help the audience keep track of where they are in the action.[1] As always in Revelation, seven is the number of completion or fulfillment: seven seals implies the divine plan in its totality, seven plagues means the full number of plagues, and so forth. The divine rule of history is accomplished; nothing is left out.

In this section of the Apocalypse the imagery becomes increasingly violent, beginning with the seals and intensifying through the trumpets and bowls. The earth itself would seem to be under attack: conquest, war, famine, pestilence; ecological devastation on a global scale; city-destroying earthquakes and fire from heaven; locust-warriors with hair like women and stingers like scorpions. At times the imagery is truly awful, in the sense of both awe-inspiring and repellent. The opening collect for the Anglican liturgy for Ash Wednesday begins: "Almighty and everlasting God, who hatest nothing that thou hast made and dost forgive the sins of all those who are penitent."[2] But the God of the Apocalypse may easily appear as the one who hates everything he has made, and with a vengeance. A superficial reading of the book may simply confirm our worst personal and collective nightmares concerning God.

The task of interpretation, of course, means going beyond superficial readings to engage the work at a deeper level. When we do this, we discover that there are in fact very good reasons underlying John's use of shocking, violent, catastrophic language.[3] Revelation is not written from the perspective of those in power, but from the perspective of an unimportant community of "nobodies" at the margins of Roman society. How could they picture the kingdom's coming other than as a radical upheaval of existing conditions? John is writing as the inheritor of traditions in which such language was entirely conventional: the prophets, with their warnings concerning the coming Day of the Lord, as well as Jewish apocalyptic traditions concerning the messianic woes, which shaped the teaching of Jesus himself. Moreover, John is more concerned with what God is doing for the faithful than with what he is doing to outsiders, and we should avoid inferring that because the former are saved the latter must be lost.[4] Finally, the violent language and imagery in Revelation are used to portray, in terms no one could mistake, the coming of the justice of God, with all that implies concerning his setting right of every historical evil. In Dostoevsky's *The Brothers Karamazov*, Ivan Karamazov famously says that the suffering of just one child—say, a small girl beaten senseless

1. David Barr, "The Apocalypse of John as Oral Enactment," *Interpretation* 40 (1986): 243–56. Chiastic outlines of Revelation likewise dispense with the sevens as large-scale structural elements.

2. *The Book of Common Prayer* (New York: Church Publishing House, 1979), 166.

3. The rest of this paragraph draws on the helpful excursus entitled "Interpreting Revelation's Violent Imagery" in Boring 1989: 112–19.

4. Boring 1989: 117 points out this holds true for many metaphorically charged passages in scripture, such as these lines from Ps. 91:7: "A thousand may fall at your side, ten thousand at your right hand, but it [harm, violent death] will not come near you." Boring notes that such language "does not presuppose a logical system within which inferences about the fate of the ten thousand that fall at your right hand can be made."

by her father—would be sufficient reason to reject God, heaven, and the whole business. Is not Revelation's picture of a God who refuses to let the tormentors escape with impunity an answer to Ivan, an affirmation that God is not simply sentimentalized love but the executor of justice on earth?[5]

Yet when all has been said, it must be admitted that these middle chapters remain rough going. Revelation is disconcertingly unsentimental in its portrayal of both God and evil. Indeed, much of the therapeutic force of the Apocalypse may well be to purge us of some of our fantasies concerning God. Rowan Williams writes that if one such fantasy is that of God as the classic Freudian father, "an authority figure who could sort out all our problems, who is always there on hand to help us out of situations where we would otherwise have to take responsibility," the opposite danger might be that of "projecting on to God the characteristics of an idealized mother, always accepting and soothing."[6] On the one hand, God the ultimate daddy, endowed with magical power to make everything right; on the other hand, God the great mommy, accepting us "just the way we are."[7] It should be evident that both fantasies are grounded in a mixture of fear, self-love, and the seemingly infinite human capacity for self-deception.

The genius of Revelation, we might say, is that it helps to purge us of these and other such fantasies concerning God. God is not whatever we would like him to be. God is God. He is the Creator and *Pantokratōr* glimpsed in the heavenly worship—power indeed, but not power at human disposal and control—and he is also the Lamb, the slaughtered victim-as-victor. If the image of the all-powerful Creator frees us of our sentimentalism concerning God, the image of the Lamb of God should free us of our fear. If there is a hermeneutic for interpreting the violent passages in Revelation it can be only the cross. "How could it be said more clearly," writes Jacques Ellul with penetrating insight, "that all that is read afterward [i.e., in the judgments of the seals, trumpets, and bowls], all these abominable things, are under the cover, under the signification, under the embrace of the love of the Lamb. And nowhere else. That all is situated *in* the cross of Jesus Christ, that these texts must not be read in themselves but only by relation to that love which sacrifices itself for those who hate it" (1977: 123, emphasis original).

6:1 We return now to the unfolding narrative, which proceeds without interruption from the worship of the Lamb to his opening of the sealed scroll. The Lamb removes the first of the seven seals. When he does so, one of the living creatures (we are not told which) cries "Come!" in "a voice like thunder." This

---

5. For a profound exploration of the relevance of Revelation to Dostoevsky's work, and in particular to Ivan's "Legend of the Grand Inquisitor," see Travis Kroeker and Bruce Ward, *Remembering the End: Dostoevsky as Prophet to Modernity* (Boulder, CO: Westview, 2001).

6. Rowan Williams, *Tokens of Trust: An Introduction to Christian Belief* (Louisville: Westminster John Knox, 2007), 15, 19–20.

7. See sociologist Marcia Witten's illuminating study of contemporary Protestant preaching, entitled *All Is Forgiven: The Secular Message in American Protestantism* (Princeton: Princeton University Press, 1993).

cry is repeated by a different *zōon* at the opening of each of the next three seals. Since the living creatures embody the vitality and diversity of creation, we must understand this "Come!" as an expression of eschatological hope on the part of all creatures. It is analogous to Paul's picture of creation's eager longing for the revealing of the children of God (Rom. 8:19). The creatures' utterance also foreshadows the church's cry of "Come!" that will be heard near the end of the Apocalypse, as the Spirit and the bride join in inviting the coming of the bridegroom (22:17). This is a good reminder that we are still in a liturgical setting. We are about to enter the realm of human history, and yet history itself is not a flat, predictable, purely horizontal state of affairs; it is through and through determined by the eschatological creativity of God.

6:2–8 The answer to the creatures' cry of "Come!" is the appearance of the famous four horsemen of the Apocalypse. Viewed simply in dramatic terms, this is one of the great set pieces in all of scripture. The riders have taken their place in the Western religious imagination, most famously, no doubt, in Albrecht Dürer's rendering of the scene in his Apocalypse woodcuts. Dürer brilliantly captures the sheer energy and grim determination embodied in the horsemen. The figures surely shaped Tolkien's conception of the black riders in *The Lord of the Rings*, the human kings who serve the enemy and who seem, like the fourth rider here, to be the embodiment of death itself. Echoes of their hoofbeats can even be heard in Bob Dylan's cryptic lyrics in "All along the Watchtower": "Outside in the distance / A wild cat did growl / two riders were approaching / the wind began to howl." Who are these riders? We are not told; all we are left with is a mood of ominous apocalyptic expectation. This is typical of modern and postmodern versions of apocalypticism, which differ from their classical counterparts in not specifying which God is about to appear on the horizon.

The direct Old Testament source of John's picture is Zechariah, where the prophet is shown four men on horses of different colors—God's messengers or advance scouts: "These are they whom the LORD has sent to patrol the earth" (Zech. 1:10). The messengers return to report that the earth is at rest. The language of this passage is similar to that used later in Zechariah to interpret the meaning of the seven lamps: "These seven are the eyes of the LORD, which range through the whole earth" (4:10). The riders in Revelation are certainly not the seven eyes of YHWH. They are creaturely agencies, principalities and powers of the kind that shape human existence. Nevertheless, they resemble the eyes in that they are agents of God's providential will on earth. John indicates this through his use of the word *edothē* ("it was given"), referring to the tasks assigned each of the riders (Rev. 6:2, 4, 8).

As for the riders individually, their identities initially seem straightforward. The first rider embodies the spirit of imperial conquest, as symbolized by the bow and the crown. (The crossbow was the weapon of choice of the Parthians, the empire on the eastern edge of the Mediterranean that represented the one real threat to Roman hegemony.) The second rider symbolizes war or civil strife.

The third represents famine. The neat symmetry of the sequence is broken at this point, as a voice suddenly cries out from the midst of the living creatures: "A quart of wheat for a denarius, and three quarts of barley for a denarius, and do not harm the oil and wine!" (6:6).

If the four animals' special responsibility is creation, then this voice suggests how the gifts of creation are turned into commodities priced out of the reach of ordinary people. The world being what it is, luxury items like oil and wine are not affected (Caird 1984: 81). Finally, the fourth rider represents pestilence, a common meaning of the Greek word *thanatos* ("death"). Viewed from this perspective, the actions of the last three horsemen are the fruit of the first. It is the lust for empire that brings all these terrors in its wake. This reading tends to stress the role of human agency: war is a human activity, engaging the energies and imaginations of whole populations in a combined effort to defeat the enemy.

Yet there is more going on here than simply a Johannine critique of Roman imperialism. We can also read the sequence backward, from the perspective of the fourth rider: "And I looked, and behold, a pale horse! And its rider's name was Death, and Hades followed him." This fourth, climactic horseman seems to sum up the other three: he is permitted "to kill with sword and with famine and with pestilence." But this means that the real power at work in all these terrors is death itself, the power who has been signaled as early as 1:18 as God's final enemy. This reading emphasizes not human agency but suprahuman powers that inflict ultimate harm on creation. If God is the maker, then death is the great unmaker. Here death assumes the role of a character, an "I"—cosmic evil personified. There are different ways to picture this. Thus Dürer depicts the fourth rider as a skeletal old man, while William Blake, in his 1800 painting *Death on a Pale Horse* (now in Fitzwilliam Museum, Cambridge), shows him as a surprisingly robust and attractive figure. Death seems strangely alive—but then Blake is a romantic, and romanticism is always tempted in the direction of valorizing death.[8] If Blake's image captures death's power, Dürer's is more faithful to the biblical horror in the face of death.

So is death God's enemy or servant? He is both, as we saw in relation to the two-actor and three-actor dramas.[9] Ultimately death is the enemy: at the end of Revelation he will be cast into the lake of fire (20:14). Penultimately, however, this very enemy is God's servant, the executor of judgment, a key instrument in God's providential rule over history. That is why both he and the other riders are

---

8. Modern existentialism is a particular form of the romantic impulse, keeping death constantly at one's side as a way of making life more compelling, honest, and authentic. The danger of such a death fixation is that one will ultimately succumb to the siren song of nihilism in the form of suicide. This is a constant theme in the novels of Walker Percy, which are marked by the struggle between the modern death wish and the Christian/Catholic affirmation of life's goodness.

9. This paradox is most intensely focused at the cross: "Dying you destroyed our death" (*Book of Alternative Services*, Anglican Church of Canada, 1985); cf. John Donne's famous line: "Death, thou shalt die."

said to be "given authority [*exousia*]." In a fallen world, death has the function of setting a limit on the human project. Perhaps this explains the odd inclusion of "wild beasts of the earth" among the fourth horseman's instruments of terror (6:8). These beasts (*thēria*) are a reminder that there are powers in this world other than humans. They prefigure the demonic beasts who will haunt the later chapters of Revelation.

The riders, then, combine elements of both human and suprahuman agency. Conquest and war are human actions, famine is the result of natural causes but is usually compounded by injustice, while death/pestilence is an evil that human beings both suffer and commit. Revelation has no theodicy to help us to sort all this out into neat piles. It simply knows that history in its present form is not history as God wills it, and that even the history that God does not will is subservient to his larger purpose. Creation and history are dark riddles; we understand very little of what goes on around us. But the suffering creation also longs for the disclosing of the children of God. Revelation has a nice way of making this point: it is the four animals, representatives of creation, who call out "Come!" Although in context this cry is an invitation to the horsemen, it also anticipates the church's cry of "Come, Lord Jesus!" for only through the event of the Lord's coming will the shadows that mar the present eon be dispelled.

With this perspective in mind, we can revisit the identity of the first rider. The consensus in ancient interpretation of this passage is that the horseman represents Christ himself, the same "white rider" who appears much later in the book (19:11). In the words of Victorinus:

> For after the Lord ascended into heaven and opened all things, He sent the Holy Spirit, whose words the preachers sent forth as arrows reaching to the human heart, that they might overcome unbelief. And the crown on the head is promised to the preachers by the Holy Spirit. The other three horses very plainly signify the wars, famines, and pestilences announced by our Lord in the Gospel. (*Commentary on the Apocalypse* 6.1–2, quoted from ANF 7.350)

This reading also helps make sense of the symbol of the bow. If the bow is in the hand of Christ, then it cannot be the crossbow. It can be only the bow of the Noachic covenant. The word for "bow" in this passage is *toxon*, the same word used in God's promise to Noah after the flood (Gen. 9:13 Septuagint). Moreover, surely this passage needs to be read in light of the rainbow bending over God's throne in Rev. 4:3, even if a different term is used there (*iris*, the more usual Greek word for "rainbow"). Christ holds the bow that signifies his Father's faithfulness to the earth. It is as the embodiment of a new covenant, both affirming the one made with Noah and going beyond it, that Christ rides forth into history.

The figural sense according to which the first horseman is Christ does not, to be sure, simply displace the literal sense of the image. The four riders form a quartet and so belong together as agents of evil; Albrecht Dürer was among the first artist to grasp this point. If the first rider resembles the hero of the story, this is because even his violence will be bent to the will of the true "white rider," the Messiah who wields no earthly weapon but only the sword of the word.

To the extent that the riders are human agencies, we must think of them as powers, forces, systems, and institutions that elude our grasp, that outrace and outwit the human capacity to control. This has been in multiple ways the lesson of modernity: the more we think we can control the world through intelligence and the extension of technique, the more out of control the world seems. "For I do not do the good I want, but the evil I do not want is what I keep on doing" (Rom. 7:19). The principalities and powers may be thought of as the social form assumed by this Pauline dilemma. The powers may not, to be sure, simply be demythologized by treating them as alienated forms of human agency. They are more than that. They are precisely *principalities and powers*, created yet rebellious, other than human; they enslave us from without. Nevertheless, they exercise their dominion in and through the social, political, and technological forces that humans have summoned into being. If it is not quite true that "we have met the enemy and he is us," it is true that the powers are capable of subverting our human capacities and turning them against us. The powers are occupying forces, yet we collaborate with them.

Yet whatever the extent of the powers' dominion, they cannot wrest us from the Creator's hand. God penultimately hands human beings over to the rule of the powers only so that he may ultimately reclaim them for lives of covenant fellowship. The powers do not win in the end. But they are given a certain scope; they are allowed to ride forth in the time between the first and second comings of Christ. The time of the church is the time of God's patience with the world, although from the disciple's point of view this time is experienced as the patient endurance of suffering.

6:9–11 Of the seven seals, these first four are the best known, no doubt because the four horsemen of the Apocalypse are so dramatically and powerfully rendered. But there is also a sense in which they constitute a kind of set piece. The four horsemen form a stereotyped group, entering and leaving the stage almost before we realize it (several of John's septenaries exhibit this four-plus-three pattern). With the fifth and sixth seals, by contrast, the pace slows down. If the horsemen symbolize God's general rule over history, the next two seals get *inside* history, gesturing at the *telos*, the goal, the divine mystery hidden beneath history's surface. We would expect the actual disclosure of that purpose to come with the opening of the seventh seal. But for now, what do the fifth and sixth seals have to tell us?

The contents revealed when these two seals are opened are obviously meant to form a sharp contrast. Both describe particular human communities: those who have been "slaughtered for the word of God" and the people denoted as "the earth-dwellers." What joins them together is that both stand in a distinctive relation to the Lamb. The martyrs are linked to him through the use of the verb

101

"slaughtered" (*esphagmenōn*, a perfect participle just as at 5:6) and by the mention of their blood. They cry out to God for vengeance on their foes. By contrast, the earth-dwellers cry out to the rocks and mountains, seeking protection from God and from the terrifying "wrath of the Lamb." It is the great day of reckoning, and in the face of God's righteous judgment who can stand upright?

We can ask two questions concerning the souls of the martyrs: where are they, and who are they? John says that they are "under the altar," as if he assumes his listeners will instantly know what he is talking about. This is the first mention of a heavenly altar in the Apocalypse. The Jerusalem temple had two altars: an incense altar where incense was burned before YHWH and the far more important altar of sacrifice. In the present passage the emphasis falls on sacrifice, underscoring the likeness between the martyrs' death and that of the Lamb. As for the souls' location "under" the altar, this is where blood sprinkled or spilled upon an altar ends up; the pouring of blood at the base of the altar is frequently prescribed in the book of Leviticus (Lev. 3, 4, 8, 9). This blood represents the departed life force of the dead beast or human being: "The life [soul, *psychē*] of every creature is its blood" (Lev. 17:14 Septuagint).

But the souls of the martyrs are restless. They rightly harbor a sense of outrage toward their persecutors: who would not be outraged? But if their death is a participation in the Lamb's sacrifice, as the whole tenor of this passage suggests, then surely they are not simply engaged in a personal vendetta. The martyrs are restless on account of their "fellow servants and their brothers" (Rev. 6:11) and beyond them on account of the world that remains unredeemed. The martyrs are not content simply to "go to heaven"; it is the earth they want, a redeemed creation in which God's goodness and justice prevails.

The sacrificial imagery is not irrelevant to the interpretation of this passage. David Bentley Hart suggests that in the pagan world the practice of sacrifice implied the surrender of something in this life (e.g., the sacrificial animal, ultimately representing the worshiper himself or herself) in order to obtain something better in the next. What would religion be if it were not essentially otherworldly? But in the case of Israel, Hart maintains, any such flight into pure transcendence was excluded. Keenly aware of just how much it had been given by God, bound in a covenant that was intimately personal, Israel had the audacity to demand a restitution that would be more than pie in the sky by and by, but a return of body and land apart from which the gift would not be what it is: "Hence Israel does not turn toward the eternal heights of the numinous to recuperate its 'investment,' but toward the eschatological horizon to find the gift restored as it was given: it cries out for vindication of the just, for the return of the murdered, for resurrection."[10]

When Rachel refused to be consoled for her lost children, it was not some heavenly consolation she desired, or even other children as a replacement. She

10. David Bentley Hart, *The Beauty of the Infinite: The Aesthetics of Christian Truth* (Grand Rapids: Eerdmans, 2003), 352.

wanted precisely *these children*. God's covenant with Israel was unimaginable apart from life in the body, apart from which no personal communion or praise of God would be possible (Ps. 88:10–12). Israel's convictions concerning God's faithfulness led inexorably, then, toward the hope of the resurrection of the individual and, with it, hope for the transformation of the entire world order. A direct line leads from the doctrine of the resurrection to the apocalyptic expectation of a new heaven and a new earth.

The memory of the martyrs has historically played an important role in the Christian imagination. It is extremely important that the martyrs not be sentimentalized. They are not always especially good, virtuous, or innocent folk. Ironically, to idealize the martyrs, or victims generally, is to rob them of their common humanity. What makes murder so terrible is not that the victims are virtuous, but that it is murder, the taking of human life in contravention of the law of God. By analogy, we might also say that what constitutes a martyr is not necessarily possession of the Christian virtues, although many martyrs have possessed these in abundance, but rather his or her witness to Jesus Christ. Indeed, William Cavanaugh argues that it is not so much a person's subjective intention that makes him or her a martyr—motives may well be ambiguous—as simply the church's recognition of a life that shows forth the reality of Jesus.[11] Paradoxically, the death of the martyr serves as a confirmatory sign that the world belongs not to the principalities of the present age, but to God.

John does not tell us just who these souls under the altar are. Surely they include Stephen and other Christians killed in the early days of the church in Palestine, as well as those killed in the Neronian persecution of the 60s. They must include Antipas of Pergamum, the one martyr actually named in the Apocalypse. John sees his death as a first installment in the coming great tribulation. But the indefinite character of the reference "those who had been slain for the word of God and for the witness they had borne" allows us to extend it to situations far beyond what John was able to imagine. To be slaughtered for the word of God is to share in the Lamb's victory. As such it is an apocalyptic event. Cavanaugh notes that when Stephen is about to be stoned, he raises his eyes to heaven and declares, "Behold, I see the heavens opened" (Acts 7:56), a declaration fully at home in the world of Revelation. Martyrdom, writes Cavanaugh, "is a bridge between heaven and earth not because the martyr is soon to travel one way to her eternal reward, but because heaven has been brought to earth in the form of one who, in imitating Jesus the Christ, has cheated earthly death of its sting. A martyr is one who lives imaginatively as if death does not exist."[12] This seems exactly right. It is no accident that the vision of the souls under the altar immediately follows the riding of the four horsemen, embodying death-in-the-form-of-empire. As a matter of historical

11. William T. Cavanaugh, *Torture and Eucharist: Theology, Politics, and the Body of Christ* (Oxford: Blackwell, 1998), 64.
12. Ibid., 65.

fact the martyrs have died: death has defeated them. And yet it is not death who emerges victorious in this exchange, but the martyrs, whose Lord has "the keys of Death and Hades" (Rev. 1:18). In a world where resurrection has happened, it is impossible to maintain the conviction that death is in charge.

The coda to the vision of the martyrs is that they are given white robes (a foreshadowing of the kind common in Revelation; cf. 7:9) and told to "rest yet a little time until the number is filled of their fellow slaves and their brothers who are to be killed as they were" (6:11 in Lattimore 1979: 262). There will be still more martyrs before the end comes. This does not mean that there is an absolutely fixed and determined number of the saints, and in fact the Greek does not even use the word "number" here. But the tribulation is finite. It will soon come to an end, not only quantitatively ("a little longer") but in the qualitative sense of perfection or telos. The filling out of the ranks of the elect belongs to the fulfillment of all things that God is bringing about.[13] We should not miss the performative force of what John is saying to the churches. He is not just saying "there will, as a matter of fact, be more martyrs," but "the souls under the altar already share in the Lamb's victory—be ready to join them!"

6:12–17 We now come to the sixth, penultimate seal, which ratchets up the energy. John's gaze shifts once again to earth, where he beholds the standard signs of apocalyptic upheaval: a great earthquake, eclipses of sun and moon, the stars falling to earth "as the fig tree sheds its winter fruit when shaken by a gale," even the sky itself rolling up like a scroll. That last metaphor would have been especially vivid for the first hearers of Revelation: imagine the sky snapping shut like this scroll I am holding (Barr 1998: 87)! The imagery is at once terrifying and strangely beautiful. If in seals 1–4 we see the trauma wrought by history or empire and in seal 5 the fate of the *ekklēsia*, then the sixth seal bears witness to the cosmic dimensions of God's saving action in Christ. It is instructive to compare this passage with Jesus's own account of the end in Mark's Gospel, where the darkening of the heavenly bodies constitutes the "great tribulation" in the proper sense, as opposed to the "beginning of the birth pains" marked by "wars and rumors of wars" (Mark 13:14–27; cf. 13:5–13).[14] We might speculate that this sequence is echoed in the progression we see in Revelation from the political-historical (the four horsemen, souls under the altar) to the cosmic (the events of the sixth seal). Yet in the imagination of both Jesus and the seer, no strong distinction is to be made between these two realms. Nature and history are equally caught up in God's apocalyptic invasion of the world in Jesus Christ.

13. In the order for the Burial of the Dead in the 1662 Book of Common Prayer, the priest petitions God "that it may please thee, of thy gracious goodness, shortly to accomplish the number of thine elect, and to hasten thy kingdom." This phrase does not appear in the 1789 Book of Common Prayer or in subsequent U.S. Prayer Books.

14. See Brant Pitre, *Jesus, the Tribulation, and the End of Exile: Restoration Eschatology and the Origin of the Atonement* (Tübingen: Mohr, 2005), 511–12.

Far more important than this standard catalog of apocalyptic destruction, however, is the cast of human characters who appear at the opening of the sixth seal. Their existence has been foreshadowed at the opening of the fifth seal, where they are called "those who dwell on the earth." In the present passage John names them more explicitly: "the kings of the earth and the great ones and the generals and the rich and the powerful, and everyone, slave and free." This list, dominated by images of wealth and power, stands in contrast to the martyrs seen in the previous vision. Wealth and power were also major concerns of the letters to the seven churches. The *ekklēsia* is summoned to identify with the powerless martyrs rather than with the upper echelons of Greco-Roman society. To be an earth-dweller is to have a large investment in the present order of things. Later in the Apocalypse, John will denote this same set of realities using the code word "Babylon."

At the same time, it is important to see that not everyone on this list is rich or powerful. While the first five items may be construed that way, the last two cast a very wide net, encompassing "*everyone*, slave and free." That the list contains precisely seven items can hardly be an accident. This is the human world in all its fullness, comprising rich and poor, prince and priest, slave and free. "Seven conditions of life are named, covering the whole fabric of society from the Emperor down to the meanest slave" (Swete 1908: 94). The list is dominated by the powerful because they are the ones who set the tone for the society as a whole; for better or worse, they get to fashion the world everyone else has to live in. Moreover, it apparently belongs to the human condition to aspire to power like this. Even the poor are not immune to the temptation, although the teaching of Jesus suggests that they are more likely to see through the illusions to which the rich are prey. Still, what the rich are enslaved to, no one is immune from; thus the list expands at the end to include "everyone, slave and free." True to the larger realism of the Bible about sin, the passage acknowledges both the real distinctions within human society and the general, universal condition that none of us escapes.

The universal character of this scene is underscored by the clear allusion it makes to Gen. 3, where Adam and Eve hide from YHWH after succumbing to the serpent's lures. The verbal echo is exact: just as Adam and Eve "hid themselves from the presence of the LORD" (3:8), so the earth-dwellers call on the rocks and mountains to "hide us from the face of him who is seated on the throne" (Rev. 6:16). Acting in a way appropriate to their name, the earth-dwellers summon the earth itself to come to their aid. The geological imagery echoes Isaiah's oracle of doom, describing the day when

> the idols shall utterly pass away.
> And people shall enter the caves of the rocks
>   and the holes of the ground,
> from before the terror of the LORD,
>   and from the splendor of his majesty,
>   when he rises to terrify the earth. (Isa. 2:18–19)

Yet if the earth-dwellers' desire is at one level to conceal themselves, their cry carries another, darker overtone: the wish for self-annihilation. And so we can invoke yet a third intertextual echo, the words of Jesus to the "daughters of Jerusalem" on the way to the crucifixion: "For behold, the days are coming when [your children] will say, 'Blessed are the barren and the wombs that never bore and the breasts that never nursed!' Then they will begin to say to the mountains, 'Fall on us,' and to the hills, 'Cover us'" (Luke 23:29–30). This death wish is really just the ultimate consequence of "hiding from the face of God," for to hide from God's face, to be cut off from his gracious presence, is nothing less than to die. The earth-dwellers' terror before the Creator is such that they would *un*make the life he has made and given them. Better to die, it would seem, than to fall into the hands of the living God.

If the earth-dwellers' problem were simply "god" in the abstract, then perhaps the situation might after all be managed. The gods and idols of human construction have their own dangers, but generally they are at our beck and call. They can be called upon when a bit of transcendence is needed, and conveniently put away again once the danger is past. What strikes fear in the earth-dwellers' hearts, however, is the God who refuses to be so managed, the God who has come threateningly near in the apocalypse of Jesus Christ. The earth-dwellers thus seek to hide not just from "the face of him who is seated on the throne" but from "the wrath of the Lamb, for the great day of their wrath has come, and who can stand?" (Rev. 6:16–17).

The wrath of the Lamb! This is indeed an unexpected twist. That the Father should be wrathful is not a totally unfamiliar idea, especially in the kind of theology where "gentle Jesus meek and mild" stands between sinful humanity and the Father's judgment. On this reading, Jesus is the purely passive and human victim who absorbs or deflects the Father's anger. The problem with this view is the sharp tension it seems to posit between the divine anger and the divine love, as also between the persons of the Trinity. It is much better to say that the divine wrath is the form that God's love assumes when it encounters resistance on the part of the creature; it is the divine "no" to the plight of humanity in this "present evil age"; and so Christ appears on the same side as the Father, as equally the agent of God's love *and* his judgment. Jesus Christ is the judge—what conviction could be more fundamental to the whole New Testament witness?—and therefore, inevitably and necessarily, the executor of the wrath and judgment of God.[15]

The earth-dwellers see this truth clearly, although they draw a disastrously wrong set of conclusions from what they see. They are right in speaking not only of the wrath of the Lamb but of "their" wrath, that is, the anger of the Father and

---

15. This is true, even if we also go on to say that the Son of God executes the divine judgment against sin and death by undergoing it himself—the "judge judged in our place," as Karl Barth puts it in *Church Dogmatics*, vol. 4.1, ed. G. W. Bromiley and T. F. Torrance (Edinburgh: Clark, 1956), 211.

the Son together.[16] They are, further, correct in their supposition that the coming of God and the Lamb must spell the end of the world in its present constitution. Who can stand in the great day of their wrath (6:17)? The question answers itself: no one. Revelation's indictment against fallen, idol-crazed humanity is as sweeping and universal as that of Paul, who quotes scripture to prove his case that "none is righteous, no, not one" (Rom. 3:10).

Surely the source of the earth-dwellers' terror is more real and immediate than simply a vague sense of being plagued by a troubled conscience. They fear Christ's power (his incarnation as the Lion, we might say) because they have previously done violence to him as their victim, as the Lamb. Having murdered the Lamb or his followers, they naturally fear that when he comes in power he will avenge himself. The church knows that "when he [Christ] was reviled, he did not revile in return; when he suffered, he did not threaten, but continued entrusting himself to him who judges justly" (1 Pet. 2:23). But the earth-dwellers do not know this. This is why they seek to protect themselves, hiding, seeking shelter, like Adam and Eve in the garden. If what Christ represents is God's decisive turning toward the world in grace, mercy, and peace, then the dwellers on earth seem doomed to turn away from this turning, misunderstanding God's righteous judgment as an expression of his hatred. If we were to imagine such turning away being extrapolated into eternity, this would be one way of picturing damnation.

From this point, we could easily imagine the story moving swiftly toward its divinely willed resolution. The opening of the sixth seal would culminate in the destruction of the earth-dwellers. The opening of the seventh seal would form the climax, announcing the salvation of the elect and the final coming of God's kingdom. Everything would achieve the kind of crystalline clarity we expect from apocalyptic literature, which is known, after all, for its stark dualisms: believer and nonbeliever, saved and lost, church and world. This would be a D. H. Lawrence–style reading of the Apocalypse, with the eschatological line being drawn with stark clarity right in the midst of history.

How odd, then, that this moment of absolute crystal clarity never arrives—at least not within the framework of the seven seals. Not only is the opening of the seventh seal delayed while John narrates a long, apparently unrelated vision (Rev. 7), but even the sixth seal itself leaves us hanging. John leaves us with the image of the dwellers on earth cowering in fear and terror, crying out for the rocks and caves to cover them and asking "who can stand?" in the opening of the *sixth* seal. In John's numerological schema, six is the number of penultimacy, the next to last, the time before the end. It is therefore the appropriate number for describing history—the situation in which all readers and hearers of Revelation find themselves.

16. A textual variant in 6:17 says "his" wrath; but this is clearly a harmonization with the phrase "the wrath of the Lamb" in 6:16. "Their" is the reading chosen in NA[27]; see Bruce M. Metzger, *A Textual Commentary on the Greek New Testament*, 2nd ed. (London: United Bible Societies, 1994), 668.

If, however, we find ourselves at the moment not of the last things, but of the next to last, this means there is still time—time to acknowledge the crucified not as our enemy but as our hope. This is not to say that we have infinite time, because time, by its very nature, is finite. The book is framed on either end by the stern announcement that "the time is near" (1:3; 22:10); this must be taken seriously. But for now, there is still time. One of the ways in which the Apocalypse subverts our expectations is that it shows us a God who, although decidedly impatient with evil, is extraordinarily patient with his creatures. Such patience is not weakness, but the counterpart to God's holiness, justice, and wisdom. He executes judgment on the world precisely in order to reclaim the world from the powers of death and hades. In the Lamb's death and life, that judgment has already been executed, in humanity's favor; would that the earth-dwellers understood that!

The fifth and the sixth seals, with their paired images of the martyrs and the earth-dwellers, may be seen as forming a kind of icon of the church and the world. Each bears a particular relationship to the Lamb. The church suffers with him, having responded to his call to follow in the way of the cross. But the church often betrays its own identity. Instead of seeking the way of lowliness, it tries to make its home among "the kings of the earth and the great ones . . . and the rich." For this reason, we cannot restrict the meaning of the phrase "the earth-dwellers" to Roman or other persecutors of the church (a theme emphasized throughout Minear 1968). Christians, too, can behave like earth-dwellers. The struggle between church and world runs right through the church itself. If the fifth seal functions as an invitation to the community, the sixth seal serves as a warning: "Don't betray the testimony of Jesus by aligning yourself with the forces of the present age!" And if the church is often all too worldly in the way it lives and speaks, the world itself is not forgotten by God. God's judgment of the world is a sign that he has not abandoned it. The sixth seal is dark and troubling—and there will be far darker passages still to come—but it is not without hope. Somewhat curiously, church and world find themselves in much the same position: awaiting the judgment of God and the Lamb.

REVELATION 7

THE GREAT TRIBULATION

And now I stand here on trial because of my hope in the promise made by God to our fathers, to which our twelve tribes hope to attain, as they earnestly worship night and day.

—Acts 26:6–7

Who shall separate us from the love of Christ? Shall tribulation, or distress, or persecution, or famine, or nakedness, or danger, or sword? As it is written, "For your sake we are being killed all the day long; we are regarded as sheep to be slaughtered." No, in all these things we are more than conquerors through him who loved us.

—Romans 8:35–37

The vision in Rev. 7 is one of the famous interludes that periodically interrupt the flow of the Apocalypse. David Barr calls them "satellite incidents," episodes spun off from the main story line and that serve as a kind of commentary on the action, although without actually advancing the plot (1998: 76). These interruptions force the hearer/reader to pause and consider more deeply what is really going on in this story. The overall theme of the present vision is that of the elect and consummated people of God, displayed as the two panels of a great diptych (7:4–8 and 7:9–17).

7:1–3 As the prelude to that scene, however, John narrates a vision of four angels standing at the four corners of the earth, waiting attentively to receive their instructions from on high. Four is the number of the cosmos, of created totality, as we saw with the four living creatures in the heavenly worship. Charged with power over the elements of earth, air, water, and fire,[1] these angels have been granted authority to restrain or set loose the fury of God's judgment upon the world.[2] In the present vision, the instrument of that fury is the typhoon, a wind capable of laying waste both earth and sea (7:1). The scope of the threatened destruction would seem to be unlimited. It is, therefore, somewhat surprising that among all the living things that could be named, John singles out trees for special attention (7:1, 3). This small detail lends an odd touch of pathos to the scene: trees are especially vulnerable to the power of wind. They here serve as a particular emblem for the devastation that would befall all of creation, should the four angels at last unleash the four winds.

The whole force of the passage, however, lies in their *not* doing so—at least not yet. A fifth angel arises out of the east, the place of dawn and rebirth, bearing in his hands "the seal of the living God" and instructing the four angels not to unbind the winds until the slaves of God have been "sealed . . . on their foreheads" (7:3). Seals were ubiquitous in the ancient world, signifying on the one hand ownership—a decree marked with the monarch's seal could be taken as bearing the full weight of his authority—and on the other hand secrecy and proof against tampering. (The Lamb's seven-sealed scroll illustrates both principles.) It is no surprise, then, that the metaphor of the seal appears frequently in early Christianity to denote the new life in Christ. As the imperial seal showed what belonged to the emperor, so the Christian "seals" of baptism and the Holy Spirit showed what belonged to God (2 Cor. 1:22; Eph. 1:13; 4:30; cf. Rom. 4:11). To be sealed with the Spirit is to be marked as God's own, to be elected, set apart, and so safely delivered through the waters of judgment. This reminds us of the pregnant question posed by the earth-dwellers at the opening of the sixth seal: "For the great day of their [i.e., God's and the Lamb's] wrath has come, and who can stand?" (Rev. 6:17).

Those "who can stand" in the day of judgment, clearly, are the chosen and righteous of God. This is the theme of the double vision that follows. As in the coming forward of the Lion/Lamb, so the present vision involves a sequence of hearing and seeing: first John hears the number of those sealed, "144,000, sealed from every tribe of the sons of Israel" (7:4), and then sees "a great multitude that no one could number, from every nation, from all tribes and peoples and languages" (7:9).

7:4–8 The key to understanding this vision is to read it holistically and interactively: each part sheds light on the other. We begin with the 144,000. Some are scandalized that the number of the saved in Revelation should be so small. In words that could have been written by D. H. Lawrence, the great pragmatist

1. At 14:18 we encounter an angel who tends the sacred fire, at 16:5 an angel of the waters.
2. The verb *krateō*, used of the angels' action of "holding back" the winds, has the same root as *Pantokratōr*, literally "the one who holds all things," the Almighty.

philosopher Charles Peirce wrote that the New Testament is a story of increasing bitterness, until in the last book "its poor distracted author represents that all the time Christ was talking about having come to save the world, the secret design was to catch the entire human race, with the exception of a paltry 144,000, and souse them all in a brimstone lake."[3] But surely Peirce misses the point. The number 144,000 is not meant to be taken literally; rather, it must be understood in light of John's overall scheme of numeric symbolism. It is the product of 144, or twelve times twelve (the twelve tribes of the sons of Israel multiplied by the twelve apostles of the Lamb; cf. 21:12–14), and a thousand, which in terms of biblical imagination denotes a vast cohort. Whatever else we may say about it, 144,000 is meant to be a large number, though evidently not as large as the "great multitude" in the scene that immediately follows (see Boring 1989: 130).

But whether the sealed are few or many, the gathering has an undeniably Israelite character. The sealed of God—who else could this be but his people Israel? So much is clear from the vision itself, with its careful enumeration of the twelve tribes of the sons of Jacob. The only question is whether the 144,000 are "spiritual" Israel, meaning the church, or in some sense Israel after the flesh, the people of God prior to Messiah's coming or the ongoing Jewish element within the church. Writing in the third century, Bishop Victorinus embraced the last of these options: he saw the 144,000 as representing specifically Jewish Christians.[4] There are two major problems with this reading. First, in Rev. 14 we will once again meet the 144,000, and there it seems clear that they represent all those who would "follow the Lamb wherever he goes," Jew and Gentile alike (14:4). Second, it is hard to imagine that the two parts of this vision are really meant to refer to discrete groups. As John hears of the Lion but sees the Lamb, and as the Lion and the Lamb are one, so he hears the roll call of the tribes but sees the great multitude, with the strong implication that the second vision is a deepening or commentary of the first. It is the unanimous witness of the New Testament that the church *is* Israel (e.g., Gal. 6:16; 1 Cor. 10; Eph. 2:12, 19; 3:6; 1 Pet. 2:9–10), the same elected and beloved people of God who were delivered from Egypt, though now under the conditions of the messianic age and with the addition of the Gentiles to Abraham's children after the flesh.

Yet while this is a great part of the truth, it is not all the truth. The strength of Victorinus's interpretation is that even if we make the claim that the church *is* Israel, we must not do so in such a way that real, living Jews become simply irrelevant. The dark side of the understanding of the church as Israel is the long history of supersessionism, which may be most simply stated as the idea that, if the church is God's people, the Jews are no longer so. This "replacement theory" has had disastrous theological and political consequences over the centuries,

3. Charles S. Peirce, *The Essential Peirce: Selected Philosophical Writings*, ed. Nathan Houser and Christian Kloesel (Bloomington: Indiana University Press, 1992), 365.
4. Arthur William Wainwright, *Mysterious Apocalypse: Interpreting the Book of Revelation* (Nashville: Abingdon, 1993), 28.

does not seem warranted by scripture, and has been widely repudiated in recent Christian theology.[5]

I do not believe, however, that the Apocalypse commits us to any such supersessionist theory. If what John sees are the twelve tribes of the sons of Israel, this says nothing per se about the composition of this people, whether Jew or Gentile or some combination thereof. Like other New Testament writings, Revelation is not trying to answer questions that arose only after the final separation between the church and the synagogue. What we can say is that Israel's historic twelve tribes form a fitting emblem of the church for two reasons: (1) because they represent the people of God insofar as they have been purged and purified (note the absence of Dan, a tribe viewed with suspicion in both early Jewish and Christian sources);[6] and (2) because they constitute an army. Surely Bauckham is right that the enumeration of the 144,000 must be understood as a military census and that the tribes are being mustered for their battle against God's enemies at the end of the age (1993b: 76–80). Indeed, this picture of the church as an army corresponds exactly to Christ's identity as the Lion of Judah, a warrior-king like his ancestor David.

7:9–12 Yet just as the announcement of Christ the Lion gives way to the vision of the slaughtered Lamb, so too does the roll call of the tribes yield to something far more wonderful: "After this I looked, and behold, a great multitude that no one could number, from every nation, from all tribes and peoples and languages, standing before the throne and before the Lamb, clothed in white robes, with palm branches in their hands, and crying out with a loud voice, 'Salvation belongs to our God who sits on the throne, and to the Lamb!'" (7:9–10).

What John sees is an *ochlos*, translated in ESV as "multitude," but perhaps rendered more simply as "crowd." It is the same word used in the Gospels to denote the common people who swarmed excitedly around Jesus (Mark 14:43; 15:8; Matt. 27:20). Moreover, this crowd is drawn from "every nation, from all tribes and peoples and languages" (Rev. 7:9; cf. 5:9; 11:9; 13:7; 14:6; 17:15). In the poetic formula of Henry Swete, this phrase used repeatedly in the Apocalypse "found a daily illustration in the polyglott [sic] cosmopolitan crowd who jostled one another in the agora or on the quays of the Asian seaport towns" (1908: 100). A few years ago I found myself waiting for a flight at Pearson International Airport in Toronto, watching the polyglot, cosmopolitan crowd jostling for position at the ticket counters. The computers were down and many flights were being canceled, making the scene even more chaotic than usual. I often find crowds depressing,

---

5. See Bruce D. Marshall, "The Jewish People and Christian Theology," in *The Cambridge Companion to Christian Doctrine*, ed. Colin Gunton (Cambridge: Cambridge University Press, 1997).

6. There is no single, decisive ordering of the twelve tribes in the Old Testament, although the listing in Gen. 49 is perhaps the most common. John's list is idiosyncratic mainly in its exclusion of Dan, a tribe that the church fathers associated with the antichrist (e.g., Irenaeus, *Against Heresies* 5.30.2).

but on this occasion there was something oddly exhilarating about the scene. I noticed a few men wearing yarmulkes. The presence of Jews was a quiet reminder that there is a central thread to the human story and that it is made up of God's covenant with Israel, to which the Gentiles, too, have been added in Jesus Christ. When the heavenly city comes, its name will be Jerusalem, and it will receive "the glory and the honor of the [Gentiles]" (21:26).

In Rev. 4–5 we saw the heavenly worship around the divine throne continually expanding, from the cherubim and elders to countless angels to "every creature" in the cosmos (5:13). If that is the cosmic liturgy, the present scene is the liturgy of the nations, the *Internationale* of redeemed humankind. Although the crowd is multilingual, it is nonetheless able to cry aloud with one voice to God and the Lamb (7:10). Unity and difference, the one and the many, are here depicted as being mutually reinforcing rather than competitive. It is now the nations' turn to lead the worship of God, and when they sing their hymn the cherubim, elders, and angels respond with a doxology of their own: "Amen! Blessing and glory and wisdom and thanksgiving and honor and power and might be to our God forever and ever! Amen" (7:12).

Creaturely reality in the Bible is *ek*-centric: to find one's center in God is, paradoxically, to be freed to be uniquely and oddly one's self. Gathered around the divine throne, the tongues of all creatures are loosed to find their own peculiar parts in the cosmic song.

7:13–17 As in the scene of the Lamb's presentation in Rev. 5, so here too the meaning of the vision is brought out by a dialogue between John and an elder. The elder asks John: "Who are these, clothed in white robes, and from where have they come?" In what amounts to a polite confession of ignorance John replies, "Sir, you know." The elder then identifies this white-robed army as "the ones coming out of the great tribulation," those who have "washed their robes and made them white in the blood of the Lamb."

"Tribulation" (*thlipsis*) is one of the great themes of the Apocalypse, as we have already seen in the discussion of the seven churches and the seven seals. The present vision invites us to penetrate more deeply into the meaning of this key term. If, up to this point, the meaning of *thlipsis* has been centered on suffering or even punishment (cf. 2:9–10), now we see that the distress of God's people is in fact their passage from death into life. Their suffering is a cleansing, a clothing, perhaps even an investiture in office corresponding to the Lamb's own. By virtue of his high-priestly work they themselves have become a kingdom of priests, standing "before the throne of God, and serv[ing] him day and night in his temple" (7:15). The Lamb's death thus marks the birth pangs of the new creation, so that to be his follower and witness is to participate in the life he brings.

We now step back to examine the two parts of the vision synoptically. This is a vision of the people of God, the saints; but is either of these groups to be identified with the church? We might well doubt it. One of the more curious features of the Apocalypse is the complete absence of the word *ekklēsia* in the main body of the work, between the close of the letters to the churches (3:22) and the concluding lines (22:16). Dispensationalist interpreters have an ingenious explanation for this omission. The church is not mentioned, they argue, for the simple reason all the Christians have been raptured into heaven! But a more serious reason for this silence presents itself. As the oracles to the churches indicate, the *ekklēsia* is indeed the audience of Revelation, and in a quite literal sense the congregations are hearing the book read aloud. The prophecy does not, however, simply reproduce their empirical ecclesiality, answering history (the time of the old eon) with more history. The churches are being shown a *novum*, the new thing that is coming, life on the far side of the great tribulation that is coming over all the world. In this sense we might say that the subject matter of the vision is not the church present and visible, but the eschatological people of God. The vision is not of what the churches are, but of what they are called to become.

But unless we think of the eschatological church as a Platonic ideal, floating free of all time, space, and struggle, then we must go on to say that it is precisely *the churches* whose destiny John narrates. It is as if he were saying to them: this is who you are, this is your life. Has he not told his hearers that they are participants in "the tribulation and the kingdom and the patient endurance that are in Jesus" (1:9; cf. 2:9–10)? By virtue of Christ's victory, they are already kings and priests to God. By virtue of his victory once accomplished, they are the victors. But they are all this in the mode of hope and of promise. "Become what you already are" is generally bad advice, if we consider who we are in ourselves. Spoken to those whose identity is sealed by Christ's promise, it is the very best advice possible.

The language of sealing is prominent in the first half of the vision, and now perhaps we are in a better position to see why. Signet rings aside, the ultimate origin of the sealing imagery is the story of the exodus, in which YHWH commands the people to smear the blood of the paschal lamb on their doorposts as protection against the angel of death. Centuries later, Ezekiel would tell how a scribe passed through faithless Jerusalem, marking a remnant so that they might be spared in the massacre about to descend on the city (Ezek. 9).[7] By virtue of its sealing, Israel/the church is both identified as God's own and offered protection from the coming apocalyptic ordeal. Sprinkled with the blood of the Lamb, called out of "Egypt" (Rev. 11:8), the people of God are drawn inexorably into the event of his Passover.

The countless multitude, by contrast, are those who have their passage through the Red Sea already behind them. They have "washed their robes and made them white in the blood of the Lamb" (7:14). From Count Nikolaus von Zinzendorf and the Wesleys onward, the evangelical Pietist tradition has made the blood of Christ into a major focal point of Christian devotion; it became a way of talking about his "passive righteousness" displayed at the cross. To be washed in the blood

---

7. Commentators regularly note that this "mark" or "sign" would have been the letter *tau*, written in later Hebrew script as + or X—the sign of the cross.

of the Lamb was thus to make this righteousness one's own. What this tradition misses, to some degree, is the character of discipleship as public confession of faith leading to martyrdom: in Rev. 7 it is not the individual, but the *people of God* who wash their robes and make them white (the color of victory) in the Lamb's blood. In this sense, the vision of the church as Israel in 7:4–8 serves as an important check on affect-centered, sentimentalized theologies of the cross. On the other hand, what this tradition gets right is the conviction that the Lamb's death seals a profoundly personal bond between him and his followers, a mutual participation or *communio*. A theology so assimilated to the conventions of polite society that it can no longer speak eloquently about Christ's blood is, to that extent, sadly impoverished.[8]

The question is sometimes raised whether John expected all Christians to be martyrs, or whether he saw the latter as, so to speak, an elite group within the larger church. I am not sure that this distinction would have made much sense to John. Rather than beginning with Christians and asking whether some are martyrs and some are not, John begins with the apocalyptic reality of the Lamb. It is *his* Passover that stands at the book's center. But since Christian existence is a participation in Christ, clearly the Lamb's followers must in some way share in his death, whether through martyrdom or some other means; death is in any case implicit in baptism.[9]

No one escapes the great tribulation. The real question for contemporary Western Christians is whether we view martyrdom as an exotic relic from an age long past, or whether we stand in solidarity with the martyrs who are even now offering up their costly witness. In many places in the world, the bodies of Christians continue to be a site of contestation between the present and the coming eons. This is not to deny that others suffer too, often grievously; but it is where the world's agony first claims us. The communion of saints is a communion in Christ's apocalyptic sufferings. We may conveniently ignore this fact, but only at the cost of ignoring the one who claims the martyrs' bodies as his own: "Saul, Saul, why are you persecuting *me*?" (Acts 9:4; 22:7).

At the outset of this chapter, John sees an angel rising from the east bearing the seal of the *living* God. This is the only time in the work this phrase is used. Why does it appear here? It is first of all appropriate as a reminder that the God of Jesus Christ is the true God, to be contrasted with all false and constructed idols, the gods who lead only to death (1 Thess. 1:9). But it also alerts us to God as essentially living; God has and is life; this is at the heart of the mystery of the slaughtered and risen Lamb. To be sealed by this God means to be made a participant in a life

8. George Hunsinger, *Disruptive Grace: Studies in the Theology of Karl Barth* (Grand Rapids: Eerdmans, 2000), 361–63.

9. A baptismal subtext seems to run through all of Rev. 7, both in the theme of "sealing" in 7:4–8 and in the motif of "washing" in 7:9–17, although admittedly it is the robes, and not the saints, who are washed in this passage. No doubt the white-robed saints in Revelation influenced the early Christian practice of baptism, which often involved clothing the baptized in white robes.

that, while not immune from death—for Jesus himself was not—is yet victorious over death, hades, and their allies in this passing eon.

All of this has taken place in the interlude caused by the strange delay between the sixth and the seventh seals. With the close of this vision the sequence resumes. We move on to explore the climax of the sequence.

REVELATION 8–9

OUT OF THE ABYSS

Nothing is going to happen in this book. There is only a little violence here and there in the language, at the corner where eternity clips time.

—Annie Dillard, *Holy the Firm*

The opening of the first six seals occurs at a rapid pace, with one event following another in dizzying succession; as readers we perhaps feel a bit disoriented. The vision of the 144,000 and of the great multitude offered a chance for us to catch our breath. In place of the world unmade, we see the church victorious. In place of the terrors of history, we catch a glimpse of that glorious future toward which all of history is headed.

8:1 The act of sealing was done for a purpose: in order to buy time, so that God's saints might be protected against the four winds of destruction. Earth's reprieve from judgment has been only temporary. Surely the opening of the seventh seal will mean the completion of God's secret plan, the coming of the end, the climax of the story. The "time" first announced at 1:3 is at hand. In light of these expectations, what actually happens next may seem a bit of an anticlimax: "When the Lamb opened the seventh seal, there was silence in heaven for about half an hour" (8:1).

There is good reason for this silence, however. What can the contents of the sealed scroll be, if not the word of God, disclosed by the one who *is* that Word himself? And although the word of God will be spoken regardless of whether we hear it, the church's hearing of the word depends on our being receptive: silence is the presupposition of listening. Dietrich Bonhoeffer makes the point in the famous opening lines of his Christology:

Teaching about Christ begins in silence. "Be silent, for that is the absolute" (Kierke-gaard). This has nothing to do with mystical silence which, in its absence of words, is, nevertheless, the soul secretly chattering away to itself. The church's silence is silence before the Word. In proclaiming the Word, the church must fall silent before the inexpressible: Let what cannot be spoken be worshipped in silence (Cyril of Alexandria). . . . To speak of Christ means to keep silent; to be silent about Christ means to speak. The proclamation of Christ is the church speaking from a proper silence.[1]

The Lamb himself is silent in Revelation. For him to have a speaking role would be superfluous, since the entire work is his speech and he himself is the embodied speech-act of the Father. The term "half an hour" has no obvious mystical or symbolic meaning, although Henry Swete's simple explanation is attractive: "Half-an-hour, though a relatively short time, is a long interval in a drama, and makes an impressive break between the Seals and the Trumpets" (1908: 107). We can perhaps imagine the lector pausing at this point for dramatic effect: the hearers naturally want to find out what will happen next. While time may be scrambled in the Apocalypse, it still rehearses a story, like our own lives, a sequence of happenings that can only be lived and told in time.[2]

8:2 After the half-hour pause a new septenary begins, this time seven trumpets blown by "the seven angels who stand before God." These angels are no doubt the seven archangels of Jewish tradition, bearing the impressive names Uriel, Raphael, Raguel, Michael, Sariel, Gabriel, and Remiel.[3] Of these seven, only Gabriel and Michael appear in the New Testament (Gabriel in Luke 1:19, 26 and Michael in Rev. 12 and Jude 9). In the present setting there is no need to name these angels, because their only role is to blow the trumpets: their identity is absorbed into their function. John underscores this subordinate status by employing the divine passive voice: seven trumpets "were given" (*edothēsan*) to them. The angels blow their trumpets, but it is God whose power and wisdom causes them to do so.

8:3–4 Before the blowing of the trumpets, however, John describes the actions of yet another angel, who is given incense to mix with the prayers of "all the saints." The temple in Jerusalem had, in addition to the altar of sacrifice, an altar of incense, a point already noted in connection with the fifth seal (6:9–11).

---

1. Dietrich Bonhoeffer, *Christ the Center*, trans. John Bowden (New York: Harper & Row, 1966), 27. Bonhoeffer's view of mystical experience is, to be sure, rather stereotyped.

2. Other reasons have been adduced for the silence in heaven: time for the prayers of the saints (8:4) to ascend upward to heaven, or a "sabbath rest" like the one that, according to Jewish tradition, will precede the coming of God's kingdom. Thus 2 Esdras (4 Ezra) 7:29–34: "After those years my son the Messiah shall die, and all who draw human breath. Then the world shall be turned back to primeval silence for seven days, as it was at the first beginnings; so that no one shall be left" (NRSV).

3. Tobit 12:15 speaks of Raphael as "one of the seven holy angels who present the prayers of the saints and enter into the presence of the glory of the Holy One" (RSV), while Michael plays a prominent role in Dan. 10:13, 21; 12:1. The full list of seven names appears in 1 Enoch 20.

Both sacrifice and incense were sensual means for coming into the presence of YHWH, prayer clothed in bodily action, a form of "bending God's ear." The Bible sometime describes incense as a form of sacrifice: "Let my prayer be counted as incense before you, and the lifting up of my hands as the evening sacrifice" (Ps. 141:2). Mixed with the smoldering incense, the prayers of the saints—not of just the martyrs this time but of *all* the saints—rise up before the throne on high.

Brief as they are, these two references to prayer are important reminders that, in the Apocalypse, the commerce between heaven and earth moves both ways. God is the primary agent in the book: therefore the primary thrust of movement is downward, from heaven toward earth. And yet it would be wrong to say that God rules simply by fiat. If the church is called to listen to the word of God, God also listens; the prayers of his people matter to him. In the New Testament the paradigm of both human prayer and God's listening is the prayer of Jesus, who, although he is the eternal Son, prays *as a human being* to the Father.[4] The church's prayers are empowered and emboldened by the prayer of Christ. It is rather striking that, in the same passage where Paul speaks of Christ's intercession at the right hand of God, he quotes Ps. 44:22: "For your sake we are killed all the day long; we are regarded as sheep to be slaughtered" (Rom. 8:36). The "slaughter" of the faithful is their participation in the agony that heralds the coming of the new creation. It is precisely in this situation of apocalyptic distress that the Lamb intercedes for his own.

8:5 The prayers of the saints move upward, carried aloft by the incense that is the prayer of Christ himself. The same angel now fills his censer with fire from the altar and flings it downward upon the earth. There may be an echo here of Ezek. 10:2–6, in which a scribe—the same scribe who had marked the foreheads of the righteous citizens of Jerusalem—is commanded by God to scatter burning coals upon the city. After the sealing comes the event of judgment. We may also think of Jesus's apocalyptically charged words in the Gospel of Luke: "I came to cast fire on the earth, and would that it were already kindled! I have a baptism to be baptized with, and how great is my distress until it is accomplished!" (Luke 12:49–50).

The fire cast upon earth by the angel is accompanied by thunder, voices, lightning, and earthquakes, calling to mind the atmosphere of God's appearing to Israel on Mount Sinai. This is the language of theophany.[5] Now, at last, the silence that accompanied the opening of the seventh seal is broken. The time has come for the blowing of the seven trumpets.

8:6–12 What happens next might be called a "controlled descent into chaos," as each trumpet announces a series of natural and human catastrophes on an unprecedented scale. The trumpets follow the usual four-plus-three pattern observed

---

4. A point insisted on and developed with great insight by St. Maximus Confessor.

5. These atmospheric phenomena constitute something of a set piece in Revelation. The language is repeated at 4:5; 10:3–4; 11:19; 16:18. In each instance the coming of God seems to be signified. The reader is invited to reflect on what each of these theophanies means in context.

elsewhere in the Apocalypse. The first four trumpet blasts share certain stereotyped features, showing that they belong together. The fifth and sixth trumpets mark a moment of intensification, while the blowing of the seventh trumpet is delayed by an interlude (10:1–11:14) that, like the interval preceding the seventh seal, discloses something of the mystery of the *ekklēsia*.

It is helpful to lay out the events of the first four trumpets in schematic form:

trumpet	1	2	3	4
object	earth	sea	freshwaters and rivers	sky
means	hail, fire, blood	fiery mountain cast into the sea	star named Wormwood	"striking" of heavenly bodies
effect	incineration: (a) one third of earth and of trees are burned up and (b) all grass is burned up	pollution: (a) one third of sea becomes blood, (b) one third of sea creatures die, and (c) one third of ships destroyed	poisoning: (a) one third of waters become bitter and (b) "many people" die from the water	darkness: (a) one third of sun, moon, and stars darkened, affecting (b) one third of day and night

John characteristically uses four to suggest the totality of creation. The means of destruction are extraordinary cosmic phenomena, some of which (hail, blood, darkness) are reminiscent of the plagues visited by YHWH on Egypt, while others (fiery mountain, the star called "Wormwood") suggest the primal energies of earth and sky. While the impact of these forces on earth is deadly, it is also strictly limited in scope. A third of the earth and of trees are burned, although "all green grass" is burned (perhaps because grass scorches so easily); a third of the sea turns to blood; a third of the waters become bitter; and so on. Although this is more than the one-quarter devastation inflicted when the fourth seal was opened, it is a good deal less than the total annihilation we might have expected. We find ourselves in the realm not of ultimate, but of penultimate things.

The limitation of "one third" does not make these events any less terrible to contemplate. Even more so than at the opening of the sixth seal, the fabric of creation itself seems to be torn open. The troubling question the passage raises, perhaps, is whether God considers creation to be finally *disposable*, or whether he finds a value in creatures beyond that of mere instrumental utility. Does God care for his creatures? Is God's eye really on the sparrow? Many scientists are convinced that about sixty-five million years ago, over half of then-existing species were wiped out, in a catastrophe event known as the "K-T mass extinctions." If the theory is correct, this is the event that killed off almost all the dinosaurs. Moreover, the current scientific consensus is that the extinctions were triggered by the impact of a six-mile-wide asteroid crashing into the ocean near the Yucatán

Peninsula in Mexico. This sounds uncannily like "a great mountain, burning with fire, [being] thrown into the sea."[6]

I mention this, not because I wish to posit any sort of one-to-one correspondence between Revelation and events in geological history—this would be "decoding" of the most speculative and irresponsible sort—but simply as a reminder that the world is both a very strange and a very rough place. In such a world, scenarios like the one in Rev. 8 may in fact be less the exception than the rule. If the K-T extinctions had not occurred there might not be mammals like ourselves, nor would the saurischian dinosaurs have evolved into the sparrows who are beheld, and loved, by the Father in heaven. To confess that "we believe in God the Father almighty, Creator of heaven and earth" entails the conviction that God does care for his creatures; yet such conviction is precisely an act of faith in that which is not yet seen (Heb. 11:3).

The Apocalypse narrates these events not in order to explain the way things are now, however, but to hold out the hope that *things will not always be like this.* Revelation's concern with cosmic happenings is strictly framed by its concern for the covenantal relationship between God and humankind. The world as we know it is beset by evil, sin, death, and the devil's reign of terror. The Apocalypse employs the idiom of cosmic catastrophe to describe the overturning of the present order and the coming of God's kingdom. Judgment is ordered toward mercy: thus the waters of bitterness (Rev. 8:10–11) will be sweetened by "the river of the water of life, bright as crystal, flowing from the throne of God and of the Lamb" (22:1).

8:13 As if to provide a respite for the reader from all this carnage, a brief, vivid scene intrudes in which John beholds an eagle crying: "Woe woe woe to those who live upon the earth from the voices of the trumpet still to come" (Lattimore 1979: 265). "Woe" is a familiar genre in scripture, appearing not only in the oracles of the prophets (e.g., Isa. 5:8–23; Jer. 13:27; Amos 5:18; Ezek. 16:23) but in the teaching of Jesus, whose blessings on the poor and the hungry are paired by Luke with the fierce woes he pronounces on the rich (Luke 6:24–26). Jesus also pronounced woes on the unbelieving cities of Galilee (Matt. 11:21–24) and on the scribes and Pharisees (Matt. 23:1–36; Luke 11:37–54). Like its counterpart the blessing, a woe is more than just an announcement of fact. It is "negative promissory" language, a corollary to the evangelical summons of "Repent!"[7] The prophet's vocation is not just to declare the truth but to induce repentance. That is why the eagle's cry sounds hopeful in context. Though the heavenly bodies above be darkened, the

6. Compounding the uncanniness, the Mexican name for the town nearest the impact site is Chicxulub, literally "the devil's tail." On the proposed relation between the meteorite impact and the extinctions, see Walter C. Alvarez, *T. Rex and the Crater of Doom* (Princeton: Princeton University Press, 1997).

7. The exception proves the rule. When Jesus says of his betrayer, "Woe to that man by whom the Son of Man is betrayed! It would have been better for that man if he had not been born" (Mark 14:21), he is speaking of the betrayal as a fait accompli. Judas's act is considered from the perspective of the role it plays in the economy of salvation, where the apocalyptic "must" predominates.

eagle still soars *en mesouranēmati* (literally, "in the middle of heaven"), declaring that the earth-dwellers' future is no fixed law of the Medes and the Persians. Fate does not rule; God rules. There is still time to repent and to live.

9:1–12 As always, the fifth element in John's septenaries brings with it a slowing of the action and a corresponding rehearsal of detail—this time of a rather horrifying sort. The fifth angel blows his trumpet, and a star falls from heaven, and "he"(!) is given a key to the bottomless pit, the Abyss. We do not need a precise geography of the lower regions to understand that this is a terrifying place. It is roughly equivalent to the realm of "Death and Hades," to which Christ alone holds the key (1:18). This key of hell is now "given" to the star-angel-spirit so that he might open the gates and release what lies within.

The opening of the abyss is first accompanied by smoke as from a great furnace, darkening the sun and the air. Then out of the smoke emerge swarming clouds of locusts. In Joel 1–2, locusts are likened to an invading army, ravaging crops, mowing down everything in their path; they are a sign of the coming Day of Yhwh. In John's vision this image is taken up and transformed into something even more awful: monsters of bizarre appearance, outfitted like cavalry horses, and equipped with the teeth of the lion and the sting of the scorpion. They are also quasihuman, having the faces of men[8] and the hair of women. In the world of Greek mythology perhaps the closest equivalent would be the Harpies, although Revelation's creatures seem even more grotesque than those horrible birds. The most disturbing thing about Revelation's locust-warriors is not their appearance, however, but what they are sent out to do: "They were told not to harm the grass of the earth or any green plant or any tree, but only those people who do not have the seal of God on their foreheads. They were allowed to torture them for five months, but not to kill them. . . . And in those days people will seek death but will not find it. They will long to die, but death will flee from them" (9:4–6). This is the first of the three woes announced by the eagle flying in midheaven.

9:13–19 The second woe is similar to the first. When the sixth angel blows his trumpet, a voice speaks from the altar commanding that "the four angels who are bound at the great river Euphrates" be set free. Prior to the opening of the seventh seal, four angels bound the four winds while the 144,000 were sealed. In the present passage it is the angels themselves who are bound. Whether these are the same angels hardly matters: the important thing is that their unloosing results in the execution of the judgment postponed at 7:1. Now the measured destruction described in 8:7–12 resumes, except that this time the one third of creatures killed are human beings, and the instruments of death are soldiers mounted on fabulous horses breathing fire, smoke, and sulfur. Once again there is an evocation of the plagues of Egypt: "By these three plagues a third of mankind was killed, by the fire and smoke and sulfur coming out of their mouths." John adds: "For the power

---

8. The Greek has *prosōpa anthrōpōn* ("faces of human beings"), but the martial imagery suggests that the faces may be specifically male.

of the horses is in their mouths and in their tails, for their tails are like serpents with heads, and by means of them they wound"—a postscript that seems almost gratuitous under the circumstances.

In the introduction, I discussed the idea that the Apocalypse recapitulates itself, repeating certain stereotyped patterns even as it advances forward. The relation between the seven seals and the seven trumpets provides a good illustration of this point. In the first sequence are four horsemen, in the second sequence locust-horses and the cavalry of 9:16–19. In the first sequence are four angels binding the four winds, in the second four angels bound by the river Euphrates. In the first sequence destruction is limited to a quarter of the earth, while in the second it extends to one third. The most potent correlation between the seals and trumpets, however, can be seen in the contrasting attitudes of human beings under divine judgment. The seals show the earth-dwellers cowering in fear before the wrath of the Lamb, while the trumpets describe an unrepentant humanity that refuses to heed the signs of impending doom: "The rest of mankind, who were not killed by these plagues, did not repent of the works of their hands nor give up worshiping demons and idols of gold and silver and bronze and stone and wood . . . , nor did they repent of their murders or their sorceries or their sexual immorality or their thefts" (9:20–21).

Another parallel between the seals and trumpets is helpful to understanding Revelation's mounting crescendo of violence:

> And I looked, and behold, a pale horse! And its rider's name was Death, and Hades followed him. (6:8)

> And the fifth angel blew his trumpet, and I saw a star fallen from heaven to earth, and he was given the key to the shaft of the bottomless pit. (9:1)

> They [the locusts] have as king over them the angel of the bottomless pit. His name in Hebrew is Abaddon,[9] and in Greek he is called Apollyon. (9:11)

What the fourth seal only hints at, the fifth trumpet makes explicit: the power that humankind must reckon with, the one Paul calls "the god of this world" (2 Cor. 4:4), is nothing less than the power of Satan, who rules over the realm of death. Two further clues show that we are in the realm of the demonic: (1) the transgression of boundaries, for example, the locusts combine aspects of insects, animals, and humans; in the Old Testament such mixing is frequently a sign of things unclean; and (2) sheer quantity: one of the characteristics of the demonic world seems to be its character as excess, as mindless duplication, as horde. The

---

9. Abaddon is referenced primarily in Israel's Wisdom literature (Job 26:6; 28:22; 31:12; Ps. 88:11; Prov. 15:11; 27:20). Both the Hebrew and the Greek terms mean "destruction," especially that experienced in Sheol, the realm of the dead.

devils inhabiting the Gerasene demoniac cry out: "My name is Legion, for we are many" (Mark 5:9).[10]

Later on in Revelation, we see Satan emerge as a distinct "person" in his own right (Rev. 12–13). The demonic is in some sense superpersonal, having the character of malign will and intentionality, while at the same time it is subpersonal, being less than the sum of the agencies that constitute it. The perfect picture of the demonic in modern times is the Nazi political rally, as portrayed in Leni Riefenstahl's brilliant propaganda film *Triumph of the Will*. But whether as superpersonal or subpersonal, the tendency of the demonic is toward the things of death. There is one final parallel between the seals and the trumpets: just as the kings, generals, and slaves seek death by asking the rocks and mountains to fall upon them, so the earth-dwellers seek the solace of death as a refuge from the scorpion-locusts: "And in those days people will seek death and will not find it. They will long to die, but death will flee from them" (9:6).

Honesty compels us to admit that Rev. 8–9 make for difficult reading at times. The incessant drumbeat of judgment, suffering, and torment seems to call into question faith in a God who "hates nothing that he has made" and "forgives the sins of the penitent." Even if it is true that God forgives the penitent, why should anyone turn in trust to a God who employs methods like these?

It is at just this point, however, that acknowledgment of the *penultimate* dualism of the Apocalypse—and indeed of the New Testament as a whole—proves indispensable to the task of interpretation. Revelation 9 offers an early glimpse of a theme that will become increasingly central as the story unfolds, namely, that the proximate agent of humanity's torment is not God but the demonic powers. The world of the New Testament is a world in thrall both to the evil one and to those created realities (in Paul's language, the "principalities and powers") that he commands for his service. This is by no means to deny God's ultimate sovereignty over the world, which Revelation could not be more insistent in affirming. Even such power as God's enemies exercise is only by dint of his permissive will. The four horsemen are "permitted" to take peace from the earth. The demonic cavalry are "permitted" to torment those who lack the seal of God. And in what is perhaps the most pregnant of these images, Apollyon the Destroyer is "given" the key of the bottomless pit to release the forces within.[11]

This "giving" or "handing over" of humanity to the powers is in fact a staple of the apocalyptic thought world of the New Testament. It can be seen in Rom. 1:24, 26, 28, where God "hands over" human beings to their own passions and the debasement of sin, and in Rom. 8:32 (cf. 1 Cor. 5:5), where God "hands over" his

10. Cf. Martin Luther's words in "A Mighty Fortress Is Our God": "Und wenn die Welt voll Teufel wär', und wollte uns gar verschlingen" ("And though this world with devils filled, should threaten to devour us").

11. In all these cases, the verb is the passive voice *edothē* ("he [she, it] was given").

own Son for the life of the world.[12] Here theological language comes close to its breaking point. We want to affirm that God is sovereign—what would the book of Revelation be without *that* conviction?—and also that the actions of the powers fall within the sway of that sovereignty, while avoiding the blasphemy that says that God is secretly in league with the enemy. To acknowledge such penultimate dualism, writes David Bentley Hart,

> is not to say that God's ultimate design for his creatures can be thwarted. It is to acknowledge, however, that his will can be resisted by a real and (by his grace) autonomous force of defiance, or can be hidden from us by the history of cosmic corruption, and that the final realization of the good he intends in all things has the form (not simply as a dramatic fiction, for our edification or his glory, nor simply as a paedagogical device on his part, but in truth) of a cosmic victory.[13]

What makes the Apocalypse such hard reading, perhaps, is that this paradox of assured victory and yet real conflict is stretched to the breaking point. I do not use the word "paradox" lightly. The mystery of God is a luminous mystery, and we should avoid all easy retreats into the darkness of the irrational and absurd. God is light indeed, but as Hart indicates, his light "can be hidden from us by the history of cosmic corruption" or obscured by what the apostle himself terms "the mystery of lawlessness" (2 Thess. 2:7).

These difficult central chapters of Revelation unfold under the sign of the Lamb, whose suffering on behalf of his enemies is the book's central clue to the nature of God. If God exercises patience with the world as his good creation, he shows nothing but fury for the world in its negative, fallen form as the realm of Satan's dominion—the world as "death working in all things, the power to dominate or slay, but not to make new."[14] "World" in the first sense is the world God "so loved" (John 3:16); "world" in the second sense is the world that Christ "overcame" (16:33). What we see in the visions of the seals and trumpets is the beginnings of the spiritual warfare that will become ever more visible and earth-shattering in the chapters that follow.

9:20–21 If Revelation's language concerning evil seems disconcertingly mythological at times, the book also has its ways of deflating the pretensions of the powers. We can see one of these at the very end of Rev. 9. When John writes that the earth-dwellers "did not repent of the works of their hands nor give up worshiping demons and idols of gold and silver and bronze and stone and wood, which cannot see or hear or walk," this might at first seem like a standard biblical

---

12. Rom. 8:32 uses *paredōken*, the same verb that denotes Judas's act of betrayal, his "handing over" of Jesus. On this theme, see Beverly Roberts Gaventa's illuminating essay "God Handed Them Over," in her *Our Mother Saint Paul* (Louisville: Westminster John Knox, 2007), 113–23.

13. David Bentley Hart, *The Doors of the Sea: Where Was God in the Tsunami?* (Grand Rapids: Eerdmans, 2005), 63.

14. Ibid., 65.

critique of idolatry (cf. Isa. 40:18–20; Jer. 10:1–11; Wisdom of Solomon 13–15). But in context, does not this passage say something more? The hordes of demons who fairly swarm through these chapters exercise their power only to the extent that we worship them, "construct" them, and so endow them with life. Such false worship can never withstand the coming of the one true God, to whom the Apocalypse bears its jubilant witness. Of Satan and his kingdom it can truly be said: "One little word shall fell him."

REVELATION 10

EATING THE SCROLL

And he said to me, "Son of man, eat whatever you find here. Eat this scroll, and go, speak to the house of Israel." So I opened my mouth, and he gave me this scroll to eat. And he said to me, "Son of man, feed your belly with this scroll that I give you and fill your stomach with it." Then I ate it, and it was in my mouth as sweet as honey.

—Ezekiel 3:1–3

The vision of the sixth trumpet concludes with a scene of frustration. The dwellers on earth have not repented of their ways. Not only that, but they are clearly caught up in a self-perpetuating cycle of idolatry and falsehood from which, humanly speaking, there is no escape. This is because they seek the solution to their plight in the very things that have enslaved them—the "demons and idols of gold and silver and bronze and stone and wood" (9:20). Breaking out of this vicious cycle of idolatry, bondage, and self-deception will require an energy and freedom that the earth-dwellers are incapable of providing for themselves.

That intervention will occur most obviously with the blowing of the seventh trumpet, which declares the coming of God's kingdom on earth and signals the resumption of the heavenly worship (11:15–19). Before that grand climax can occur, however, John once again inserts a delaying interlude between the sixth and seventh element in the sequence. Like the interlude that interrupts the seven seals, this one also has two parts: John's narration of his prophetic calling (10:1–11) followed by the story of the "two witnesses," a remarkable brief parable of the life of the church (11:1–13). While the two parts clearly ask to be read together, each is sufficiently rich that it makes sense to treat them separately.

10:1–2 The episode begins with the familiar "and I saw" formula, indicating the start of a fresh series of visions. This time John sees a strong or mighty angel (*angellon ischyron*) coming down from heaven. Here we see apocalypse in its specifically spatial aspect, breaking open earthly reality, creating hope where human possibilities are exhausted. After the constricting terrors of the trumpets, there is something joyful, surprising, and even cheerful about the coming of this angel. The whole scene becomes reenergized; something new is happening.

Alone among all the angels who come and go in Revelation, this mighty angel is rendered with a wealth of descriptive detail. All of his features allude to images already encountered: he is enveloped in cloud and rainbow (1:7; 4:3), his face shines like the sun (1:16), his feet are like pillars of fire (1:15), and he holds a scroll in his hand (5:1). We may think of him as a kind of fused icon of God and of Christ. Even his location, planted between earth and sea, is suggestive of God's identity as Creator of all things. His strength and radiant countenance especially evoke Christ's appearing in the opening scenes of the book. It is little wonder that the church father Primasius maintained that John had seen *Dominum Christum descendentem de caelo*, "the Lord Christ descending from heaven" (my translation from Swete 1908: 126).

The angel is, if not Christ, then a type of Christ, bringing transformative news from a world beyond this one. Yet it is *in* this world that he plants his feet—one foot on land, the realm of human habitation, and one foot on the sea, the realm of unformed chaos, the "deep."[1] At least the coastal cities of Asia Minor (Ephesus, Smyrna) existed at the boundary between ocean and land, and the island of Patmos was certainly such a liminal place. Yet just as the Lord trampled the waves of the sea (Job 9:8) and Christ walked on water (John 6:16–21), so the mighty angel has no difficulty planting his foot upon (not *in*!) the sea itself. The image is one of total mastery. In William Blake's extraordinary watercolor rendering of this scene, a young, naked, and quite virile-looking male figure towers far above the seer, shown in his usual pose with pen in hand.[2] Fire swirls around the angel's feet, while in back of him the sky glows with golden and yellow light (one senses that the sun is directly behind his head). His left hand holds the book—a modern bound book, not a scroll—while his right hand is raised toward heaven. He is enormous. Blake's rendering brings to mind the Colossus of Rhodes, the great statue that, according to legend, stood athwart the harbor of the island of Rhodes

1. In both Greek and Old Testament thought, the "Abyss" was thought of as the primordial ocean; in the Judaism of New Testament times it acquired the meaning of "underworld" or "prison for evil spirits." See Joachim Jeremias, "*Abyssos*," in *Theological Dictionary of the New Testament*, ed. Gerhard Kittel, trans. Geoffrey W. Bromiley (Grand Rapids: Eerdmans, 1964), 1.9–10.

2. William Blake, *And the Angel Which I Saw Lifted Up His Hand to Heaven*, ca. 1805, Metropolitan Museum of Art. See also Albrecht Dürer's rendering of this scene, depicting the angels' legs as literal architectural columns! As with Dürer's Lamb, the grotesqueness of the image is emblematic of the strangeness of the vision itself.

in the pre-Christian era.³ What Blake gets right about the angel is his strength, beauty, and sheer verticality: he links earth and heaven, even as he straddles the realms of both earth and sea. Like angels generally, this strong angel is an opening to another world, reminding us that there is more to the cosmos than what can be manipulated and controlled by human beings.

10:3–4 The angel's colossal size is matched by his great voice, like that of a lion roaring, a metaphor that appears in the Old Testament: "The lion has roared; who will not fear? The Lord GOD has spoken; who can but prophesy?" (Amos 3:8; cf. Hos. 11:10). The metaphor may also imply that this angel speaks with the full authority of the Lion of Judah. When the angel cries out—whether to proclaim something or simply to announce his presence, we are not told—he evokes an answering echo on the part of the seven thunders. The Greek literally says that the thunders "spoke in their own voices." This clustering of voice references reminds us that we are in the realm of prophecy. All the voices in Revelation are ultimately instruments in the hands of the one voice, the word or speech of God.

John refers to the rumbling of *the* seven thunders without explanation, as if he takes for granted that his hearers will understand the reference. Perhaps the thunders were a well-known figure of mythology, or perhaps the definite article simply serves to create a sense of insiders' knowledge, suggesting that the apocalyptic world has its own quite definite atmospherics corresponding to its strange geography. It is also possible that there is an allusion to Ps. 29, a hymn that depicts YHWH as the God of the storm and that repeats the phrase "the voice of the LORD" seven times.⁴ Revelation frequently employs thunder language to evoke the appearance of God on Sinai (Rev. 4:5; 8:5; 11:19; 16:18), but thunder is also an appropriate mode of angelic speech. When a voice from heaven addresses Jesus in John's Gospel, the people (plural for agreement) standing nearby imagine that they are hearing thunder or possibly an angel (John 12:28–29). Surely the language of thunder is the language of God.⁵

It is precisely this assumption that makes what happens next so striking. As soon as the thunders sound, John prepares himself to write; indeed the form of the Greek verb⁶ suggests that he actually began to do so, but was prevented for

3. See Morton D. Paley, *The Apocalyptic Sublime* (New Haven: Yale University Press, 1986), 85. The statue actually existed, although the claim that it straddled the mouth of the harbor is almost certainly fiction. If Blake is alluding to this statue, he may be recalling that the Colossus was a representation of Helios, the Greek sun god (cf. "his face was like the sun" in Rev. 10:1).

4. It is hard to represent sound in a visual medium. In his watercolor of the strong angel, Blake depicts the seven thunders as seven horsemen galloping through the sky in the background. The horses, with their thundering hoofbeats, serve as a visual representation of the sound. It is a clever device, even if the text makes no mention of horses.

5. The African-American spiritual "Steal Away to Jesus" contains the words: "My Lord, he calls me, he calls me from the thunder / The trumpet sounds within-a my soul / I ain't got long to be here."

6. *Ēmellon graphein* is an imperfect denoting attempt; see Max Zerwick, *Biblical Greek: Illustrated by Examples*, ed. Joseph Smith (Rome: Pontifical Biblical Institute Press, 1963), §273.

some reason. From the commands at 1:11 and 1:19 one might have thought that John was to write down everything he saw or heard. But a voice from heaven now intervenes: John is specifically told *not* to record what the thunders said, but to seal it up, an action that appears to be at odds with the overall thrust of the book toward revelation, disclosure, *apokalypsis*.

There is, however, a biblical precedent for this command. In the concluding lines of the book of Daniel, the mysterious "man clothed in linen" instructs the prophet to "shut up the words and seal the book, until the time of the end" (Dan. 12:4). In the context of Daniel, the sealing of the scroll means that the visions described by the prophet will find their true fulfillment at some indefinite time in the future. "The end" is not yet, although the shifting calculations offered in Dan. 12 suggest some uncertainty on this point. But the command given in Rev. 10 is far more radical: rather than being told to write in the scroll and seal it up, John is—in this single instance—prohibited from writing at all. The contents of the rumbling of the seven thunders will thus remain forever a mystery.

Speculation about "what the thunders said"[7] is fruitless: the clear intent of the command is that their speech form no part of the revelation entrusted to John. But rather oddly, the *fact* of John's abortive attempt to write *is* part of that revelation. Why should this be the case?

I suggest that there are two reasons for the inclusion of the episode. First, the overall theme of Rev. 10 is the vocation of the prophet, as concretely embodied in the figure of John himself. John is indeed called to write down what he sees and hears. But he is not to write indiscriminately. Not every purportedly divine voice is the specific word that binds the prophet. Far from endowing John with mantic powers of divination, his calling to be a prophet requires that he listens again and again for *that* word of the Lord that he is commissioned to speak under particular circumstances. In a somewhat analogous way, while Paul could boast of private revelatory experiences in which he heard "things that cannot be told, which man may not utter" (2 Cor. 12:4), he knew that his apostolic mandate extended only to the proclamation of the gospel (1 Cor. 2:2; Gal. 1:8). Neither the apostle nor the prophet is a free agent; he lives "by every word that comes from the mouth of God" (Matt. 4:4).

The second reason for the silencing of the seven thunders is related to the first. If they were to be included, the thunders would form yet another septenary, in continuity with the seven seals and the seven trumpets. The pattern has by this point in the book been well established. If seals can give way to trumpets, then trumpets can yield to thunders, a set of even more terrible judgments culminat-

---

7. T. S. Eliot employs this phrase as a section title in "The Waste Land," written in the aftermath of the Great War of 1914–18. Much of the language and imagery of the poem has an apocalyptic flavor, although one might say that Eliot is seeking to evoke the anti-apocalyptic landscape of modernity, where nothing genuinely new is allowed to happen. The thirst that is one of the poem's key symbols can be read as "a thirst . . . of hearing the words of the LORD" (Amos 8:11).

ing (we might easily imagine) in a decisive theophany and the final annihilation
of the earth-dwellers.

But this, of course, is precisely what does not happen. Like Sherlock Holmes's
"dog that did not bark," John's nonrecording of the seven thunders is a highly
significant event in itself. It breaks the pattern of sevens. To be sure, there is one
more septenary still to come, the seven bowls of the divine wrath: God does not
cease his activity of judgment until relationships on earth are actually rectified,
reflecting the promise of peace embodied in the covenantal rainbow. But while
God's "no" to human sin is utterly serious, it was never the point. God's "no"
stands in the service of his "yes," declared in the extraordinary affirmation that
now appears on the lips of the mighty angel:

> And the angel whom I saw standing on the sea and on the land raised his right
> hand to heaven and swore by him who lives forever and ever, who created heaven
> and what is in it, the earth and what is in it, and the sea and what is in it, that there
> would be no more delay, but that in the days of the trumpet call to be sounded by
> the seventh angel, the mystery of God would be fulfilled, just as he announced to
> his servants the prophets.

10:5–7 What could this "mystery" be, if not the gospel? And who is the
angel if not a gospel bearer, possibly even (as suggested earlier) an icon of the
one who is the very content of the gospel, Jesus Christ himself? In the book of
Daniel, the man clothed in linen raises his hand to heaven and swears "by him
who lives forever" that the time of suffering of God's people will be "for a time,
times, and half a time," after which the end will come (Dan. 12:7). By contrast, in
the Apocalypse no such postponement is envisioned. The angel says "there would
be no more delay"—literally, "there will be no more time" (*chronos ouketai estai*).
The mystery of God will be fulfilled as soon as the angel of the seventh trumpet
sounds the call. The kingdom is not the outcome of some process of struggle or
development, leading through history to the end. We have already arrived at the
end. "There will be no more time."

10:8–11 The heavenly voice commands John to take the scroll from the hand
of the angel. While the Lamb is worthy to open the scroll with seven seals, con-
taining God's plan for human history, it is only this "little scroll" that constitutes
"the Lamb's book" in the proper sense.[8] Unlike the seven-sealed scroll, this book
is the *positive* expression of God's will for his creatures, having the Lamb's victory

---

8. Bauckham 1993a: 243–57 argues that this "little scroll" is to be identified with the Lamb's
scroll, which, now that its seals have been removed, lies open for all to see. In favor of this view is
the scroll that appears in Ezek. 2–3, which resembles the Lamb's scroll in that it is "written on the
front and the back" and resembles the little scroll in being eaten by the prophet. I find this argument
ingenious but finally unpersuasive. The scrolls in Revelation have different functions in quite different parts of the book. The newness of the little scroll seems more in line with Bauckham's insight
that, after the negative results of the seals and trumpets, the sealing up of "what the thunders said"
and the appearance of the mighty angel represents something like a fresh start.

as its actual *content*. The evangelical character of this portion of Revelation is widely recognized by commentators. Thus the notes in the Geneva Bible identify this scroll as "the Gospel of Christ, which the Antichrist cannot hide, seeing Christ bringeth it open in his hand" (Kovacs and Rowland 2004: 119). Jacques Ellul concurs: "The little open scroll is very clearly this Gospel. . . . Now the great design of God is fulfilled: the Incarnation, which is this fulfillment, is realized" (1977: 78).

In obedience to the command of the voice, John steps forward to receive the book from the hand of the angel standing on sea and land. The angel says, "Take and eat it." In the parallel passage in Ezekiel, the angel simply says, "Son of man, . . . eat this scroll" (Ezek. 3:1). The double command *take and eat* is clearly a Christian formula, influenced by the traditions concerning the Last Supper in which Jesus tells his disciples to "take, eat; [for] this is my body" (Matt. 26:26).[9] The "taking" is not irrelevant to the eating. God commands that we "take" by our own action what he desires to give, a free human response to his free gift of grace. It was with deep insight that Thomas Cranmer included the words "take, eat" at the administration of Communion in his service for Holy Eucharist, to the end that the worshiper might "feed on him [Christ] in thy heart by faith, with thanksgiving."[10]

John's taking of the little scroll is "eucharistic," not in the direct sense that the scene depicts the celebration of the sacrament, but in the sense that he is being commanded to ingest the word of God, to let it enter him so as to become part of his own being. We are what we eat: being nourished by the word of God or by Torah is a frequent theme in scripture (Ps. 19:10; 34:8; 119:103; Jer. 15:16). Like physical food, the food that is the word is not necessary only for sustaining life but delightful, as Ezekiel discovers when he eats the scroll and finds that it is "as sweet as honey" (Ezek. 3:3).

Yet the intrinsic delight of the word does not make its course in the world any less conflicted. The scroll given to Ezekiel may be sweet, yet it is also covered with words of "lamentation and mourning and woe" (Ezek. 2:10). To be a prophet is to encounter resistance. In the Apocalypse, this dual aspect of the prophet's vocation finds expression in the dual character of the scroll, which while sweet to the taste makes John's stomach bitter. The gospel, although it embodies God's "yes" to humanity, is also the occasion of offense. It is vulnerable to rejection, and this rejection will be aimed not just at the message but at the messenger. The prophet's existence has the same shape as that of the church itself; both are inevitably cruciform.

Nevertheless, the accent in the present scene falls not on John's bitter stomach, but on the fact of his mission to the world: "And I was told, 'You must again

9. While only Matthew has the words "take, eat" together, all three Synoptics record the command to "take" in the context of the fellowship meal.
10. *The Book of Common Prayer* (New York: Church Publishing House, 1979), 338.

prophesy about many peoples and nations and languages and kings.'"[11] Prophesy as such is not new to John. He is known to the churches of Asia precisely in his identity as a Christian prophet. What is new, it seems, is the eschatological urgency of the situation. "There will be no more time," says the angel. Yet far from causing the church to hunker down into a sectarian enclave waiting for the end, the gift of the gospel sends the church outward into the world of peoples, nations, languages, and kings. The mighty angel crying with a loud voice is a type of Christ's prophetic office, and John's eating of the scroll a sign of the church's mission of bearing witness to the gospel, both in its life and its speech. And as the angel stands astride land and sea, so the gospel is truly a message without borders.

11. This is a good example of the blurring of voices that occurs throughout the Apocalypse. At 10:8, it is the heavenly voice that speaks; at 10:9, it is presumably the voice of the angel from whom John receives the scroll; and at 10:11, the Greek literally translated says: "And *they* are saying to me, 'You must again prophesy.'" The plural subject here could mean "the heavenly voice and the angel," or it could simply suggest an indefinite subject, virtually equivalent to the passive voice. Thus ESV: "I was told."

REVELATION 11

DEATH IN JERUSALEM

Christ is the one who has been made flesh, died and risen again in order to take away the sins of the world and to reconcile all to the Father; therefore the Church in each place, always "bearing about in the body the dying of Jesus," sharing through him in the messianic tribulations which are the mark of the continuing conflict between the reign of God and the power of evil, will also manifest in its life the victorious life of the risen Jesus (2 Cor. 4:10).

—Lesslie Newbigin, "What Is a 'Local Church Truly United'?"

The vision of the angel with the little scroll forms part of the interlude that delays the blowing of the seventh trumpet. We now come to the second part of that interlude: the tale of the two witnesses who meet their death in "the great city." Drawn in broad, almost cartoonish strokes, this minor masterpiece of biblical storytelling is a parable of the church and so stands in essential continuity with the vision that precedes it. It forms a fitting climax to the first half of the book of Revelation.

11:1–2 Before we arrive at this climax, however, we are confronted with another episode in which John himself occupies center stage. Having been told that he must "again prophesy" (10:11), John is given a measuring rod and commanded to measure the temple of God, the altar, and the worshipers inside—an action hearkening back to similar incidents in Ezek. 40–48 and Zech. 2:1–5. To measure something in this sense is to describe a clearly defined space. Thus in the older prophets, the measuring of the temple is a sign of God's sanctifying the temple or of resanctifying it following the pollutions and desecrations of the Babylonian exile. Such an act was essential, insofar as the temple marked the necessary boundary between the sacred and the profane or between the holy people of God and the Gentile nations.

But in the New Testament the "temple" is the church (1 Cor. 3:16–17; 2 Cor. 6:16–18; Eph. 2:21), whose holiness, a gift of the Spirit, derives from Christ, who is *the* temple in an unsurpassable sense (John 2:21). The temple and its worshipers are holy, therefore safe; this is why they occupy the inner court directly surrounding the altar. By contrast, the outer court is "given over" to the Gentiles (again connoting divine permission) who will not only profane it by their presence but actively "trample" on it for forty-two months. This period of time is not chosen randomly. Equivalent to 1,260 days or three and a half years, it echoes the "time, times, and half a time" of the book of Daniel, the apocalyptic period immediately preceding the day when "the shattering of the power of the holy people comes to an end" and the promises of God are fulfilled (Dan. 12:7; cf. 7:25). However Daniel may have arrived at this figure, it suits John's purposes beautifully: three and a half is a "broken seven," denoting the radical imperfection that marks the present evil age.

The letters to the churches have already shown Revelation's concern for the holiness of the *ekklēsia*, especially in relation to the pagan city. The measuring of the temple is a spatial metaphor of this holiness. It affirms that the inner court—the sanctity of the people of God themselves—will be preserved, even if the Gentiles manage to ravage the holy city and abolish its religious practices. If John was indeed a priest who fled Jerusalem following the fall of the city to the Romans in AD 70, this vision may well preserve his memory of that event, although the parable as used here points not to the past but to the future: John foresees a coming period of 1,260 days in which God will sustain the church in the face of Gentile hostility. There is a remarkable parallel to this passage in the apocalyptic discourse in Luke's Gospel, in which Jesus says: "For there will be great distress upon the earth and wrath against this people. They will fall by the edge of the sword and be taken away as captives among all nations, and Jerusalem will be trampled on by the Gentiles, until the times of the Gentiles are fulfilled" (Luke 21:23–24). But in Luke's Gospel and in Acts, "the times of the Gentiles" means the time of the church, which moves out *from* Jerusalem in a mission extending to the ends of the earth. The hostility of the nations (whether to historic Israel or to the *ekklēsia*) cannot undo their role in the divine economy or prevent their evangelization by Christ's own appointed witnesses.

11:3 Those witnesses are the primary focus of attention in the narrative that follows: "And I will grant authority to my two witnesses, and they will prophesy for 1,260 days, clothed in sackcloth." The voice—presumably the same voice the seer heard telling him to devour the scroll and to measure the temple—abruptly shifts from the mode of command into that of narration: instead of issuing instructions to John, the voice simply speaks—perhaps now with a mainly christological inflection, as suggested by the reference to "my" witnesses. The witnesses take over John's role as the primary actors in this drama.

The present story expands and deepens the account of John's prophetic commissioning in the previous chapter. The witnesses are prophets. The time of their prophecy is the apocalyptic period of 1,260 days, the same interval in which the Gentiles are permitted to trample the holy city. Here we find yet another surprising convergence with Luke's Gospel. In Jesus's inaugural sermon in his home synagogue in Nazareth, he mentions the famine in Elijah's day and gives the duration of this famine as three and a half years (Luke 4:25), a detail not found in the Old Testament traditions concerning Elijah (1 Kgs. 17–18).[1] Perhaps in Luke's reckoning, three and a half years is the right amount of time for a prophet's ministry—or for the ministry of an Elijah-like Messiah. Whereas Luke locates the prophetic activity of Jesus in a time of "famine," John of Patmos locates the church's witness in a time of apocalyptic desolation. A church that complains of living in difficult times has understood neither the captivity of the world to the powers nor its own mandate. Difficult times are just the times the gospel is meant to address.

How we preach the gospel, however, is as important as when we preach it. The two witnesses are said to be "clothed in sackcloth," the traditional sign of penance in Israel. The "sackcloth dress indicates that the attitude of the Church ... must needs be penitential and not triumphant" (Swete 1908: 135).[2] The proclamation of the gospel requires the telling of truth about human sin, including, although by no means limited to, that sin committed by the church itself. The church represents Jesus Christ to the world in the painful awareness that it will very often *mis*represent him. It is therefore clothed in sackcloth, modeling for the world that turning back toward God is the appropriate response to the gospel. Thoughtful, discerning repentance is thus a constitutive practice of the church, not because the church is not holy, but precisely because it *is* holy, and because it is called on to demonstrate its seriousness about sanctification through the practice of confession and amendment of life. In the words of the Second Vatican Council: "The Church ... clasping sinners to her bosom, at once holy and always in need of purification, follows constantly the path of penance and renewal" (*Lumen Gentium* 8).

11:4 Some of the imagery characterizing the witnesses is drawn from Old Testament sources. Thus the shutting of the heavens against rain suggests Elijah, while the turning of water to blood and the calling down of plagues upon one's enemies is reminiscent of Moses in Egypt. It would be wrong, however, to try to identify the two witnesses with nameable individuals. They are rather to be seen as types

---

1. The period of three and half years for Elijah's famine is also found in Jas. 5:17. For the comparison that follows I am indebted to Minear 1968: 295 (in a stimulating chapter entitled "Comparable Patterns of Thought in Luke's Gospel").

2. The ellipsis in this sentence conceals a qualification: according to Swete, the church's penitence is appropriate only "during the prevalence of paganism, if not to the end of her course on earth." Swete clearly identifies the apocalyptic three and a half years with the time of the church's persecution prior to Constantine. Would it not make more sense to identify this time with the whole period of the church's historical existence, in which it is called to fasting/penance (cf. Mark 2:20)?

or figures of prophecy. Everything they do and suffer, they do and suffer together; they are the "prophetic company" in its smallest possible cohort. Moreover, there are hints in the passage that more is going on here than just the representation of the prophet's calling. The witnesses are initially called "the two olive trees and the two lampstands that stand before the Lord of the earth," language drawn from the same fertile passage in Zechariah that has already shaped John's seven eyes/ seven lamps imagery (Zech. 4). In Zechariah, the olive trees are Joshua the high priest and Zerubbabel governor of Judea, the first representing the priesthood, the second the kingship. These are clearly messianic figures, although they lived in an age that, while crucial for Israel's future existence—the return from exile, the rebuilding of the temple—fell far short of any visions of messianic fulfillment. Joshua and Zerubbabel point beyond themselves to the one who would combine the offices of prophet, priest, and king, a "Joshua" (Yeshua, Jesus) who as God's anointed (the olive tree) sheds his light on the entire world (the lampstand).

The present vision, of course, speaks of *two* lampstands and olive trees. The whole tenor of this passage is messianic and christological, and yet the immediate subject of the vision is not Jesus Messiah per se, but the way the church displays his story in the form of its witness. Under the Torah, the agreement of two witnesses was required in order for testimony to be considered valid (Deut. 19:15). In the time of the new covenant, two is the number of the fundamental cell of the Christian mission, reflected in Jesus's sending of the twelve and the seventy-two to preach the good news and to cast out demons (Mark 6:7; Luke 10:1; cf. "where two or three are gathered in my name" in Matt. 18:20). The church lives by and in its action of testimony. The confluence of the imagery of lamps and olive trees suggests, perhaps, that the oil of testimony will never be exhausted, that the church's lamp will perpetually be replenished by the one who is himself God's anointed. The church testifies to Jesus, whose life and death are one great act of testimony to the Father in heaven. And so we can say that *God* is the ultimate object of the church's testimony, a point made explicit when it is said that the two lampstands/olive trees are stationed "before the Lord of the earth." Christ and the Father are one, so that to be the ambassador for either one is to be the ambassador for both: "It is to the Gospel of God that the Church bears witness, and the Gospel of God is simply Jesus crucified, but attested Son of God by his rising again from the dead."[3]

That simple, fundamental movement characterizing Jesus's story, passing from crucifixion to resurrection and from death to life, is fully on display in the remarkable little narrative that follows. It can be seen as a drama unfolding in three broad acts.

11:5-6 Act 1 opens with the two prophets already enjoying spectacular success. Any foolish enough to offer resistance to them soon learns with whom they are dealing: "If anyone would harm [these prophets], fire pours from their mouth

3. D. M. MacKinnon, *The Church of God* (Westminster: Dacre, 1940), 32.

and consumes their foes. If anyone would harm them, this is how he is doomed to be killed." Again we are reminded of Elijah, whose ability to call down fire from heaven led to a bloody climax: the slaughter of the prophets of Baal (1 Kgs. 18:40). Combining the miraculous powers of Elijah with those of Moses, the two witnesses move through the world like an irresistible force. A superficial reading of this story suggests that it offers a rather horrifying justification for Christian violence against the pagan world.

It does nothing of the kind. Rather, the narrative renders the life history of the witnesses in deliberately bold, exaggerated strokes, the intent of which is not to valorize the human messengers, and certainly not to underwrite violence, but to glorify the God of heaven. The church *is* sent out into the world with an extraordinary power at its disposal. But it is the power of the word of God, a word that in scripture is referred to as a "consuming fire" (Heb. 12:29; cf. Deut. 4:24) and of which it is said that it will "not return to [God] empty" (Isa. 55:11). The career of the two witnesses in this first act corresponds to the time of Jesus's earthly ministry, in which he enjoyed unparalleled success against his foes (e.g., the Scribes and Pharisees) and in which he was widely celebrated for the liberating, authoritative power of his preaching: "And they were astonished at his teaching, for he taught them as one who had authority, and not as the scribes" (Mark 1:22). Despite the hyperbole, the Apocalypse is not being ironic when it attributes such authority to the church, which like its Lord speaks "in demonstration of the Spirit and of power" (1 Cor. 2:4).

11:7–10 Act 2 describes a great reversal: "And when they have finished their testimony, the beast that rises from the bottomless pit will make war on them and conquer them and kill them." This statement is jarring, not just because nothing in the narrative so far prepares us for it, but because of the understated, almost matter-of-fact tone in which it is said. It is as much as to say, this is just how things are. The church that speaks with Pentecostal tongues of fire will in the course of time confront the beast from the bottomless pit, and just as surely the church will lose this confrontation. There is nothing glorious, heroic, or tragic about the church's destiny as it appears under this description. The death of the saints is simply reported as the inevitable outcome of act 1: just as *Christ's* mission of proclaiming God's kingdom led to his violent death at the hands of his enemies, so the *church's* mission cannot but be greeted by a similar fate. All this is the normal fate that can be expected by prophets. No wonder the scroll, so sweet to the taste, turns bitter as soon as it reaches John's stomach!

What follows can be described only as a ritual of public humiliation. The bodies of the prophets will lie in the square of "the great city that symbolically [i.e., spiritually, *pneumatikōs*] is called Sodom and Egypt, where their Lord was crucified." The bodies will be exposed to the gaze of onlookers from all peoples, tribes, tongues, and nations. Having been denied the simple human decency of burial, the witnesses are clearly no longer human but simply objects, to be discarded in the streets like so much trash. They are the despised enemy, who do not deserve the respect and care with which we honor our own dead. This is the first mention in Revelation of the "great city," the primary focus of attention in Rev. 17–18, as well as of "the beast" (*to thērion*), the monster from the sea who makes a memorable appearance in Rev. 13. Such foreshadowing is typical of the Apocalypse, which is constantly dropping hints and allusions that are later developed into full-blown themes.

11:11–13 Act 3 narrates the reversal of the reversal. The "three and a half days" of the witnesses' humiliation marks the apocalyptic period of the church's persecution and distress, although it also hints dimly at Jesus's own three-day sojourn in the tomb. But the time of suffering is finite. Using language evocative of Ezekiel's valley of the dry bones, John writes that "a breath of life from God entered [the witnesses], and they stood up on their feet, and great fear fell on those who saw them" (cf. Ezek. 37:10). Once again John mentions the spectators' gazing on the witnesses, a detail he returns to in an almost obsessive way.[4] It is not only the prophets' verbal testimony that makes them into witnesses, but that they speak in the language of the body, showing forth in their own bodies the *martyria* of Jesus himself. In much the same way Paul describes his own apostolic existence, humiliated, foolish, hovering near death, as a kind of visible demonstration of the gospel: "Like men sentenced to death, . . . we have become a spectacle [*theatron egenēthēmen*] to the world, to angels, and to men" (1 Cor. 4:9). Or: "For we who live are always being given over to death for Jesus' sake, so that the life of Jesus also may be manifested in our mortal flesh" (2 Cor. 4:11).

This understanding of the church's showing forth of Christ crucified as the life of the world must be kept very far, of course, from any notion of manipulation or technique. The church cannot manage its engagement with the world toward the attainment of predictable results. The two witnesses are not in control of their fate. They are, rather terrifyingly, out of control. As Paul's use of the term *theatron* suggests, the church is engaged in a kind of guerilla theater, a company of amateurs with scant resources and but little time for rehearsal, charged with performing the story of Jesus in the streets of the great city. The church is always more or less making things up as it goes along. This leaves room for a great deal of ingenuity and discernment with respect to context—the performance will look a little different in Santiago as compared to Nairobi, in Singapore City as compared to Montreal—while leaving the basic shape of the drama unchanged. The church, if it really is the church, cannot fail to live out the script of dying with Christ in the great city. It has been anointed for just this mission.

Where and what is "the great city"? John tells us that "spiritually" the city is called Sodom, synonymous in Jewish tradition with ultimate wickedness, and Egypt, the place of slavery and oppression. If we then ask what the city is called at the literal sense, there can be only one answer: historical Jerusalem. It was in Jerusalem and nowhere else that the witnesses' Lord "was crucified." The concrete

4. Cf. 11:9, where the verb is *blepō*, and 11:11, 12, where the verb is *theōreō*.

particularities of Jesus's life and death bestow meaning on all other particular stories, anchoring them in the larger story of God's purposes, not dissolving them into mere shadows but freeing them to serve precisely as *witnesses* to God's grace in Jesus Christ.

The great city, then, is neither one particular city (Rome, say) nor all cities in all times and places. It is rather the name we give to all those particular stories in which human beings rise up in opposition to the rule of God, seeking to dispose of God (and safeguard their own autonomy) by murdering his appointed messengers. What we see in the tale of the witnesses is nothing less than the *deepening of human solidarity through the practice of violence*, a point powerfully underscored by John's picture of individuals from all "peoples and tribes and languages and nations," coming together to celebrate the prophets' death. As God and the Lamb were the infinitely attractive focus of the creatures' gaze in the heavenly worship, so the bodies of the two prophets are at the center of a kind of antiliturgy, a festive occasion that even involves the giving of gifts: "Those who dwell on the earth will rejoice over them and make merry and exchange presents, because these two prophets had been a torment to those who dwell on the earth" (11:10). Human community is in fact being created here, although of a particularly vicious and demeaning sort. The bonds of fellowship are cemented by the blood that flows through the streets of the city.[5]

The narrative does not, however, assign direct responsibility for the witnesses' death to the inhabitants of the city. The one who does the actual killing is "the beast that arises from the bottomless pit." The citizens merely celebrate the results of the beast's action, which they believe has released them from their torment. While it would be too simple to say that this relieves the earth-dwellers of all responsibility, it does situate their violence within a larger framework of cosmic opposition to the Lamb. As in the Passion Narratives in the Gospels, the work of evil in Revelation is distributed among both human and suprahuman agents, but the primary emphasis falls on the demonic element.

More important than the work of either humans or angels, however, is the action of God. It is *God* who acts in the death and resurrection of the witnesses, just as it is God who acted in the death and resurrection of Christ. And as was the case with Christ, God's vindication of the witnesses is not limited to their personal salvation, their escape into heaven out of a fallen world. Their vindication has an

5. John's portrayal of the city calls to mind René Girard's theory of the scapegoat, according to which all human society can be traced back to an original act of violence, in which existing social tensions were discharged and unity achieved through the murder of an innocent victim; see René Girard, *Things Hidden since the Foundation of the World*, trans. Stephen Bann and Michael Metteer (Stanford: Stanford University Press, 1987). We have been creating scapegoats ever since. Girard argues that it was Jesus's great achievement to expose this mechanism for what it is: "You will know the truth, and the truth will set you free" (John 8:32). But what Girard advances as a general theory of social strife, the Apocalypse describes as simply the reaction with which the world greets the Lamb and his followers.

effect *in* the world: "And at that hour there was a great earthquake, and a tenth of the city fell. Seven thousand people were killed in the earthquake, and the rest were terrified and gave glory to the God of heaven" (11:13).

This event as such falls not in the realm of ultimate, but only of penultimate things. Unlike Christ's resurrection, it does not itself constitute the dawning of the new age. But it is an event *in* the dawning of the new age. If the penultimacy can be seen in the death of the seven thousand—a sobering outcome on anyone's reckoning—the eschatology can be seen in these seven thousand being only a tenth of the city and in "the rest," over sixty thousand souls, repenting and giving glory to God (in sharp contrast, 9:20 explicitly states that the bulk of humankind did not repent of their idolatry). The witnesses' donning of sackcloth and ashes was not in vain. The church's ministry has a real impact on the world in this time between the times. But the achievement of this result requires that the prophets' preaching of the word, which did not succeed in converting anyone, be sealed by their death—in the Apocalypse, the means of participation in the Lamb's victory. As in relation to Paul, the apostolic preaching must be performed in the key of the cross, so that there is a real congruity between the message and the messenger.

What kind of story is this? Although we have seen death at the hands of the beast and the unseemly gazing of the earth-dwellers on the dead bodies of the prophets, the overall tenor of this story is remarkably hopeful. It has more in it of comedy than of tragedy. The pattern of total success/total failure/total vindication is a showing forth of the power of the gospel. The last glimpse we catch of the earth-dwellers is their gazing upward as the witnesses ascend to heaven "in a cloud"—the same place from which Christ will return! The witnesses' death is the affirmation of their life and so stands as a sign of hope even for the great city.

11:14 If we were tempted to confuse these next-to-last things with the end itself, a voice suddenly intrudes to correct our error: "The second woe has passed, behold, the third woe is soon to come." This brings us back to earth quickly; we are still in the midst of the three woes announced by the eagle, which are coordinated with the three concluding trumpet blasts (8:13; 9:12). We would expect that the seventh, climactic trumpet blast would bring the whole sequence to its terrifying conclusion.

11:15–19 But once again, the Apocalypse confounds our expectations. Instead of a woe, what follows is the resumption of the heavenly liturgy: a celebration of the victory of God as it is accomplished in the death of his prophets. Voices in heaven sing the words sung by millions each Christmas (how many know it is from Revelation?) as part of the "Hallelujah" chorus in Handel's *Messiah*: "The kingdom of the world has become the kingdom of our Lord and of his Christ, and he shall reign forever and ever."

Few would think of this "establishment" musical composition as having to do with theological politics, but the meaning is plain. "The kingdom of the world," that is, the world insofar as it constitutes itself as a sphere of power independent of God, has become the kingdom of Israel's God and his Messiah. The great city

and the other cities of this world are no longer under the dominion of the powers of evil. Even before the end, they have come under the dominion of God; the
doxology in 11:17–18 clearly speaks of an act already accomplished.[6] John has
prepared us for this change in perspective in the story preceding, which partway
through (11:11) shifts from the future tense into the aorist, indicating completed
action. Having their death already behind them, the witnesses no longer confront
the kingdom as a future but as a present reality. The change is also signaled by a
subtle modification in Revelation's familiar language concerning God. Rather than
praising God as "the one who is and who was and who is to come," as in previous
uses of the formula, the elders address him as the "Lord God almighty, who is
and who was. . . ." In this highly charged eschatological context, the phrase "is to
come" no longer applies. The coming of God gives way to his actual arrival on the
scene. We are not surprised when the entire episode concludes with a Sinai-like
theophany complete with lightning, thunder, hail, and earthquake, while the
heavenly temple opens to disclose the ark of the covenant within.

This theophany brings us full circle. Part II of Revelation began in Rev. 4, with
John's vision of the heavenly worship—a temple scene, if also an imperial court
ceremony—and proceeds through the judgments of the seals and trumpets to
the episode in which John measures the temple and its worshipers. In all of this,
the Apocalypse displays its powerfully vertical character. It is "about" God and
God's world. The revelation of this world is mediated by angels blowing trumpets
and standing astride land and sea. It would be hard to imagine a more emphatic
expression of the holiness, righteousness, and otherness of God than is found
in this second of John's great stories, which describes the remaking of the world
according to God's perfect will.

But now the temple in heaven is *opened*. Despite everything we have seen, God
does not simply stand against the world in judgment. The Lamb is the Lord of
history, but he is also the door (cf. 3:8, 20; 4:1) who has opened the way into the
holy of holies; he has entered "heaven itself, now to appear in the presence of God
on our behalf" (Heb. 9:24). The vision of the ark of the covenant, at the precise
moment when the servants of God are said to receive their heavenly reward, is a
sign indicating "the restoration of perfect access to God through the Ascension
of the Incarnate Son" (Swete 1908: 145). The covenant with Noah signified by
the rainbow (Rev. 4:3; 10:1), the covenant with Israel embodied in the ark, the
new covenant realized once for all in Jesus's flesh—all these are signs of the peace
that has been established between heaven and earth. If the events of the seals and
trumpets serve to create a sense of claustrophobic pressure and constraint, with
God, as it were, closing in on the world, the opening of the temple suggests a space

6. ESV's "you have taken your great power and *begun* to reign" is an attempt to bring out the
force of the inceptive aorist, used with verbs like "reign" that denote an ongoing state. God assumes
his reign (an event taking place at a specific moment in time) but then continues to reign. See
Max Zerwick, *Biblical Greek: Illustrated by Examples*, ed. Joseph Smith (Rome: Pontifical Biblical
Institute Press, 1963), §250.

marked by holiness, mutuality, indwelling, *koinōnia*. In Christ that mutuality has already been established. It awaits its final realization amid the streets, dwellings, and marketplaces of the great city.

In the meantime, what the great city does have is the church, a community that, as depicted in the story of the witnesses, subsists essentially in its mission. The church follows Jesus Christ out into the world. As a community of prophecy it participates in Jesus's own ministry as Spirit-borne prophet, speaking the gospel in the midst of the city. As a priestly people it summons the world to the worship of the true God, as against the false gods who promise so much but who actually enslave. As a royal people it testifies to God's gracious rule, summoning Israel, and all the nations, to the acknowledgement that "the kingdom of the world has become the kingdom of our Lord and of his Christ." While the story of the witnesses does not say everything that needs to be said about the church, it does serve as a rough script for the improvised guerilla theater that the *ekklēsia* is called on to perform, in a role that combines extraordinary power with infinite vulnerability. Part of God's grace to the church is that it does not have to have everything worked out in advance; this is part of its essential humanity. It need only entrust itself to the God who raises the dead, as he once did in that city "where their Lord was crucified." It need only be a witness.

PART III

✚ FALLEN IS BABYLON ✚

REVELATION 12

DAUGHTER ZION DELIVERED

Great is the Baptism that lies before you: a ransom to captives; a remission of offenses; a death of sin; a new birth of the soul. . . . But there is a serpent by the wayside watching those who pass by: beware lest he bite you with unbelief. He sees so many receiving salvation, and is seeking whom he may devour. You are coming in unto the Father of Spirits, but you are going past that serpent.

—St. Cyril of Jerusalem, *Catechetical Lectures*

From Rev. 4 onward, the reader has shared John's vantage point in heaven, from which he looks down to see judgment being visited on earth. Beginning with Rev. 12 comes a shift in perspective. Now John seems to be looking *up* at heaven, the great dome of the sky functioning as a kind of projection screen, on which he sees a parade of what he calls *sēmeia*: signs, omens, portents. People in the ancient world were in general far more attuned to the sky than we are. The sky was seen as an intelligible reality, to be scrutinized (like the entrails of animals) for the light it shed on human destiny or even the affairs of the gods: "We saw his star when it rose and have come to worship him" (Matt. 2:2). In the Jewish apocalyptic tradition it was believed that the end would be accompanied by terrifying events in the sky, eclipses and meteors, falling stars and the shaking of heaven. Such cosmic imagery was employed not only by the prophets (e.g., Joel 2:30–31) but by Jesus himself (e.g., Mark 13:22; Matt. 24:24; cf. John

4:48).[1] If the beginning saw the creation of sun, moon, and stars, then surely the end would be heralded by their wrenching transformation.

12:1–4 Not only does John see signs in heaven, but these signs tell a story, revolving around two great antagonists: a woman, clothed in splendor and yet crying out in the agony of her labor pains, and a monstrous red dragon, with seven heads and ten horns and wearing a crown on each of his heads. The primary story in Rev. 12 is the dragon's pursuit of the woman. This narrative is interrupted by 12:7–12, an account of heavenly warfare between the dragon's forces and the armies of the archangel Michael. As we read this entire sequence, we should be attentive to possible relations between the internal story and the framing narrative; each sheds light on the other.[2]

The dragon's identity is more straightforward than that of the woman, so I will treat him first. Besides, he is best dealt with quickly. The dragon is, of course, a figure for Satan, an identification that John makes explicitly at 12:9. He is red because this is the color of blood and of warfare (cf. 6:4). He is seven-headed because he is evil to the maximum degree and because evil is essentially pluriform: "My name is Legion, for we are many" (Mark 5:9). He wears crowns because he has pretensions at kingship and because he is indeed the leader of an army (Rev. 12:7). Finally, he is represented as a dragon or serpent because he is a cosmic being, a creature from the dawn of time, the *ancient* serpent (12:9). The dragon is very old. He is not as old as God, who alone is eternal and without rivals. But he is older than humanity; he seems to have been there already when Adam and Eve were placed in the garden. While the man and woman were unquestionably at fault for their disobedience, they were responding to a power of chaos that, while not woven into the fabric of creation by God, yet seems to infect creation as we know it. Evil is "always already there," a surd factor that must be both reckoned with and constantly resisted.

How literally should we take this dragon/serpent imagery? When John says that the dragon is the one who is "*called* the devil and Satan," he betrays an awareness that there is no single, definitive way of representing this surd factor. We should bear this in mind as we examine other representations of evil in the Apocalypse, like the beasts from the land and the sea (Rev. 13) or the "three unclean spirits like frogs" (16:13). Of course all this language is imaginative, metaphorical, and deeply inadequate in many ways. On the other hand, this does not mean that we could dispense with the metaphors in favor of some literal form of language. Both God and the devil outrun our ability to depict them, although for opposite reasons. God is too real for our minds to encompass, while the devil is an ontological negative, always hovering at the border of unreality, although his effects in our world are real enough.

---

1. John's Gospel characteristically applies the idiom "signs and wonders" to events in Jesus's own ministry.
2. A good example of this intercalating technique is found in Mark 5, where the healing of Jairus's daughter is interrupted by the story of the woman with a flow of blood.

But why should we dwell on this nasty creature, when the vision opens on a note of such loveliness and splendor? John sees "a woman clothed with the sun, with the moon under her feet, and on her head a crown of twelve stars." She is the first in a series of powerful female figures who dominate the later chapters of the Apocalypse: the Great Whore in Rev. 17 (the antithesis of the woman here) and the bride of the Lamb in Rev. 21 (who is in some ways the woman's double). The woman in our passage is resplendent. Her attire distantly recalls the description of the Shulamite maiden in the Song of Songs: "Who is this that looks forth like the dawn, fair as the moon, bright as the sun, terrible as an army with banners?" (Song 6:10). Albrecht Dürer depicts the woman as a pretty German Madonna, standing demurely with her hands clasped in prayer. William Blake's watercolor does a much better job of capturing the woman's essential radiance, beauty, and power. He depicts her in high romantic style, with arms outstretched and golden wings spread to fly at the very moment of the dragon's attack.[3]

Yet perhaps Blake is just a touch too romantic. This woman is no sun goddess. Her garment of light is a gift, bestowed by the one whose face is "like the sun shining in full strength" (Rev. 1:16; cf. 10:1). "This woman is clothed with the sun," writes Heinrich Bullinger, because the "scripture calleth Christ the sun of righteousness, and light of life. Saint Paul commandeth the church to put on Christ. He therefore is the light, the life and righteousness of the church: by Christ is covered the nakedness of the church: Christ is the ornament and beauty of the church, through him it shineth in the world." Bullinger takes the moon symbol to mean that "all courses and alterations of times, and what so ever is mutable and corruptible in this world, all affections also and infirmities, the church treadeth under her feet."[4]

The woman, then, is the church or more broadly the people of God, as suggested by the crown of twelve stars, echoing the imagery of twelve tribes and twelve apostles elsewhere in Revelation (7:1–8; 21:14). Traditional interpretation sees her signifying Israel under the old covenant. Thus Victorinus writes that the woman is "the ancient Church of fathers, and prophets, and saints, and apostles, which had the groans and torments of its longing until it saw that Christ . . . had taken flesh out of the selfsame people" (*Commentary on the Apocalypse* 12.1, quoted from ANF 7.355). More specifically, we can see her as "Daughter Zion," the personification of Jerusalem often mentioned in the writings of the prophets. At times Daughter Zion is portrayed in distinctly unflattering terms. She is shown as disgraced, humiliated, and punished, a wife/daughter whom YHWH has cast off; even her labor pains are a sign of her vulnerability at the

---

3. The posture of woman and dragon in Blake's picture can be construed as an attempted rape, although there is no hint of that in John's story.

4. Heinrich Bullinger, *A Hundred Sermons Vpo[n] the Apocalips of Iesu Christe: Reueiled in Dede by Thangell of the Lorde, but Seen or Receyued and Written by Thapostle and Eua[n]gelist S. John* (London: John Day, 1573), 349.

hands of her lovers, who now lie in wait to kill her (cf. Jer. 4:31). Elsewhere in the Old Testament, however, Daughter Zion emerges as a sympathetic and hopeful figure, restored to a place of honor and entitled to "put on [her] beautiful garments" as for a festival.[5]

In his famous study of the Apocalypse, Austin Farrer speaks of the "rebirth of images" that takes place in the book.[6] The phrase is especially apt in the present context. In the apocalyptic atmosphere of the New Testament, the Old Testament image of Daughter Zion is reborn, we might say, as an image of cosmic birth pangs. Paul famously writes that "the whole creation has been groaning together in the pains of childbirth until now" (Rom. 8:22), while in John's Gospel Jesus comforts his disciples by saying: "When a woman is giving birth, she has sorrow because her hour has come, but when she has delivered the baby, she no longer remembers the anguish, for joy that a human being has been born into the world" (John 16:21). He is referring, of course, to his death.

The woman clothed with the sun in Rev. 12 is all these things. She is Israel, Zion, Jerusalem, the church, the whole creation groaning in apocalyptic agony. Jacques Ellul writes:

> She is, very obviously, first of all, *the* woman, corresponding in heaven to Eve: which is confirmed by the fulfillment of the prophecy of Genesis concerning the hatred between Eve and the serpent, the victory of her posterity won over the serpent, and the latter's fall (12:9). But in addition the woman is surely Zion and Israel, who engender the Messiah and the believers. Further, she is very clearly Mary; or rather, the celestial reduplication of Mary, mother of the little child. (1977: 85, emphasis original)

While it might be objected that the woman cannot be the church, given that she gives birth to the child rather than deriving from him,[7] the objection misses the essential unity of God's people across time. As Israel, the woman brings forth the Messiah. As the church, she gives birth to the multitude of Messiah's brothers and sisters; hence the reference to "the rest of her offspring, on those who keep the commandments of God and hold to the testimony of Jesus" (12:17). The people of God are Israel in that it keeps the commandments (*mitzvot*) of God, and they are the church in that it offers testimony to Jesus. But whether in the old covenant or the new, the people of God is a maternal reality, bringing forth children by water and the Spirit, reshaping them after the image of Christ. Thus Paul writes in his angry-tender letter to the Galatians: "My little children, for whom I am again in the anguish of childbirth until Christ is formed in you" (Gal.

---

5. Isa. 52:1–2 also contains the promise that "no more [shall] come into you the uncircumcised and the unclean," echoed in Rev. 21:27. See also Isa. 66:7; Mic. 4:10; Ps. 87:5.

6. Austin Farrer, *A Rebirth of Images: The Making of St. John's Apocalypse* (Westminster: Dacre, 1949).

7. This is Ellul's objection, in the passage immediately following the quotation given above.

4:19).[8] The Apocalypse offers a perhaps surprising testimony to the motherhood of the church.[9]

12:5 The woman's giving birth to *disciples*, however, comes to expression only later on in the passage (Rev. 12:17). John's primary concern is to describe the birth of her firstborn, called "a male child, one who is to rule all the nations with a rod of iron." While the description is sparse, it is enough to send us back to the great messianic psalm that speaks of God's anointed ruling the nations with an iron rod (Ps. 2:7–9). But consider what this means. If the child's destiny is to rule the earth, he represents an ultimate threat to the dragon's ambitions. What identity does the devil have, other than the sheer, untrammeled exercise of power? If the woman's son wins, Satan loses everything. Like King Herod, who is in some ways his earthly representative, the devil knows that he must rid himself of this rival while he still has the chance. It is a wonderfully tense moment in the story: will the terrible monster succeed in devouring the newborn baby? Or will the baby grow up to be the mighty prince he is destined to be?

And yet, oddly, the dramatic tension is resolved almost as soon as it is stated: the child is miraculously snatched from the dragon's mouth and carried up to God and his throne. This almost comical anticlimax reminds us that we are not in a dualistic universe where good and evil confront one another as equals. We are in the realm of creation and gospel. There is an element of risk here, to be sure. In the first letter of Peter we are told that the devil prowls around "like a roaring lion, seeking someone to devour" (1 Pet. 5:8). In Rev. 12 this "someone" is the Messiah himself, who, precisely by virtue of being human, is also vulnerable. In this sense the story of the child's birth and rescue may be considered a close call for the human race. But *this* Messiah is also the Son of God, and as such he is sovereign over every enemy. The dragon's jaws snap shut, but they come up with nothing but air!

When the child is said to be "caught up to God and his throne," the Greek verb is *harpazō* ("to carry off, take by force"). It is the same verb used by Matthew

---

8. Bede cites this Galatians passage in his commentary on Rev. 12: "The Church, in a spiritual sense, both brings forth those with whom it travails, and ceases not to travail with them when already born. As she herself says, 'My little children, of whom I travail in birth again, until Christ be formed in you.'" See Bedae Presbyteri, *Expositio Apocalypseos*, Corpus Christianorum: Series Latina 121A, ed. Roger Gryson (Turnhout: Brepols, 2001), 387; English translation from Edward Marshall, *The Explanation of the Apocalypse by Venerable Beda* (Oxford: Parker, 1878), fragments of which are available online at apocalyptic-theories.com. For a wonderful treatment of maternal imagery in Paul, see the essays in Beverly Roberts Gaventa, *Our Mother Saint Paul* (Louisville: Westminster John Knox, 2007).

9. This conviction is as much a part of the Reformation tradition as it is of Catholicism. Thus John Calvin says that "there is no other way to enter into life unless this mother [the church] conceive us in her womb, give us birth, [and] nourish us at her breast. . . . Away from her bosom one cannot hope for any forgiveness of sins or any salvation"; *Institutes of the Christian Religion*, ed. J. T. McNeill, trans. F. L. Battles, Library of Christian Classics 20–21 (Philadelphia: Westminster, 1960), 1016 §4.1.4. One can find equally strong expressions in the writings of Luther.

to describe those who would lay violent hands on the kingdom (Matt. 11:12) and by Paul to describe the saints being carried off to meet Christ on his return (1 Thess. 4:17; 2 Cor. 12:2, 4). In short, it is the "rapture" word, so beloved of Protestant dispensationalists.[10] Our present passage is the only "rapture" described in Revelation, and it speaks neither of Christians nor of the end, but of Christ's own ascent to the right hand of power. A rapture in the popular understanding of the term would make no sense at all in the Apocalypse. Instead of the saints going up, the city of God comes down.

But if Christ ascends to God's right hand, when does this event take place? Clearly not at his birth, but at his ascension. The birth in this story is a metaphor for Jesus's death, the necessary prelude to his assuming power as Lord. This linkage is consistent throughout the New Testament. "Truly, truly, I say to you, unless a grain of wheat falls into the earth and dies, it remains alone; but if it dies, it bears much fruit" (John 12:24; cf. 16:21).[11] Jesus's death is his entry into the only true life, the life of God.

12:6 What links Jesus's destiny and the church's destiny in Rev. 12 is the theme of ultimate safety, despite the terrors of this world. After she has given birth, the woman flees into the wilderness, where she has "a place prepared by God, in which she is to be nourished for 1,260 days"—the by now thoroughly familiar apocalyptic period (→11:1–3, 9, 11). It is an image of remarkable tranquility. Although the woman is harassed and persecuted, she is always protected. Daughter Zion is "delivered" in a double sense: she is conducted safely through childbirth, and she is rescued from the clutches of the evil one. She is delivered of a child, and she undergoes a deliverance even greater than that which took place at the Red Sea. The woman is not only sheltered, she is *nourished*—possibly an allusion to the Eucharist, the *viaticum* or "way bread" that sustains the church on its journey.

12:7–9 The story of war in heaven interrupts the flow of the woman-dragon sequence. Indeed, the reader who skipped directly from 12:6 to 12:13b might not even notice that anything was missing. But in fact, the tale of heavenly warfare encapsulates the major theme of this section of Revelation; it could even be seen as a summary of the whole book *in nuce*. It would be a mistake to ignore it.

Once again, the dragon is a central character in the drama. But this time his antagonist is the archangel Michael, who like Satan himself commands an army of angels; this is a rather different role for angels from what we have seen up till now. Once again the situation is ripe with dramatic possibilities. Surely this would be one of the high points in any film version of the Apocalypse, filled with elaborate, Tolkien-like battle scenes, fantastic displays of swordplay between the two main characters, and lots of gore.[12] It would win the Oscar for special effects.

---

10. Cf. Hal Lindsey, *The Late Great Planet Earth* (New York: Bantam, 1973).

11. On the birth-for-death imagery see Raymond E. Brown, *An Introduction to the New Testament* (New York: Doubleday, 1997), 791.

12. According to theological tradition, angels are purely spiritual beings and so could not suffer physical harm. But I doubt this would stop a determined Hollywood scriptwriter.

Yet in fact, John's account of the conflict shows remarkable restraint. All he tells us is that "the dragon and his angels . . . [were] defeated"—literally, "lacked the power" or "did not prevail"—and that "there was no longer any place for them in heaven." The Greek word translated "place" here is *topos*. Earlier we were told that the woman has a *topos* in the desert prepared for her by God. Now we hear that the dragon and his angels have lost their *topos*. Even if such a place was once theirs, they have forfeited it. God refuses to make peace with evil. He will not tolerate it in his house (heaven), and while the dragon enjoys something of a second career on earth, we are assured that this reprieve is strictly temporary and that the dragon's days are numbered: "His time is short" (12:12).

Mention of the devil's "time," however, raises an important question: *when* is all this happening? On the one hand, talk of the dragon's losing his "place" in heaven suggests that the story takes place in some primordial time before the fall, perhaps even before time itself. Jewish traditions concerning the pretemporal fall of the angels are reflected elsewhere in the New Testament (2 Pet. 2:4; Jude 6). The theme is memorably developed by John Milton in his epic *Paradise Lost*. If evil is "always already there," it is even truer that God eternally refuses to make peace with it. We cannot exclude such cosmic-primordial overtones altogether.

12:10–12 Yet even if we say that Satan's defeat occurs in some sense before the dawn of time, the *reason* for that fall lies *in* time: the Lamb's victory and his followers' faithful participation in that victory. This becomes clear in the declaration that immediately follows Satan's expulsion:

> And I heard a loud voice in heaven, saying, "Now the salvation and the power and the kingdom of our God and the authority of his Christ have come, for the accuser of our brothers has been thrown down, who accuses them day and night before our God. And they have conquered him by the blood of the Lamb and by the word of their testimony, for they loved not their lives even unto death."

Some commentators are embarrassed that it is not Christ, but the archangel Michael, who wins the victory over Satan. This makes it sound as if Christ required angelic assistance to do his work. Such worries are too literal minded and miss the bifocal vision of the Apocalypse. "St. Michael and all angels" (as their feast day is called) are both a reality in themselves and a figure for Jesus and his followers. It is the Lamb's victory, and only as such an angelic victory before the world began, and the saints' victory enacted between now and the parousia. St. Michael is thus a figure of Christ, a point made by Heinrich Bullinger, who reminds us that this whole vision began with talk of "signs" or "tokens":

> But forasmuch we heard in the beginning, that these were tokens, they must needs signify and betoken other things. I suppose here therefore to be signified, Christ the head of his church, king and protector with his memberss [sic], apostles, martyrs, and faithful. Nother [neither] is it a rare thing, that Christ should be figured to us by angels: but is even most accustomed, that angels are called the ambassadors of

God, and the faithful servants of Jesus Christ. Christ therefore head of the church and the faithful members of Christ, fight against the Dragon, yet after a diverse sort [in different ways]. For Christ overcame him alone in the combat without help of any creature, whilst in temptations he discomfited him at the last, and also by dying on the cross and rising again from the dead, he also brake his head. This is the only, true and singular victory: whereby afterwards are obtained the victories of Christ's members, gotten of that general fight wherein Christ fighteth not now only hand to hand with the devil but all the members of Christ at all times under Christ their captain fight against the devil, and in the virtue or victory of Christ, fight and overcome: as we shall hear by and by in that song of praise.[13]

Once again, we see the temporal blurring and dislocation that is so characteristic of the book of Revelation. In the words of the liturgy: Christ has died, Christ is risen, Christ will come again. It is all one victory, but temporally dispersed, in such a way that a real history is permitted to unfold between the first and second comings.

It will be noticed, perhaps, that this way of telling the story treats historical evil primarily as a reaction to God's prior initiative. Satan is cast out of heaven, and *therefore* he is exceedingly angry, knowing that his time (*kairos*) is short.[14] Having no place in heaven and only a limited amount of time on earth, the devil is afraid, a point made by the letter to the Hebrews when it explicitly links Satan with the fear of death (Heb. 2:14–15). The truth is that Christ holds the keys of both death *and* hades. The devil's only recourse, then, is to make his way through the world as a teller of outrageous lies. That is why our passage calls him "the deceiver of the whole world" and "the accuser of our brothers." He deceives the whole world with the fear of death, causing men and women to distrust the Creator who has given them life. He accuses "our brothers" by spreading the false rumor that their life and witness mean nothing to God, that a life devoted to God is a life wasted, and that they therefore would have been better off worshiping idols, whose payoff, after all, is much more tangible and immediate. The devil is the original bearer of false witness.[15] His lies are legion, like his multiple personalities. At the social level, they include all the stratagems of deception and doublespeak by which corporations, governments, and the vast enterprises of technocracy seek to keep people from a knowledge of the truth. These powers understand all too well that if the truth were known, their time, too, would be uncomfortably short.[16]

13. Bullinger, *Hundred Sermons*, 356.
14. Cf. Luke 4:13: "And when the devil had ended every temptation, he departed from him until an opportune time [*kairos*]."
15. "When he lies, he speaks out of his own character, for he is a liar and the father of lies" (John 8:44). This characterization of Satan points back to his role in earlier Jewish tradition as God's "prosecuting attorney," a picture reflected in the book of Job.
16. William Stringfellow, *An Ethic for Christians and Other Aliens in a Strange Land* (Waco: Word, 1973), 97–106, lists the following "stratagems of the demonic powers": (1) the denial of truth, (2) doublespeak and overtalk, (3) secrecy and boasts of expertise, (4) surveillance and

But while the devil is a tireless worker, "accus[ing our brothers] day and night before our God," we know that his lies will ultimately prove ineffective. We know this because he is no match for Jesus Christ, the true witness, the one who tells us the truth about us by claiming us as God's own. And because Christ speaks the truth, the Christian, too, is summoned to a vocation as courageous truth-teller. She does this first of all by bearing witness to the gospel, but also through a quiet passion for truth in everyday life. "You shall not bear false witness against your neighbor" (Exod. 20:16). This commandment of the law is also integral to the gospel. Whenever the Christian refuses to go along with the devil's lies, she confirms her love both of the true witness and of the neighbor who suffers the burden of false witness. The "necessity" of lying is grounded in the structures of the old eon. But that eon is passing away. In a world where truth (Christ) is victorious, there is no reason not to speak the truth.

12:13–17 The dragon angrily stalks off in search of other victims. Shrewdly realizing that "if he cannot directly attack the Woman's Son, he can hurt the Son through the Mother," he mounts an attack on her (Swete 1908: 157). Surely she will prove an easier target? Yet once again, the prey turns out to be maddeningly elusive. The woman is given eagle's wings and flies to her *topos* in the desert, where she is to be nurtured for "a time, and times, and half a time," the apocalyptic period of the church's suffering.[17] This time, however, the desert refuge proves less effective, as the dragon spews out a flood of water to sweep the woman away—a reversal of Israel's safe passage through the Red Sea. The dragon would summon up the primeval forces of chaos to drown his enemy once for all.

12:15–17 Water being the devil's instrument, it is striking that precisely the *earth* should now rise up to the woman's aid. Surely this episode is among the most baldly comic in all of Revelation. The dragon has already been thwarted twice, the first time when the child was snatched up to heaven and then again when the woman flew away.[18] Now the earth opens up her mouth and swallows up the dragon's mighty flood.[19] This third frustration is perhaps the most humiliating

harassment, (5) exaggeration and deception, (6) cursing and conjuring, (7) usurpation and absorption, (8) diversion and demoralization.

17. Cf. Exod. 19:4, where the eagle's wings belong to God, and Isa. 40:31, where it is the saints who are said to "mount up with wings like eagles." Commentators both ancient and modern seek to find particular meanings in these wings. Bede sees here a reference to the Old and New Testaments, while Hippolytus finds an allusion to the hands of Christ stretched out on the cross.

18. It is perhaps irreverent, but if one wanted an analogy from popular culture for the dragon's frustration, one could do worse than to recall Wile E. Coyote's hapless pursuit of the Road Runner.

19. The dragon's flood is an instance of the exodus motif that runs throughout Revelation. David Barr notes, however, that there is no parallel for what is said of the earth here: "All other biblical references to the earth opening her mouth have to do with destruction not rescue. Also unparalleled is the notion of one woman rescuing another (earth being in Greek a feminine noun with a feminine pronoun)" (1998: 125). To be sure, the grammatical gender of *hē gē* would not in itself be sufficient to identify earth as a "she," any more than the gender of *die Gabel* in German means that forks are female. It is a matter of context. The earth "came to the help of the woman." Earth

of all. Like many an occupying power throughout history, the devil is forced to discover that conquering is easier than ruling, that the locals cannot be trusted, and that it is hard to stop them from giving aid and comfort to the partisans. It is a frustrated and hungry dragon who goes off to "make war on the rest of her [the woman's] offspring, on those who keep the commandments of God and hold to the testimony to Jesus." This outcome once again has comic overtones—does the dragon really think this new campaign will be any more successful than his previous ones?—while being at the same time completely serious. The reader knows that more blood will be shed before the church's warfare is over.

There is a larger theological point to be made here. We have seen that the term "earth" often carries negative connotations in the Apocalypse, as in the often repeated phrase "the dwellers on earth." In the context of this parable, however, earth appears as helpful and sympathetic. While Revelation's Jewishness is such that it would not be wise to construe the earth as a divinity, our passage surely conveys a sense of the earth's status as part of God's good creation. While they may rule the earth in this present evil age, Satan and his allies cannot actually succeed in rendering the world "demonic"—a deeply comforting thought.[20] Because of this, however, the church can from time to time expect to find allies in unexpected places. John Howard Yoder famously writes that "people who bear crosses are working with the grain of the universe." He goes on to say that "one does not come to that belief by reducing social process to mechanical and statistical models, nor by winning some of one's battles for the control of one's own corner of the fallen world. One comes to it by sharing the life of those who sing about the Resurrection of the slain Lamb."[21] It is not the securely established, but the persecuted church that is in the best position to see how the grain of the universe lines up.

The woman clothed with the sun is a polyvalent figure, being at once Israel, Daughter Zion, Mary/the new Eve, and the church. But why this intrusion of maternal and birth imagery at just this point in the book? If the "birth" recounted in 12:1–5 is at heart the paschal mystery of Christ's death, this death is nevertheless undergone by the Son of God in his human flesh, "born of woman, born under the law" (Gal. 4:4). If the predominant image in the story of the two witnesses is that of Christ's death and resurrection, the theme of the present episode is that

---

appears here as an agent in the narrative, not as an impersonal object. It seems not unreasonable, then, to see this character as being female: "mother earth." The suspicion is strengthened by the overall mythic tone of Rev. 12, as well as by the presence of important feminine characters (the heavenly woman, the great prostitute) throughout this section of the book.

20. A thought powerfully captured in Gerard Manley Hopkins's sonnet "The Grandeur of God," which begins with a catalog of the ways in which human beings have despoiled the earth, but ends by affirming that we cannot undo the gift of creation itself: "And for all this, nature is never spent; / There lives the dearest freshness deep down things." The reason for this freshness is the continually renewing activity of the Spirit: "Because the Holy Ghost over the bent / World broods with warm breast and with ah! bright wings."

21. John Howard Yoder, "Armaments and Eschatology," *Studies in Christian Ethics* 1 (1988): 58.

of the incarnation, "the total union of the *whole* of man with the *whole* of God" (Ellul 1977: 85, emphasis original). Christ's victory is not achieved in some realm of pure spirit and only afterward applied to the world. Having assumed creaturely flesh, he brings life to creation from within. The entire atmosphere of the vision has something of the cosmic about it, displaying the reality of Jesus as the one who has defeated the powers and who unites heaven and earth in his own body. From ancient times, the safeguard of his true humanity has been the doctrine of Mary as the Theotokos or God bearer, a scandal to all those who feel it necessary to keep God at a safe distance from the world.

But because God has not kept his distance and because the Messiah is born and dies in history, the church exists to insure that he is not lacking in younger sisters and brothers. In its "Marian" dimension, the church is our mother. It brings forth children into a dangerous world, a world in which its adversary, the devil, is always seeking new victims to devour. At the center of the vision in Rev. 12 is the figure of warfare, Michael and his angels fighting against the devil and his angels. Let the reader understand: Christ and his followers against the powers! The vision concludes on an ambiguous note, with a clear indication that the warfare continues even up to the present day: "The dragon became furious with the woman and went off to make war on the rest of her offspring" (12:17). Who else can "the rest of her offspring" be but the present hearers of the Apocalypse, whether in the *ekklēsiai* of the first century or in the missionary congregations of the twenty-first?

The picture of the church that emerges from Rev. 12 is of a harassed, threatened, and quite vulnerable community. Vatican II famously spoke of the church as the "pilgrim people of God" (*Lumen Gentium* 64). That phrase should not be taken to mean progress along a series of tourist stops following a safe, well-established route. In the medieval world, setting forth on pilgrimage was a dangerous activity; the church's existence can be no less so. There will, of course, be certain signposts, markers left by past pilgrims to guide us across a forbidding landscape. For these we can only be grateful. This does not change the church's movement through the world having the character of improvisation, a constant relying on the grace of God rather than a mastery marked by total control. That the church *can*, however, rely on God's grace means that we can have confidence in the church surviving (and even flourishing) despite all the assaults of the evil one. In traditional language, this is the Christian conviction concerning the "indefectibility" of the church. Truly the gates of hell will not prevail against it (Matt. 16:18).

That the church can and must rely on God does not exclude the possibility of its receiving all manner of help from creaturely sources, providing it does not confuse the latter with the help it receives from the Creator himself. Here as throughout the Apocalypse, chief among these sources is the ministry of the holy angels. If the angels in Rev. 12:7–12 are primarily a figure for the church's own warfare, as Bullinger maintains, they are also, I think, simply themselves. The angels of God fight on our behalf. Though the world be temporarily under the rule of the principalities of this age, there are countervailing forces at work, constantly reminding the church that God has not abandoned his creation. Some of these forces may be extraordinary, even angelic, powers, while others are of a more earthbound sort. The earth itself comes to the woman's aid! But either way, the church should know that it is not alone in its battle with the principalities. As Elisha said to his servant, "Do not be afraid, for those who are with us are more than those who are with them" (2 Kgs. 6:16).

Dietrich Bonhoeffer expressed the same thought in a modern idiom, in a poem entitled "Powers of Good" written from his Berlin prison cell in the waning days of 1944. It expresses a serene confidence in God's providential care of the world through the good powers, evidence of an unseen world:

> The powers of good surround us in wonder,
> Comforted and kept beyond all fear,
> So I will live with you in these days
> And go with you to meet the coming year.
>
> The old year still fills our hearts with terror.
> We carry still the burden of these evil days.
> O Lord, give our chastened souls your healing
> For which you have so gracefully created us.
>
> But, should you offer us instead the bitter cup
> Of suffering, filled to the brim and overflowing,
> We will accept it gratefully without flinching
> From your good and ever-loving hand.
>
> While all the powers of good protect us
> Boldly we'll face the future, come what may.
> At even and at morn God will befriend us
> And never fails to greet us each new day![22]

22. Dietrich Bonhoeffer, *Letters and Papers from Prison*, ed. Eberhard Bethge (New York: Macmillan, 1972), 400–401.

REVELATION 13

THE BEAST AND THE SAINTS

As I looked, this horn made war with the saints and prevailed over them, until the Ancient of Days came, and judgment was given for the saints of the Most High, and the time came when the saints possessed the kingdom.

—Daniel 7:21–22

In some older biblical translations, such as KJV, Rev. 12:18 reads: "And I stood upon the sand of the sea," indicating John's location as he observes the horrors of the next vision. But the manuscript tradition that attests this reading is poor.[1] The far more likely reading is: "And he [the dragon] stood on the sand of the sea." The sentence, then, marks a transition between two phases of the dragon's activity: his failed pursuit of the woman into the wilderness and his new strategy of waging war on "the rest of her offspring." These offspring are nothing other than the assemblies that form the audience of Revelation.

The dragon continues to be a powerful presence throughout the next part of the book, although now his manner of working is hidden and indirect. The devil has a multitude of servants. In the Gospels he is called "Beelzebul, . . . the prince of demons" (Mark 3:22). In Rev. 12:7–9 he commands an army of angels. Part of what makes the present passage so disquieting is that it shows how demonic

---

1. NA[27] reads *estathē* ("he stood"). The reading *estathēn* ("I stood") probably arose from copyists assimilating the verb to the first person of the next sentence: "I saw a beast rising out of the sea." See Bruce M. Metzger, *A Textual Commentary on the Greek New Testament*, 2nd ed. (London: United Bible Societies, 1994), 673. In English Bibles, Rev. 12:18 in NA[27] is variously given its own number (NRSV), included in 12:17 (RSV, ESV), or included in 13:1 (KJV).

reality proliferates. It is constantly summoning up new forms and strategies. Its names are legion.

13:1–4 As Rev. 13 opens, we are permitted to be present at the irruption—"creation" would not be the right word, since the devil does not create—of a particular form of the demonic into the human world. Standing on the shores of the sea, the dragon summons an ally out of its chaotic depths. Heinrich Schlier makes the arresting proposal that the dragon, when he looks into the sea, beholds his own image, which then takes on an objective reality of its own. Knowing and loving himself, the dragon brings forth the beast.[2] And indeed, there is a strong correspondence between these two monsters even at the level of appearance. Both have seven heads and ten horns. Both wear crowns, the dragon on his heads and the beast on his horns. The physical resemblance between the two is a sign of their spiritual equivalence. The beast, however, is subordinate to his master: thus the dragon is said to give to the beast "his power and his throne and great authority. . . . And they worshiped the dragon, for he had given his authority to the beast, and they worshiped the beast, saying, 'Who is like the beast, and who can fight against it?'" (13:2, 4).

The repeated use of the word "authority" in this chapter (13:2, 4, 5, 7, 12) is a clue that we find ourselves in the sphere of the political. Such is also signaled by the animal imagery in 13:2, comparing the beast himself to a leopard, his feet to a bear's feet, and his mouth to a lion's mouth.[3] The language reiterates Daniel's description of four beasts, which like John's arise from the sea. The first three are successively likened to a lion, a bear, and a leopard, while the fourth is a ravaging and devouring monster who sports ten horns. The allegory is transparent: Daniel tells us that the four beasts represent four kingdoms (Dan. 7:17, 23). Commentators ancient and modern see the first three beasts as symbolizing the Babylonian, Median, and Persian empires, while the fourth signifies the Greek empire of Alexander the Great. The ten horns of the latter represent the ten rulers who succeeded Alexander. The last of these, the "little horn," embodies the ruthless tyrant Antiochus Epiphanes, who sacked Jerusalem and set up an altar of Zeus in the temple of YHWH (2 Maccabees 6:1–11). It is in just this context that Daniel is granted his powerful vision of the Ancient of Days, the judge who condemns the final beast to destruction and who grants a universal kingship to "one like a son of man" coming on the clouds of heaven (Dan. 7:11–14).

2. Heinrich Schlier, *Principalities and Powers in the New Testament* (Freiburg: Herder, 1961), 76.

3. The use of animal imagery in political allegories is well known. Examples include Thomas Hobbes's *Leviathan*, George Orwell's *Animal Farm*, and Richard Adams's *Watership Down*. Of modern examples, perhaps the most powerful is Art Spiegelman's *Maus*, a graphic novel of the Holocaust in which the Jews are depicted as mice, the Germans as cats, and the Poles as pigs; see Art Spiegelman, *The Complete Maus: My Father Bleeds History/And Here My Troubles Began* (New York: Pantheon, 1996).

By the time that John of Patmos was writing, Alexander's empire and the blasphemies of Antiochus had long since been relegated to the dustbin of history. On the one hand, the Jews had resisted and outlasted these tyrants; Hanukah commemorates the fact. On the other hand, the end had clearly not yet come. In the first-century Jewish apocalypse known as 2 Esdras (4 Ezra), the seer is given a vision of a horrible three-headed eagle, so powerful that "all things under heaven were subjected to it, and no one spoke against it—not a single creature that was on the earth" (2 Esdras [4 Ezra] 11:6 NRSV). The seer explicitly identifies this eagle with the fourth beast of Daniel (2 Esdras [4 Ezra] 11:39–46; 12:11). The eagle conquers all the empires that have gone before it, institutes a reign of terror, and maintains power through deceit and cunning. Interestingly, the seer of 2 Esdras also sees the eagle as internally conflicted, with its multiple heads and wings devouring each other, until just one head is left to rule (2 Esdras [4 Ezra] 11:35). The most natural thing to suppose is that the Jewish seer is speaking of Rome. Despite its dynastic struggles in the 50s AD (the contending wings and heads), Rome's power toward the end of the first century must have seemed unstoppable. It was the true successor of Alexander, not just in terms of military success and the scope of its rule, but as the bearer of Hellenistic culture to the entire known world. It had a "civilizing mission."

In 2 Esdras (4 Ezra) 12:1–3, the eagle's power finally encounters a limit in the form of a mighty lion, who prophesies the destruction of the eagle and whose prophecy instantly comes true—a performative utterance, indeed! It is later explained to the seer that this is the Messiah who will come to liberate God's people (12:31–39). But in the Apocalypse to John, the Lion of Judah has *already* come. He has come as the Lamb. His death is the all-encompassing victory that liberates people of all nations, tribes, and languages, not just from the tyranny of Rome, but from all the principalities and rulers of the present age. The curious thing about the Apocalypse—one might also say that it is the curious thing about Christianity—is that while it resembles 2 Esdras in anticipating Messiah's future coming, it sees this coming as the fulfillment of a definitive victory that has already occurred: "Worthy are you [O Lamb] to take the scroll and to open its seals, for you were slain, and by your blood you ransomed people for God . . . and you have made them a kingdom and priests to our God, and they shall reign on earth" (Rev. 5:9–10).

Because the Lamb's victory is what unleashes eschatology in the Apocalypse, we need to understand its monsters in an eschatological way. The beast of Rev. 13 is truly the final beast, not just by being the last in a series, but by incarnating all the terrors of which political humanity is capable. That is why he displays the attributes of all of Daniel's first three monsters. He is part of the final, historical attack by the evil one on the grace of God manifested in Jesus Christ.

The parodic element in John's depiction of the beast is quite explicit. As the woman clothed with the sun gives birth to the child, so the dragon "fathers" the beast by calling him forth from the sea.[4] God the enthroned entrusts the sealed scroll to the Lamb, the dragon gives "his power and his throne and great authority" to the beast. As the Lamb is the word of God who bears true witness (19:11), so the beast wears blasphemous names on its heads and blasphemes God's name. As the Lamb lives even though slaughtered (*esphagmenon*), so one of the beasts' heads appears as if slaughtered (*esphagmenēn*), and yet its death blow was healed. A final, somewhat poetic parallel can be seen in the Greek words John employs. John might have chosen any of several words to speak of a lamb. The word he actually employs is *arnion*, which rhymes with *thērion*, the word for "beast" (Eller 1974: 79–80). Even at the aural level, the beast cannot help but mimic the one he despises.

13:5–7 The beast is, in fact, the antichrist. While Revelation does not use this word, which in the New Testament appears only in the Johannine epistles (1 John 2:18 [twice], 22; 4:3; 2 John 7), the correspondences make clear that the *thērion* is Jesus's opposite. Jesus lives and rules—that is the ultimate reality testified to by the Apocalypse. But the penultimate reality, the reality of our lived experience, seems quite different. The beast exercises authority for the full apocalyptic period of forty-two months. He makes war on the saints and "conquer[s] them"— an extraordinary statement (Rev. 13:7)! The verb *nikaō* is normally used in the Apocalypse to describe the Lamb and his followers, but here it is the beast who conquers and the saints who lose (so also 11:7). (John never says that the Lamb himself is conquered; that would truly be a contradiction in terms.) Fascinated by the beast's marvelous powers of recuperation, his "resurrection" from the dead (13:3), human beings slavishly offer themselves to the worship of the beast. In the historical competition between the worship and rule of the Lamb on the one hand and the worship and rule of the beast on the other, the beast has undeniable advantages. To all human calculations, the beast's way of doing things seemed destined to win out in the end.

The saints lose. This outcome will seem disappointing only to the extent that we embrace the beast's criteria for what constitutes success. The church that imagines it has a successful strategy for confronting the principalities and powers on their own terms had better think again. It is not only that the church, by submitting to the court of human judgment rather than to the decrees of the just judge, will lose its own soul; ironically, it will not even gain the world.

That the church has no strategy for defeating the beast should not be taken as a counsel of indifference to success as such, at the level of what might be called tactics. In the things that the church is genuinely called to do, there is nothing wrong with its wanting to do them well. A soup kitchen should be clean and well managed and genuinely help those it is meant to serve. A program of evangelism

---

4. The image of birth is especially clear in William Blake's watercolor *The Great Red Dragon and the Beast from the Sea*, which shows the beast rising from the chaotic depths into the space between Satan's legs (Blake's "dragon" mixes human and serpentine features).

can legitimately endeavor to reach as many people as possible (but this precisely should not mean segmenting the "market" so as to attract mainly young, affluent couples; such tactics reek of Babylon's ways). A church's engagement with social policy concerning abortion or stem-cell research should be well informed and well reasoned and seek to make a practical difference in the lives of human beings even outside the church. All this is to a great degree common sense; Christians make no fetish of failure.

None of this, however, changes that success must not come at the expense of Christian faithfulness in a world dominated by the powers. The utterly unsentimental witness of the Apocalypse is that, in the larger scheme of things, the church needs to be prepared to lose, not because failure is good, but because this happens to be the nature of the story in which we are involved. Moreover, it lies in the very character of the gospel that what counts as failure in human terms is surrounded and attended by the grace of God (1 Cor. 1:25). William Stringfellow writes in his great "Homily on the Significance of the Defeat of the Saints":

> Revelation 13:7 contains no melancholy message. It authorizes hope for the saints— and, through their vocation of advocacy, hope for the whole of creation—which is grounded in realistic expectations concerning the present age, enabling the church— as the first beneficiary of the resurrection—to confront the full and awesome militancy of the power of death.... This seemingly troublesome text about the defeat of the saints by the beast is, preeminently, a reference to the accessibility of the grace of the Word of God for living now. To mention the defeat of the saints means to know the abundance of grace.[5]

The hopefulness in Rev. 13, though mostly hidden under its opposite, comes to expression in a brief phrase John introduces seemingly by accident. Describing the beast's universal dominion, he writes that "all who dwell on earth will worship it"—and then not wishing to commit blasphemy, he quickly corrects himself: "Everyone whose name has not been written in the book of life of the Lamb that was slaughtered from the foundation of the world" (NRSV margin; so also KJV). The earth-dwellers will worship the beast. But those whose names are written in the book of life will not worship him. The true worship of God in the world is embodied in the *leitourgia* of those who refuse to succumb to the beast's falsehoods.

13:8 The extraordinary phrase "the Lamb that was slaughtered from the foundation of the world" deserves extended treatment. The Greek is a little ambiguous, and the phrase could be rendered grammatically so as to say something slightly less radical. Thus ESV: "Everyone whose name has not been written before the foundation of the world in the book of life of the Lamb who was slain." This reading aligns with 17:8, which speaks of "the dwellers on earth whose names

5. William Stringfellow, *Conscience and Obedience: The Politics of Romans 13 and Revelation 13 in Light of the Second Coming* (Waco: Word, 1977), 111.

have not been written in the book of life from the foundation of the world." In that passage it seems to be the book that exists *apo katabolēs kosmou* ("from the foundation of the world"), not the Lamb. But how different are these two readings in practice? Not only is the older translation still defensible from a grammatical perspective, but it seems to be logically implied in any case. All agree that it is the Lamb's book of life. And the Lamb, in Revelation, is by definition he who was slain. To shift into nonmetaphorical language for a moment, there is no Jesus who is not slain, and John is hardly imagining a "second person of the Trinity" in abstraction from the incarnation. God's electing purpose is eternal, and it *intends history*—precisely the history enacted at Golgotha and in the lives of Jesus's followers, whose names are written in his book of life.[6] It is in this sense that the Lamb has never not been slaughtered, even if his life-giving death takes place on a particular Friday afternoon outside the walls of Jerusalem.

13:9–10 A voice suddenly intrudes on the narrative, summoning the listener to attention (cf. Jer. 15:2):

> If anyone has an ear, let him hear:
> If anyone is to be taken captive,
> > to captivity he goes;
> if anyone is to be slain with the sword,
> > with the sword must he be slain.

Here is a call for the endurance and faith of the saints.

The expression "if anyone has an ear" takes us back to the letters to the churches, at the point where each assembly is addressed directly by the Spirit. Surely this is to be taken as a comment on the Lamb's book of life. Those whose names are written in the book are not some anonymous cohort of the elect. They are the listeners themselves. They are the ones who, right now, are confirming their identities *as* the elect by patiently enduring the marauding and violence of the beast. *Nostra res agitur*, says the prophet again and again: "These things concern us" in very direct and concrete ways.

13:11–15 Now John sees a second monster, this time arising out of the earth: "It had two horns like a lamb and it spoke like a dragon." In one brief stroke, John communicates the essential information that this monster, too, is an avatar of the dragon and that he pursues his ends by mimicking the Lamb. The role of this second beast is to cause people to worship the first one, a vocation he exercises by working great signs (*sēmeia*). By himself, the beast from the sea would be simply brute power, his agenda to kill and destroy all too transparent. As Hitler needed Goebbels, so the first beast needs the second to be his minister of propaganda, a master in the art of language and symbolism, charged with the task of making

---

6. This same blurring of prehistory, Jesus's history, and the church's history occurs in the story of the war in heaven in Rev. 12. Further support for the traditional rendering comes from 1 Pet. 1:20, which speaks of the Lamb being known "before the foundation of the world."

beast-worship seem plausible and attractive. Later on in the book he will be referred to as the "false prophet" (16:13). Not only does he incite human beings to make an image (*eikōn*) of the sea beast, but he breathes life into this image, "so that the image of the beast might even speak and might cause those who would not worship the image of the beast to be slain" (13:15). If Adam and Eve are fashioned in the image of God, who breathed life into them at the creation, so the second beast fashions a false image *of what it means to be human*, enticing men and women to exchange their God-given glory for a cheapened form of existence.

13:16–17 "Cheapen" is the appropriate metaphor, because what follows interestingly turns to economic questions: "Also it causes all, both small and great, both rich and poor, both free and slave, to be marked on the right hand or the forehead, so that no one can buy or sell unless he has the mark, that is, the name of the beast or the number of its name." There is a twofold meaning here. First, the beasts control the mechanisms of exchange, setting the terms for who can and cannot participate in the market. While human beings cannot help but make and produce, buy and sell, in order to live, what the beasts effect is a terrible distortion of this aspect of human life in community. The realm of economics is preeminently a realm dominated by the principalities, a theme developed in much greater detail in the Babylon vision in Rev. 18.

Even more fundamental, however, is the second point: under the beasts' reign, human beings themselves become commodities. No one can be a stakeholder in the system who does not bear the mark of the beast, written on hand or forehead. Goods are marked, cattle are marked. Human beings are generally not marked, but are the bearers of names. A person's name serves to locate that person in the context of natural family and community and also to identify him or her as *this* one and no other. But to bear the beast's mark and name is to be robbed of such identifying traits. In the beast's economy, I can buy and sell only to the extent that I am myself bought and sold (cf. 18:13). I am in principle exchangeable with any other. Moreover, the vision tells us that this condition is universal: "Also it [the land beast] causes all, both small and great, both rich and poor, both free and slave, to be marked on the right hand or the forehead" (13:16).

Stringfellow writes that the one great power underlying all the powers, even Satan himself, is death, the "moral reality which rules nations and all other principalities and powers of this world." It is death who permeates the whole of the principalities' existence.[7] Death in this deep sense can assume many forms. The branding of humans as the beast's property, thus ultimately disposable, is no less a sign of death's presence than is the literal killing of the saints. The denial of the image of God in human beings is death's work. That is why the receiving of *Christ's* name is such a momentous event in the life of the Christian (3:12; 14:11). In sacramental terms this occurs at baptism. Occurring as an event in the public

---

7. William Stringfellow, *An Ethic for Christians and Other Aliens in a Strange Land* (Waco: Word, 1973), 67.

world, baptism sets a visible, concrete limit to the reign of the principalities. It says that this man or this woman has been claimed as Christ's own forever and that nothing the powers can do can alter that fact. "I have called you *by name*, you are mine" (Isa. 43:1).

The beast from the sea attempts to mimic Christ the Lamb, and together the dragon, beast, and false prophet constitute an entire demonic Trinity parodying God, the Lamb, and the Spirit. As God gives life, generously and with overflowing abundance, so the dragon reeks of death. As Christ comes bearing the peace of God, so the beast embodies every kind of violence and bloodshed and exploitation. As the prophetic Spirit exposes the truth in all things, so the false prophet spins a web of lies, inviting us to debase ourselves by worshiping the beast rather than the Creator.

13:18 The vision concludes with an aside to the reader, which is a familiar feature of the Apocalypse: "This calls for wisdom: let the one who has understanding calculate the number of the beast, for it is the number of a man [*anthrōpou*], and his number is 666." The verses immediately preceding have equated the mark of the beast with both his "name" and his "number." Now we are told that that number has a definite value: six hundred and sixty-six (the Greek text spells it out in words). Apparently only those who possess the proper key can calculate the number correctly.

Already in the ancient church, the number of the beast was a matter of speculation among the faithful. Ancient commentators assumed, no doubt rightly, that John was engaged in the Jewish practice of *gematria*, whereby words have numerical equivalents based on the value of the letters of the alphabet. This was a common enough practice in the ancient world.[8] So what we need is a person's name whose letters add up to the mystical 666.[9] The most common guess among modern scholars is "Nero Caesar," which, if spelled using Hebrew letters (NRWN QSR) yields the requisite figure. This view is strengthened when we consider a textual variant, known to St. Irenaeus, according to which the beast's number is 616. It just so happens that this is the sum of the Hebrew characters when the final *n* is left out of Nero, the Latin form of the name (Kovacs and Rowland 2004: 148).[10] Perhaps

8. A piece of graffiti found at Pompeii reads, "I love the girl whose name is phi mu epsilon (545)" (Caird 1984: 174).

9. There have been endless attempts to identify the beast as this or that historical figure on the basis of 666. My favorite comes from a postcard I found pasted into an old commentary on Revelation in the Wycliffe College library. Dated March 15, 1940, the postcard is addressed to "President, Toronto University," and bears a South Carolina return address. It purports to show how a Hebrew, numerical rendering of the letters C. A. Hitler (for "Chancellor Adolf Hitler") adds up to the required 666. The writer, one William C. Frierson, is at least appropriately modest about his discovery: "While this proves nothing at all, it is a bit interesting just now." The commentary was in the collection of the Rev. Henry J. Cody, President of the University of Toronto from 1932 to 1945. Did Cody smile when he received this card? Or did Frierson's calculation seem all too "interesting" under the circumstances?

10. Metzger, *Textual Commentary on the Greek New Testament*, 676.

a scribe wanted to make the calculation "come out right" using the version of the emperor's name familiar to him.

That early Christians might have wanted to identify Nero as the beast should come as no surprise. He was well known as a persecutor of the young Christian movement. His cruelty was legendary. The dynastic chaos that followed his death coincided with the Jewish war of AD 66–73, an event with apocalyptic overtones in the memory of both church and synagogue. If one had to identify the beast with any particular figure in the first century, one could hardly do better than this madman-emperor.

But why should we identify the beast with a character from the mid-first century? John's vision is of a coming terror, not a figure from the past. To be sure, historians sometimes refer to a popular legend according to which Nero, returned from the dead, was poised to lead an army from the east to reclaim his empire. This might explain the "horn" that suffered a death blow and then was healed (13:3). Even so, this horn is only one among the beast's ten horns. More to the point, John's monster is bigger and more awful than any individual emperor, even one with Nero's reputation for tyranny. We are dealing with the *final* beast, the sum of all terrors, the eschatological opponent of God in his explicitly political-civic form. "The kingdom of the world has become the kingdom of our Lord and of his Christ," we heard following the vindication of the two witnesses (11:15). The beast, then, is more than simply Nero, or even the empire of which Nero was head for a time. He is the kingdom of the world, the human city, *insofar* as it embodies hatred of the Lamb and resistance to his righteous rule. To the extent that John has Nero or Rome in view, these serve simply as the parable nearest at hand for the unimaginable forms that historical evil will assume, the nearer we approach the end.

This monster is born of the dragon's anger and frustration when he failed to devour the Messiah-King. Unable to harm either the son or the mother, the dragon summons forth the beast, a false messiah endowed with the capacity to lead human beings astray. If we think of the dragon as God's cosmic opposition, then the beast is his historical counterpart, an all-colonizing empire (Daniel's beasts were a succession of empires) that will tolerate any ruler except one: the risen crucified. The beast is the antichrist, the anti-Jesus, the anti-Lamb. Even his number tells us this. Quite apart from its connection to Nero, 666 is an interesting number. In a rather obvious way, 666 triply fails to attain the seven of divine perfection or fullness (although the beast's seven heads suggest that he has a negative perfection all his own, namely as the embodiment of evil). But lying just beyond seven is eight. In early Christian typology Easter was often thought of as the "eighth day of creation," Sunday being the eighth day after the seven originally set forth in Gen. 1. Eight is the number of eschatological fulfillment. It did not take long for Christian interpreters to discover that the *gematria* value of the name "Jesus" in Greek is 888, a tripling of eschatology, in much the same way as the beast's number is a tripling of the imperfect six.[11] Jesus in Revelation is *ho erchomenos* ("the coming one"), while the beast is passing away, a creature whose origin and destiny are in the realm of death. He emerges out of the death-dealing sea and in the end will be consigned to the abyss, whereas Jesus will stay forever.

Jesus, however, is not simply at the end of history; he is *in* history. This is what we mean when we speak of the incarnation. In a secondary and derivative way, it is what we mean when we speak of his presence through the Spirit to the church. This is an important reminder in itself concerning the use of the antichrist image or more generally concerning the language of "the demonic." While the agents of Satan are certainly abroad in the world, they do not *rule* the world. God sustains his creation in spite of the threat to it represented by the lordless powers, who are not, in fact, lordless at all: Christ has triumphed over them. Alertness to the presence and activity of Satan, yes (cf. 1 Pet. 5:8); ceding territory to him, no. As the child was snatched from the jaws of the dragon, so the world itself has been delivered from the power of the evil one—in promise and in truth, if not yet in visible manifestation.

But if Christ is in history, this means that there are incursions of the final beast into the realm of history, in the form of various satanic persons or institutions who prefigure his emergence. A favorite candidate from the late medieval period onward has been the papacy, which, like the beasts of Revelation, seemed to many to combine a lamblike appearance with an actual policy of blasphemy. While this exegesis predated the Reformation, it became a staple of Protestant exegesis. "Here, then, are the two beasts," writes Luther; "the one is the empire, the other, with the two horns, the papacy, which has now become a temporal kingdom, yet with the reputation and name of Christ."[12] Heinrich Bullinger identifies the second beast with the papacy, specifically with the succession of popes beginning with Pope Boniface VIII, whose bull *Unam Sanctam* asserted the church's superiority in temporal as well as spiritual matters. For Bullinger these two spurious "keys" are symbolized by the horns of the land beast, namely "the priesthood and king-dom, which the Popes usurp to themselves, assuming that power is given them in heaven and in earth."[13] Calvin likewise belongs in this tradition. "Of old," he

---

11. The interested reader can pursue the numerological dimensions of 666 by reading the exquisitely detailed account in Bauckham 1993a: 384–452, from which parts of this paragraph are taken. Bauckham makes much of 666 as a "triangular number" as this term was understood in Pythagorean arithmetic, namely the sum of the consecutive numbers in a series. The number 666 is not only a triangle but a "double triangle," being the sum of the numbers up through 36, which is itself the sum of the numbers up through 8. While the connections Bauckham draws seem strained at times, he convincingly sketches a backdrop of ancient numerology in which speculation about the mystical properties of numbers would have been taken for granted.

12. Martin Luther, *Luther's Works*, ed. Helmut T. Lehmann (Philadelphia: Fortress, 1932), 6.484.

13. Heinrich Bullinger, *A Hundred Sermons Vpo[n] the Apocalips of Iesu Christe: Reueiled in Dede by Thangell of the Lorde, but Seen or Receyued and Written by Thapostle and Eua[n]gelist S. John* (London: John Day, 1573), 388.

writes, "Rome was indeed the mother of all churches; but after it began to become the see of Antichrist, it ceased to be what it once was."[14]

Such statements are likely to strike the modern reader as extreme, even bizarre. They must be measured against the extraordinary claims that were made on the papacy's behalf in the Middle Ages, especially as the hopes of the conciliar movement collapsed in the later part of the period.[15] Early modern Catholic theologians were more than happy to return the favor. A favorite candidate for the antichrist among Catholics was Martin Luther, the monster from the north. Had he not proved his antichristic credentials by the blasphemies he directed against Mother Church?

There are two questions to be considered with respect to the church and the antichrist. If we ask whether the church, acting at times as an all-too-human institution, be enlisted in the service of the principalities, the answer must be tragically "yes." The South African Reformed Church's decades-long support of apartheid, the persecution of Mennonites by both Protestants and Roman Catholics in the sixteenth century, the failure to speak out more forcefully on behalf of the Jews in the 1930s, the toleration of sexual abuse by clergy—all these point to the multiple ways in which the church capitulates to the reign of sin and death.

On the other hand, if we ask whether the church itself is a principality[16] or, more strongly, whether it is an agent of Satan, then we need to step back and ask ourselves just what we are saying when we make such a claim. Ephraim Radner points out that what was novel about the use of the antichrist label in the Reformation debates was the notion that the antichrist is first of all an *internal* opponent, that he has come to inhabit the bosom of the church itself. It now became possible to "accuse members within the church not only of instrumental participation in satanic deception, but of incarnating the deception itself."[17] If so, however, what else can serious Christians do but seek to separate themselves from the demonic other, now understood as our fellow Christian! Especially in Protestantism, this view of the antichrist as the enemy within has led, in effect, to a suspicion of the very idea of church and to a view of Christianity as a perpetual movement outward,

14. John Calvin, *Institutes of the Christian Religion*, ed. J. T. McNeill, trans. F. L. Battles, Library of Christian Classics 20–21 (Philadelphia: Westminster, 1960), 1144 §4.7.24.

15. Even so Catholic an Anglican as Rowan Williams writes: "The mediaeval papacy may have been a vastly significant cultural and political phenomenon, but I'd have to say that—from an Anglican, as from an Orthodox point of view—almost everything said theologically about the papacy between 1000 and 1500 is at best outrageous and at worst materially blasphemous. It may be important to understand why intelligent and (by the standards of the day) quite moderate men of the sixteenth and seventeenth centuries seriously believed the bishop of Rome to be Antichrist." Williams is not, however, saying this judgment was correct, even at the time of the Reformation, much less in relation to the papacy in our own day. See Rowan Williams, "The Future of the Papacy: An Anglican View" (London: Catholics for a Changing Church, 2000).

16. As Stringfellow has no difficulty affirming in *Ethic for Christians and Other Aliens*, 107, 78.

17. Ephraim Radner, *The End of the Church: A Pneumatology of Christian Division in the West* (Grand Rapids: Eerdmans, 1998), 74.

into a sectarian purity that we can approximate through repeated separation, even if we cannot ever quite get there.

Such ideas take us very far, I think, from the picture of the antichrist as presented by the Apocalypse. Instead of worrying about the possible presence of the antichrist in the church, the Christian community ought to be focused on the task of recognizing his activity in the world, through those fallen powers and agencies that anticipate his coming at the end of time. To do this, modern Western Christians need to overcome their naïveté with respect to the powers. The world in its present constitution is not always a hospitable or friendly place for Christ's followers. Indeed, it is not always a hospitable or friendly place for human beings, who are daily conscripted into the service of the powers. The state offers police protection and picks up the garbage, but it may also spy on its own citizens and practice torture abroad. The internet is one of the great technological achievements of our age, and yet it is well known to be a sewer, enabling child pornography and other forms of sexual predation. The media entertain us, but they also degrade. The church that exists in a state of denial about the powers will be blind to the character of the world it inhabits and will—very likely—be tempted to overconfidence about itself. Such a church will be of little use in God's resistance army.

The faithful church will be the church that is able to read Rev. 13, not hysterically and certainly not with the thought of pinning down the identity of 666 once for all, but soberly and with discernment: "This is the key: Wisdom / whoever has intelligence should calculate the number of the beast" (13:18 in Minear 1968: 109). Wisdom (*sophia*) and intelligence (*nous*)[18] are the marks of a community that knows it has no stable, once-for-all status in this life, but must negotiate the world with a combination of reason, theological insight, and street smarts. Most of all, the church's wisdom is that which comes from hearing the word of God.

John envisions a scenario in which Christians, living at the end of history, confront the ultimate incarnation of evil, the devil's last, desperate backlash against the divine mercy and judgment displayed in Jesus Christ. This is an extraordinary situation. We, on the other hand, flatter ourselves by thinking we live in ordinary times. But the extraordinary has a way of breaking into everyday life in the most unexpected ways. In a famous episode from World War II, the citizens of the village of Le Chambon—sober, conservative members of the Reformed Church of France—found themselves sheltering Jews threatened with deportation, thereby saving thousands of lives. When Pastor André Trocmé and his congregation were asked where they found the courage to take such risks, they replied, with remarkable consistency, that as disciples of Jesus Christ they could do no other. Perhaps we might say that the citizens of Le Chambon had learned to inhabit the "apocalyptic ordinary." In ways small and large, the beast's universal dominion is called into question by such actions, which do not need to win the war, but only offer up a witness to the one who has triumphed over the world and for it and who will triumph again.

18. Paul affirms that Christians are those who have "the mind [*nous*] of Christ" (1 Cor. 2:16).

REVELATION 14

THE ETERNAL GOSPEL

My life flows on in endless song above earth's lamentation;
I hear the real though far-off hymn that hails a new creation. . . .
No storm can shake my inmost calm, while to that Rock I'm clinging.
Since Christ is lord of heaven and earth, how can I keep from singing?

— Robert Lowry, "How Can I Keep from Singing?"

With the transition from 13:18 to 14:1, we experience once again a startling shift in mood and tone. What might be called "the book of the beasts" concludes on a somber note: the beast from the land makes war on the saints and kills them, while the false prophet causes the whole world to be marked with the mark of the beast (13:16). In the encounter of the powers with the people of God, it seems that the powers win.

14:1–3 Yet this is far from being the case. John looks again, this time to Mount Zion, where he sees the Lamb surrounded by 144,000 followers "who had his name and his Father's name written on their foreheads." The sheer existence of this community is a rebuke to the antichrist's ambitions to supplant God and establish a new, universal worship, centered on himself. As the earth-dwellers bear the beast's name and mark, so the 144,000 bear the names—the word "mark" (*charagma*) is not used in this context—of Jesus and the one he calls "Father."

We have met these 144,000 before. They are the same company of the twelve tribes of the sons of Israel in 7:1–8, the "Israel" half of the great double vision of the people of God. Whereas in that earlier vision the point was simply the enumeration of the tribes, as for a military roll call, here the gathered "army" is actually shown doing something. They are singing. After the unpleasant prophecy concerning the two beasts, this comes as a refreshment of sorts. We have heard no heavenly voices since the jubilation at Satan's downfall at 12:10, no liturgy since 11:16–18, and no mention of singing since the adoration of the Lamb in Rev. 5. Not since that scene of heavenly worship, perhaps, has the hearer been so awash in sound: "And I heard a *voice* from heaven like the *roar* of many waters and like the *sound* of *loud thunder*. The *voice* I heard was like the *sound of harpists playing on their harps*, and they were *singing* a new *song* before the throne and before the four living creatures and before the elders. No one could learn that *song* except the 144,000 who had been redeemed from the earth" (14:2–3).

While the metaphors are probably just meant to suggest a loud, multilayered sound, they also display a certain trinitarian order. The "roar of many waters" is the voice of Jesus (1:15). The "sound of loud thunder" is the voice of God as at Sinai (4:5; 8:5; 11:19). The "sound of harpists playing on their harps" is perhaps suggestive of the Spirit, who, like Orpheus with his lyre,[1] plays music of surpassing sweetness.

While the language suggests that the music emanates from heaven and thus from God, it is also sung by creatures before God, in his presence (*enōpion tou thronou*). John does not tell us who these singers are; the subject is an indefinite "they." Perhaps we should imagine a chorus of angels. But the identity of the singers is less important than the song itself, which is the *new* song, the song of the new and redeemed creation (5:9; cf. Ps. 33:3; 96:1; 98:1; 144:9 ["ten-stringed harp"]; 149:1; and Isa. 42:10 [with strong eschatological overtones]). Once again when John gestures toward the eschatological future, he falls naturally into language suggestive of music and hymnody. God is both infinitely worthy of praise and himself harmonious, so that the creature who exists in his presence cannot but break out into song. In the words of Robert Lowry's famous hymn: "Above the tumult and the strife I hear its music ringing / It sounds an echo in my soul / How can I keep from singing?"

What the 144,000 hear, then, is that music of the future. Indeed they are said to *learn* the new song. But, living still amid "the tumult and the strife," they learn it precisely so that they can sing it as they go into battle. The last time we saw these 144,000, they were being enumerated tribe by tribe, a military census as in ancient Israel (Rev. 7:1–8). We are thus brought back with a jolt to the present, with the present section of the Apocalypse (Rev. 6–18) being dominated by messianic and military imagery. Just as King David was both the "sweet singer of Israel" and a warrior, so the tribes mustered in this scene are at the same time both singers and soldiers. When the last things come into the midst of the next-to-last things,

1. The Greek word *kithara* is better translated "zither" or "lyre." Moreover, the Greek is alliterative. It is more like "the sound of zitherers zithering on their zithers."

conflict ensues. Represented by the 144,000, the "church as Israel" is precisely an image of the "church militant," a people engaged in a life-and-death struggle with the powers of the present age.

14:4–5 This military background needs to be kept in mind if we are not to misunderstand the description of the 144,000 that follows, namely as those "who have not defiled themselves with women, for they are virgins." The point is certainly not that the redeemed community is restricted to an elite composed of celibate males. Rather, we must imagine a situation in which ritual purity, including sexual abstinence, was required of all Israelite soldiers going into battle (Deut. 23:9–10; 1 Sam. 21:5–6). Not unlike the priest, the soldier exists in a zone of cultic holiness. The routines of everyday existence (including sexuality) are set aside, so that one may concentrate totally on the difficult task at hand. The image is male, as befits an army in the ancient world; but the application of the image extends also to female disciples of Jesus. One can equally imagine a community of female religious of whom it could be said that "they have not defiled themselves with men, for they are virgins." Moreover, it is not only celibate Christians who are called to practice such soldierlike service and devotion. The call to holiness applies to all the faithful, married and celibate alike.

The most important thing about these warriors is not their virginity per se, but that they "follow the Lamb wherever he goes." This interesting phrase shows how easily the lamb as a cultic or priestly image fades over into the image of Christ the King. In the history of Western art, the Lamb, a figure of Christ's suffering, is usually seen bearing the flag of victory. Whereas previously in Revelation the Lamb has been pictured at the center of a cosmic worship, now we see him on the move, marching out to meet his enemies. His followers go with him. They do not fear the places they will journey through or the enemies they will encounter, so long as they are with the Lamb.

The image is thus one of discipleship. This is the first of three occasions in Revelation where the verb *akoloutheō* denotes the existence of Christians.[2] It is later said of those who die in the Lord that "their deeds follow them"—an arresting image (14:13). Likewise, toward the end of the book we see the armies of heaven following the word of God into battle (19:14). Discipleship in the Apocalypse is supremely active. The disciple is utterly available to the Lord, a responsible agent with a specific role to discharge in the service of Christ. Yet discipleship is also, by its very nature, a passion, a dying or self-offering at the altar of God. And so the metaphor once again shifts back to sacrifice. The 144,000 are the "firstfruits," the first—but as the language implies surely not the last—of all the human race to be redeemed out of the old eon into the new creation. As with any Old Testament sacrifice, the offering to be presented must be pure. Thus John adds that "in their

---

2. At 6:8 *akoloutheō* describes hades accompanying death; at 14:8–9 it describes a sequence of angels.

mouth no lie was found, for they are blameless." The witnesses of the true witness must themselves be truthful.

14:6–7 Three angels appear, each bearing a message that offers a kind of commentary on the vision just seen. The first of these is the most important. Like the eagle of the three woes, this angel is said to fly "in midheaven" (RSV and NRSV; ESV has "directly overhead"), the zenith where he can be easily seen and heard (cf. 8:13). But instead of crying woe, the angel proclaims "an eternal gospel": "Fear God and give him glory, because the hour of his judgment has come, and worship him who made heaven and earth, the sea and the springs of water." To whom does he announce this message? Not to the Lamb's followers. These have already heard the gospel and are living its consequences. Rather, the message is spoken "to those who dwell on earth, to every nation and tribe and language and people." As the similar sequence in Rev. 7, John's vision of a limited group (144,000) is followed by the use of a catholic formula: every nation, tribe, and so on. In Rev. 7, however, it is clear that the countless multitude *are* the eschatologically redeemed, whereas in the present passage the hearers must still *become* this.

On a first hearing, this "gospel" may not sound terribly gospel-like. The form of speech is not the promissory language so beloved by the Reformers. It is not a declaration of God's unconditional pardon of the sinner. Rather, it comes in the form of a command: fear God and give him glory. Law and obligation would seem to trump deliverance and release.

Yet to accept this distinction too readily would reflect a rather thin understanding of what the gospel itself is. What makes the gospel liberating is not simply that it delivers us from the oppressive voice of the law, but that it liberates us for God. The gospel is liberating because it is true; it is the Creator's own word to his creatures. And because it is true, it inevitably makes a claim upon us. That is why the gospel can at times take the form not only of outright declaration ("Christ is risen") or of promise ("this is my body, given for you") but of law or command ("love your neighbor as yourself"). As Karl Barth put it, the law itself is a form of the gospel.[3] The claim it makes on us is a gracious claim.

But the content of the gospel is Jesus Christ. What makes the gospel more than simply law is its being based on the reality of God's apocalyptic action in Jesus. Thus the angel's message says that because the hour of his judgment has come, *therefore* fear God, give him glory, and worship him as the giver of all good gifts. Already as our Creator, God has made us and set us within a habitable world, "heaven and earth, the sea and the springs of water." All this is good news. There is no one to whom this good news does not apply. It is, remarkably, good news for "those who dwell on earth," a phrase that so often has negative connotations in the Apocalypse. Here it is used in a hopeful way. The gospel announced by the first angel is not only eternal, it is universal.

3. Karl Barth, *Church Dogmatics*, ed. G. W. Bromiley and T. F. Torrance (Edinburgh: Clark, 1957), 2/2.509.

14:8 A second angel follows closely on the first, declaring, "Fallen, fallen is Babylon the great! She has made all nations drink of the wine of the wrath of her fornication" (NRSV).[4] While the fall of Babylon does not become a major theme until later in the book, John here plants the seed of that idea, using his typical device of foreshadowing. For now, it is enough to know that Babylon's demise is the inevitable corollary of the good news just announced by the first angel. If God is faithful—meaning, if God is God—then Babylon cannot stand. The judgment of God spells the end of the human city in its present chaotic state. A new city in which justice and peace embrace will need to rise on its ashes.

14:9–11 The impossibility of agreement between God and evil attains a terrible clarity in the passage that follows. A third angel appears, declaring that whoever receives the mark of the beast will be forced to "drink the wine of God's wrath, poured full strength into the cup of his anger." The beast's worshipers will be "tormented with fire and sulfur in the presence of the holy angels and in the presence of the Lamb." Their suffering will last unto ages of ages (*eis aiōnas aiōnōn*), and "smoke" from a fire will never go out (cf. 18:18; 19:3). If the glory of God is expressed in the song of the new creation, the anger of God is expressed in the eternal torment of those who worship the beast.

Like the message of the second angel, this declaration foreshadows events later in the book (20:10–14). The picture it offers is not pretty. To readers such as D. H. Lawrence and C. S. Peirce, Revelation's teaching about hell offers clear evidence of being the product of a sick, vindictive mind, determined to draw very precise boundaries between the saved and the lost. "We" (insiders, true Christians) will soon be playing harps in heaven. "They" (earth-dwellers, worldly folk) will soon be getting exactly what they deserve. On this reading, God is for the elect only to the extent that he is against—eternally against!—someone else.

The Apocalypse is not a sentimental book, and it would be wrong to try to take the sting out of passages like these simply because they shock or offend. But we should at least try to be as lucid as possible concerning what the offense entails. A beginning can be made in noting that the three angelic declarations are cumulative. The message of the first angel, bearing the "eternal gospel," is an invitation to believe the good news that Israel's God and not the beast is Lord over creation. Significantly, it is directed to "every nation and tribe and language and people," in short, the earth-dwellers (14:6). The message of the second angel reinforces that point. Not only is God Lord over all things in principle, he has actually established and secured his lordship by overthrowing Babylon, an event here declared as an accomplished fact. Although in terms of the narrative Babylon's fall still lies in the future, the Lamb's victory means that we can be bold enough to treat it as an event in the past. After all, the reader already knows that Satan is living on borrowed time (12:12). Although we are not told to whom the second angel's words

---

4. The phrase "fallen, fallen is Babylon" comes from the oracle against Babylon in Isa. 21:9; the language about Babylon forcing others to drink of its wine comes most directly from Jer. 51:7.

are spoken, we can assume that these, too, have an unrestricted audience, as the reference to Babylon's hegemony over "all nations" suggests (14:8).

The messages of all three angels are eschatological in the sense that they describe the divine action of grace that will inevitably hasten the coming of the end. The message of the third angel, however, is eschatological in a more precise sense. It assumes the perspective of an observer who lives after Babylon's and the beast's demise, and it envisions—impossibly and horribly—a situation in which some continue to worship the beast anyway. In a case such as this the preaching of the gospel (first angel) and the announcement of the end of the old régime (second angel) have been in vain. In love with gods who do not really exist and who certainly don't exist anymore, the beast-worshipers suffer from the perpetual unreality of what they have made of their own lives. Moreover, they cannot help but do so *in God's presence*, not because God delights in human suffering, but because there is finally *no such thing* as a life lived apart from God, as the lost now discover to their horror. Jacques Ellul writes with great perception:

> It is not the Lamb and the Elect in the presence of whom, etc., but: the damned suffer in the presence of the Lamb. Which means expressly that it is the becoming aware, the knowledge of who Jesus Christ is, that is the essential point of the suffering of these "rejects." . . . The judgment at this moment is then: to be what one has actually wished to be, but seeing in the light of God what it was. (1977: 176)

At this moment in the book, the notion of Christ as the "true witness" stretches almost to the breaking point, for what he bears witness to here is those who have (eternally, it would seem) rejected him.

14:12 Eschatological language is prophetic language. And the natural setting for prophecy is the church. While the messages of the first two angels are directed to the earth-dwellers, the third is more properly understood as a dispatch to the Lamb's followers, warning them of the consequences of abandoning their posts. The words that come next confirm this view: "Here is a call for the endurance of the saints, those who keep the commandments of God and remain loyal to Jesus" (my translation). John of Patmos would not be the only early Christian writer to utter dire admonitions against apostasy. The author of Hebrews, too, warns that for those who follow Christ and then spurn him there is no repentance—a harsh word, although he softens it by saying he expects "better things" of his readers (Heb. 6:4–10; cf. 12:25).

14:13 If the rhetoric of Hebrews combines strictness with gentleness, in Revelation it is all strictness. Having received the word of truth, Christians are actually in greater danger of damnation than are others. Yet a softening of sorts follows. After the three angels have delivered their several messages and exited the stage, a heavenly voice intervenes, always a sign that something new is about to happen: "And I heard a voice from heaven saying, 'Write this: Blessed are the dead who die in the Lord from now on.' 'Yes!' says the Spirit, 'that they may rest from their labors, for their deeds follow them!'" (ESV slightly modified).

This is the first time John has been commanded to write since the conclusion of the letters to the churches (in 10:4 he was expressly told not to write down what the seven thunders said). Even more significant, it is the first time a blessing has been uttered since the one spoken on the listeners at 1:3. From this point forward the blessings will multiply, with five more being spoken between now and the end of the book, adding up to the mystical seven (16:15; 19:9; 20:6; 22:7, 14). This is the first of only two occasions when speech is attributed directly to the Spirit, and it is the first cry of "yes" or "amen" since the scene of worship at 7:12. The "amen," too, will sound with increasing frequency as we near the end of the book.[5]

Since the command to write in Revelation is consistently presented as issuing from Christ, we may imagine the dialogue in 14:13 as a call and response of sorts between Christ and the Spirit. What Christ utters, the Spirit confirms. And what Christ utters is a blessing on *the dead*. The dead! In the Bible death is depicted as the realm of curse, terror, taboo, separation from God and from the consolations of human community. Whatever else the dead may be, they are surely not blessed. But now we hear, "Blessed are the dead, blessed are those whose dying displays the victory of the Lord of life." This is a small but significant turning point in the narrative of the Apocalypse. While many terrible things still lie ahead, the blessing spoken on those who die *in the Lord* suggests that Satan, the beast, and the other agents of death will not prevail. In the contest between death and life, life—the new, eschatological life in the Spirit—wins. Having just received the ultimate warning, the hearers now are given the ultimate word of encouragement.[6]

14:14–20 The words "blessed are the dead" form an appropriate transition to the next vision. John looks and sees "one like a son of man, with a golden crown on his head, and a sharp sickle in his hand." This Son of Man can only be Christ (cf. 14:1). While the Son of Man in the opening Christophany was clothed in glory, he did not bear a crown. This may simply be a variation in imagery, or it may indicate that in the present vision Christ is shown in his specifically royal-messianic office (as is also the case with the crowned figure in 19:11–13).

The sickle tells us that it is harvest time, a New Testament image for the end of days with deep roots in Israelite prophecy (Mark 4:26–29; Matt. 3:12; Luke 3:17; 10:2; John 4:35; Rom. 1:13; Isa. 18:5; 24:13; Jer. 51:33; Hos. 6:11; Joel 3:13). An angel appears, telling the sickle bearer to begin the task of reaping the harvest of the earth. While it may initially seem strange for Christ to be

5. Rev. 16:7 and 22:20 (both using *nai*, "yes"); 19:4 and 22:20 (both using *amēn*). This is obscured in the ESV rendering of 14:13, which begins, "'Blessed indeed,' says the Spirit."

6. Johannes Brahms uses the words "blessed are the dead who die in the Lord henceforth" as part of his *Requiem*, a requiem Mass that was intended to comfort and not terrify. It therefore excludes the medieval hymn *Dies Irae* or "day of wrath." While some passages in Revelation are as harsh as anything found in the *Dies Irae*, Brahms could hardly have chosen a more hopeful text than Rev. 14:13.

receiving instructions from a mere angel, the anomaly disappears when we note that the angel is seen coming "out of the temple," the place where the Father dwells invisibly between the cherubim. Jesus warns that even the Son does not know the day or the hour when the end will come, but the Father alone (Matt. 24:36). If the pattern familiar from Matthew's Gospel is followed here, then the wheat (the elect) would be gathered into the barn, while the weeds (the reprobate) would be burned, bringing history to its swift apocalyptic conclusion (13:24–30).

John, however, says nothing of weeds or of chaff. He simply says that the Son of Man swings his sickle and "the earth was reaped" (Rev. 14:16). The imagery suddenly shifts, and now it is no longer wheat but the vine that is being harvested. The agent of this second harvest is an angel, who is instructed by yet *another* angel (again proceeding from the altar and rather obscurely said to possess power "over the fire") to swing the sickle and cut down the heavy-hanging clusters of grapes. The image is literally a bloody one: "And the angel put forth his sickle on the earth, and gathered from the vine of the earth and put the grapes in the great press of the anger of God. And the press was trampled outside the city, and the blood from the press came up to the bridles of the horses, for sixteen hundred furlongs" (14:19–20 in Lattimore 1979: 275).

We thus have two images of reaping—first of wheat, then of grapes. Like other such doublets in Revelation, this one forces us to ask about the relationship between the two images. One possibility is that the wheat harvest represents the positive side of judgment, while the grape harvest represents judgment in its negative aspect. In favor of this view is the lack of any mention of chaff. The wheat is a figure for the elect, while the trodden grapes, rising high as the horses' bridles, symbolize the blood of the lost. Later in Revelation we will hear that Christ treads "the winepress of the fury of the wrath of God the Almighty" (19:15), a saying that appears expressly in connection with his iron rule over the nations (cf. Isa. 63:3–6; Joel 3:13). Julia Ward Howe's "Battle Hymn of the Republic" picks up on this imagery: "He is trampling out the vintage where the grapes of wrath are stored." If the grain safely stored represents the friends of God, then surely the grapes of wrath must signify his enemies.

The image of blood, however, is a remarkably multivalent one in Revelation. On the one hand, blood is a sign of death (Rev. 8:3; 16:3–4), especially the death of the prophets, saints, and martyrs, on which the great whore Babylon is said to be "drunk" (16:6; 17:6; 18:24). On the other hand, the blood of the martyrs is their participation in the life-giving blood of Jesus (5:9; 7:14; 12:11). And while blood may be a sign of death, the dead are not cut off from the Lord's blessing. Finally, John provides us with an important geographical clue. He tells us that the winepress is located "outside the city," which can be none other than the great city Jerusalem, the place "where their Lord was crucified" (11:8). Here we find a trace of the church's memory that Jesus was crucified outside the gates of Jerusalem, a tradition widely attested in the New Testament (John 19:17, 20; Mark 15:20; Matt. 27:32; Heb. 13:12–13).[7]

The apocalyptic imagination is characterized by its "bifocal vision." Although, among the powers of this world, Babylon is the greater shedder of blood, this image fuses in John's mind with the blood of the slaughtered Lamb and of his followers. Christ's death thus becomes the definitive Christian interpretation of the words spoken by YHWH in Isaiah:

> I have trodden the winepress alone,
>   and from the peoples no one was with me;
> I trod them in my anger
>   and trampled them in my wrath;
> their lifeblood spattered on my garments,
>   and stained all my apparel. (Isa. 63:3)

Christ, then, is both the harvester and the harvested, he who treads the vintage and he who is trodden upon by the powers of this world. He is "the trampled grape, the wine poured out, the dead for all the dead, the condemned for all the condemned" (Ellul 1977: 179). The blood of Christ is a sign not of death but of life. Moreover, the sheer quantity of the blood that flows from the winepress— "as high as a horse's bridle, for 1,600 stadia"—suggests the extraordinary scope of Christ's act of self-offering. Four is the number of the cosmos, of creation; four squared indicates absolute intensification; four squared multiplied by one hundred indicates that this blood is sufficient to drown an empire. As the armies of Pharaoh were swept away by the waters of the Red Sea, so the demonic powers and their agents will be swept away not by military prowess but by the life-giving blood of the Lamb.

As so often, the Apocalypse mixes its metaphors. That there should be mention of cavalry horses in the midst of an image of harvesting reminds us where Rev. 14 began—with the Lamb on Mount Zion, rallying his troops for the battle to come. While Christians are indeed warriors of a sort, they are also firstfruits, an initial offering to God out of a much greater harvest, whose full extent we cannot even begin to imagine.

---

7. Caird 1984: 192 points out that Matt. 21:39 and Luke 20:15 recast Mark's parable in Mark 12:8 so as to have the owner's son killed outside the vineyard.

REVELATION 15

THE SONG OF MOSES
AND THE LAMB

Then Moses and the people of Israel sang this song to the LORD, saying,
"I will sing to the LORD, for he has triumphed gloriously;
    the horse and his rider he has thrown into the sea.
The LORD is my strength and my song,
    and he has become my salvation.
The LORD is a man of war
    the LORD is his name."

                —Exodus 15:1–3

Like the first half of John's Gospel, the second half of Revelation could easily be described as a "book of signs" (*sēmeia*). So far we have encountered two such signs: the woman clothed with the sun, indicating Eve/Israel/Mary/the church, and her adversary the great red dragon, indicating the devil. We have also seen how the beast from the land leads people astray by performing signs and wonders.

15:1 Now John beholds another sign in heaven, this one described as "great and amazing": seven angels entrusted with seven plagues, known as the last plagues, "because the anger of God is fulfilled in them" (Lattimore 1979: 275). The seven plagues are contained in seven bowls. This is the last of the four great septenaries (the others being the churches, seals, and trumpets) that help guide the listener through the maze of the Apocalypse. As a prologue to the pouring of the bowls, John describes a series of preparatory actions involving "the tent of witness in heaven" (15:5–8). Since these actions are really part of the plague sequence itself, discussion of them will be deferred to Rev. 16.

15:2 Before the unleashing of the plagues, however, John narrates a brief, vivid moment of jubilation and triumph—in effect, a postscript to the vision of the 144,000 gathered with the Lamb on Mount Zion. The seer beholds "what appeared to be a sea of glass mingled with fire." This is no doubt the same crystal sea that he saw spreading out before God's throne in an earlier vision (4:6). Standing beside this sea are those who have emerged victorious from their encounter with the beast. It is telling that John does not attribute this victory to the saints themselves. A literal rendering of the Greek would be: "those who are conquerors [present tense] from the beast and from his image and from the number of his name." Luther said that the gospel can be found in the pronouns, but here the gospel is contained in the preposition *ek* ("from, out of"), suggesting the saints' *ex*-odus from their Egypt-like captivity under the beast. Having passed through one "red sea," flowing with the blood of Christ (14:20), the martyrs pause beside another sea, that of the primeval waters of creation. These are now tamed, serene, a source no longer of violence but of peace. On the first Christmas, wrote John Milton, the tumultuous sea for once "had quite forgot to rave / While birds of calm sit brooding on the charmed wave."[1] John of Patmos tells us that the sea where the conquerors stand is similarly charmed, perhaps by the pentecostal fire with which it is said to be "mingled" (15:2).

15:3–4 The exodus forms a kind of subtext throughout the Apocalypse, present yet hidden under multiple figures, hints, and allusions. But now the theme is stated in an unambiguous way. The song sung by the sea, John tells us, is none other than "the song of Moses, the servant of God, and the song of the Lamb." The original song of Moses was a hymn of victory and a war song (Exod. 15:1–3). This song is traditionally sung at the church's Easter vigil, celebrating Christ's resurrection as the definitive paschal (Passover) victory over sin, death, and the devil.

But while the church may and must sing this song, it is not the song sung by the conquerors at the sea of glass. A new exodus literally demands a new song, celebrating not just Israel's deliverance from Egypt or even the resurrection, but the submission of *the nations* to God's righteous rule. "Who will not fear, O Lord, and glorify your name? For you alone are holy. All nations will come and worship you" (15:4). The twofold mention of *ta ethnē* in the present hymn serves as a reminder of Revelation's catholic-cosmic trajectory, the divine action drawing people from all nations, tribes, and languages into the acknowledgment of God as *Pantokratōr* and Lord.

What joins the song in Exodus with the song of the Lamb is not just the theme of victory, however, but the importance that both songs accord to the *name* of God. Whether in the form of the Tetragrammaton Yнwн, or the formula "who

---

1. John Milton, "Ode on the Morning of Christ's Nativity." Surely the term "birds of calm" alludes to the Spirit brooding over the waters in Gen. 1.

was and who is and who is to come," or the name of Jesus, the name of God is a powerful indicator of his holiness. God is holy and singular, as well as gracious and loving. The life and death of the Lamb may be seen as the act in which God glorifies his own name, a kind of "yes" to himself, on the basis of which the nations are summoned to add their own "yes" in the form of an eternal *sanctus*. "For your righteous acts have been revealed" (15:4). Once again we see the crucial role played by the first commandment in the Apocalypse. This is yet another reason why the song of the Lamb does not render the song of Moses obsolete, but rather confirms and intensifies it.

REVELATION 16

THE CUP OF GOD'S WRATH

Jesus drinks the bitter cup,
 The winepress treads alone,
Tears the graves and mountains up
 By his expiring groan:
Lo! the powers of heaven he shakes;
 Nature in convulsions lies,
Earth's profoundest center quakes,
 The great *Jehovah* dies!

> —Charles Wesley,
> "God of Unexampled Grace"

The traditional view is that the Apocalypse in some ways recapitulates itself. But recapitulation is more than simple repetition; it is intensification. Events are moving toward their climax. The day of reckoning can no longer be deferred. "The time is near" (1:3).

For this very reason, the sequence of seven plagues—the last of the four great septenaries—is also among the book's darker, more troubling episodes. If God is bringing the present evil age to an end, then the inhabitants of that age will inevitably experience a great contradiction, affecting not just their outward circumstances but their own souls. The wrath of God brings to light things long hidden. It exposes truths that the earth-dwellers would prefer to suppress. The revelation of the divine wrath presses God's opposition to the world almost to the breaking point, leading us to think that, even if God does not quite hate everything he has made, he at least despises a great deal of it.

All the more reason, then, to remind ourselves that *the* determinative agency throughout these chapters remains that of the slaughtered Lamb. He is the executor of God's judgment, in the seven plagues no less than in the seals and the trumpets. The crucified reigns—graciously and justly. If it is not always obvious how this is so, these affirmations remain utterly central to anything even pretending to be Christian faith. This knowledge allows us to read passages like the seven bowls not only with a certain equanimity but even, I might say, with a growing sense of excitement. Surely much of the power of the Apocalypse resides in its being simply a very good story. The seals, the trumpets, now the bowls—where is it all going, and when will it all end? When will the promised liberation finally occur? What will happen to the earth-dwellers and to the conquerors? What, for that matter, will happen to us?

15:5–16:1 The beginning of the bowls sequence is marked by one of Revelation's regular returns to temple imagery. Like the angels of the trumpets, the angels of the bowls do not presume to act on their own authority. Their action is authorized by God. Both sequences are preceded by symbolic actions—the casting of a fiery censer onto the earth in the first instance, the angels receiving the bowls from the four living creatures in the second—that underscore the solemnity of the events about to unfold. While the general milieu in both cases seems to be "the heavenly temple," at the outset of the bowls sequence the reference is more specific:

> After this I looked, and the sanctuary of the tent of witness [*ho naos tēs skēnēs tou martyriou*] in heaven was opened. . . . And one of the four living creatures gave to the seven angels seven golden bowls full of the wrath of God who lives forever and ever, and the sanctuary [*ho naos*] was filled with smoke from the glory of God and from his power, and no one could enter the sanctuary until the seven plagues of the seven angels were finished. Then I heard a loud voice from the temple [*ek tou naou*] telling the seven angels "Go and pour out on the earth the seven bowls of the wrath of God." (15:5–16:1)[1]

Not just the temple, but "the sanctuary of the tent of witness in heaven." This surprising, somewhat archaic-sounding phrase recalls Israel's wilderness wanderings, when the divine presence would periodically descend on the tent of witness/meeting. On such occasions, not even Moses could enter the tent (Exod. 40:34–35; cf. Rev. 15:8). There is something supremely appropriate about John's use of this imagery at just this point. The heavenly tabernacle is not Herod's temple located on earth—a temple that John doubtless knew, but that now lay in ruins. The Judaism of the synagogue likewise understood that there was no returning to this temple. The "tent of meeting" is, rather, the eschatological communion

---

1. ESV translates *naos* in this sequence as both "sanctuary" and "temple." The ambiguity is perhaps inevitable, given that John is playing on imagery of both the wilderness tabernacle and the Jerusalem temple(s).

established by God with humanity in Jesus Messiah, the tent "not made with hands, that is, not of this creation" (Heb. 9:11), the Word who became flesh and "tabernacled" among us (John 1:14).[2] Whether as tent or as temple, Christ is the place of divine indwelling, both locus of holiness and meeting place. Yet the action of judgment requires a kind of suspension of this function for the duration of the seven plagues: "No one could enter the sanctuary until the seven plagues of the seven angels were finished" (Rev. 15:8). This does not mean that Christ, as judge, is no longer the Savior, no longer gracious. It does mean that his saving activity will for a brief time take the form of a sheer, uncompromising "no" to all in creation that opposes God. Stated differently, the true worship of God—the very purpose of the tabernacle—cannot be resumed until the world is actually remade, renewed, and purged of every evil.

An air of finality attends the progression of the seven bowls. Unlike the septenaries of the seals and trumpets, here we find neither a four-plus-three structure nor an interlude that delays the coming of the climactic element. The flow of events is uninterrupted, unless one counts the mysterious voice that intrudes at 16:15, and this outburst has the opposite effect of a delay, making the time seem more urgent. As commentators never fail to point out, the bowls sequence also differs from that of the trumpets in the sheer scale of the havoc envisioned. While the trumpet blasts effect the destruction of "only" a third of the earth and of its inhabitants, no such limit is set in the case of the plagues. They are the "last" plagues in the precise sense that, beyond them, no further event of tribulation will be required to effect God's purposes for his creation. The judgment of the world is real, but it is finite. God does not will to be forever in opposition to the world he loves, but speaks against it only that he may speak for it out of his powerful love. "The LORD is merciful and gracious, slow to anger and abounding in steadfast love. He will not always chide, nor will he keep his anger forever" (Ps. 103:8–9). The plagues are poured out so that a world may come into being in which plagues are no more.

We are not there yet, however. It remains for us to explore the seven bowls themselves in greater detail. Even more so than in the case of the trumpets, these curses roughly recall the plagues of Egypt, as seen in this side-by-side comparison:

Seven Bowls (Rev. 16)	Egyptian Plagues (Exod. 7–12)
1. sores	sixth plague
2. blood—the sea	first plague
3. blood—rivers and springs	first plague
4. scorching heat	—

---

2. In John 1:14 the verb *skēnoō*, a cognate of *skēnē* ("tent"), denotes Christ's "pitching his tent" in human flesh. The same verb is used in Rev. 7:15 and 21:3 to refer to God's sheltering presence in the midst of his people.

Seven Bowls (Rev. 16)	Egyptian Plagues (Exod. 7–12)
5. darkness	ninth plague
6. river dries up/frogs	second plague
7. earthquake/hailstones	seventh plague

Clearly the correlation is a very loose one. Rather than setting forth a one-to-one equivalency between the two sets of plagues, the vision reflects a basic judgment that "this" (the eschatological judgment of the world in Christ) is like "that" (God's liberating action on behalf of his people at the Red Sea). The vision thus sustains the exodus theme already noticed. Just as the goal of the exodus was not the death of the Egyptians, but Israel's deliverance, so the purpose of the bowls is not the destruction of humanity but the gathering of a people. Comparing the plagues of Revelation to the story of the exodus shows that the gathering of the faithful on Mount Zion and the song of the Lamb *precede* John's vision of the seven plagues. If Exodus shows things in chronological order, the Apocalypse shows them in teleological order. The way (through tribulation and judgment) is ordered toward the goal (communion with God, as realized in the life and death of the Lamb). If the nations, those who "bore the mark of the beast and worshiped its image" (16:2), are to become the people of Israel's God, then they must be liberated from their enslavement to the powers. One cannot serve both God and the beast.

16:2–7 The theological heart of the bowls sequence is to be found in the third, sixth, and seventh bowls, each of which John expands on with significant commentary. (By contrast, the first, second, fourth, and fifth bowls give the impression of being rather formulaic.) When the third angel pours out his bowl on the rivers and springs of water, "the angel in charge of the waters"[3] declares: "Just are you, O Holy One, who is and who was, for you brought these judgments. For they have shed the blood of saints and prophets, and you have given them blood to drink. It is what they deserve!" To which "the altar" answers: "Yes, Lord God Almighty, true and just are your judgments!" (ESV slightly modified).

At the heart of this remarkable call-and-response is an affirmation of the divine justice. On the one hand, the angel in charge of the waters acknowledges the cosmic rightness of God's judgment on evil. The natural world is not just a neutral, amoral backdrop for the actions of spiritual and moral beings. The unjust shedding of blood violates cosmic order itself.[4] God has fashioned the world as a cosmos, an ordered totality, into whose fabric righteousness is woven like a thread.

3. In this context, the angel seems to be the spirit who rules the watery parts of creation, here speaking on behalf of creation as a whole. The righteousness of God is not simply of interest to humans, but is cosmic in its scope; thus creation's eager expectation of the revelation of the children of God in Rom. 8.

4. At 15:7 the seven angels are given their seven bowls by one of the four living creatures, likewise representatives of creation.

If the cries of victims are not forgotten by the angels and natural forces, still less will they be forgotten by God himself.

And they are not forgotten. "The altar" that speaks in this passage must be a metonym for the martyrs at rest beneath the altar, whom we last heard petitioning God for justice at the opening of the fifth seal (6:9). Seeing the anger of God poured out on those who have shed their blood, they declare that they are satisfied. God had told the martyrs to wait. They have waited—perhaps a short time, perhaps a very long time, at least as these things are measured in human terms. But either way, the wait is not infinitely long. "We shall overcome," wrote Martin Luther King Jr., "because the arc of the moral universe is long, but it bends toward justice."

To the reader's relief, John does not depict God's vengeance on the evildoers as an actual shedding of blood. He does, however, employ the rather horrible image of drinking blood. The evildoers are deserving, worthy, of such punishment.[5] There must be some kind of final reckoning, in which the victimizers will be brought face to face with their accusers and made to "drink" their blood (acknowledge, internalize, confess the value of the lives they have slaughtered). None of this means that *the church* is in any position to avenge the blood of victims, tempting as this possibility may be. Karl Barth writes that while "we certainly hear the cry of those who were slain for the Word of God, . . . we do not read of Christians playing any active part in the judgments on the world that is hostile to God and his people. . . . Patience and faith are what the saints have to oppose to this world."[6] Or as St. Paul writes in an equally apocalyptic context, the Christian foregoes vengeance in order to "leave it to [literally, 'make room for'] the wrath of God" (Rom. 12:17–19).

16:10–11 The fifth bowl is narrated only briefly, but it provides a crucial piece of information: the divine wrath is poured out on the throne of the beast himself. Because human beings are under the spell of the beast, they curse or blaspheme God (Rev. 16:9, 11, 21), blasphemy being a central aspect of the beast's identity (13:1). While the note about people gnawing their tongues in anguish is repellent, it offers a kind of dark testimony to a central Christian conviction concerning human creatures: they are made for the praise of God. The use of the tongue to curse God is deeply *unnatural*, setting the human person in fundamental contradiction to himself or herself (Jas. 3:9). Interestingly, the usual context for the word "tongue" in the Apocalypse is God's calling a people out of "every nation, . . . all tribes and peoples and tongues," that is, languages (Rev. 7:9; cf. 5:9; 11:9; 17:15). Although the beast cannot finally sever the bond between God and his creature—even when we curse, we have God's name on our lips—he can so warp the creature so that it hates the one who made it. The destruction of the beast's

5. The phrase "it is what they deserve!" may be literally translated "they are worthy [of it]!" possibly an ironic echo of the Lamb's being "worthy" of all worship.
6. Karl Barth, *The Christian Life: Church Dogmatics*, vol. 4/4: *Lecture Fragments*, trans. Geoffrey W. Bromiley (Grand Rapids: Eerdmans, 1981), 208.

kingdom will put an end to this intolerable situation, once more freeing the tongue and all the members for the praise of God.

16:12–16 Of all the plagues, the sixth is the most complex, offering remarkable testimony to the complexity of the forces at work in human existence. The first thing we notice are "the kings from the east." The historical commentaries usually gloss these kings as Parthians, the great empire to the east—beyond the Euphrates—that offered the only real threat to Rome's hegemony; and that is enough to help us unpack the image. Up to now we might have imagined a purely binary situation, in which the beast and his armies are arrayed against the armies of God, as in the battle between St. Michael and Satan in Rev. 12. But the presence of the kings from the east shows that the beast's rule does not go unopposed, even in the world of the nations. Like Cyrus of Persia enabling the liberation of the Jews from Babylon, the kings from the east are important not because they are virtuous, but because they are instruments of God's providential rule. They end up doing the Lord's bidding despite themselves—an ironic outcome, familiar to any good reader of the Bible. Moreover, they act only by God's sufferance. The same God who made a way across the Red Sea at the exodus, now dries up the Euphrates to prepare the "way" (*hodos*) for the kings from the east.

As the book moves toward its conclusion, the military theme becomes ever more insistent. The dragon now mounts his counterattack. Vanquished in heaven, he makes a last desperate bid for dominance on earth:

> And I saw, coming out of the mouth of the dragon and out of the mouth of the beast and out of the mouth of the false prophet, three unclean spirits like frogs. For they are demonic spirits, performing signs, who go abroad to the kings of the whole world, to assemble them for battle on the great day of God the Almighty. . . . And they assembled them at the place that in Hebrew is called Armageddon. (16:13–14, 16)

Although the dragon, the beast, and the false prophet have been on the scene since Rev. 13, this is the first time they explicitly appear as a kind of demonic anti-Trinity, a parody of God the *Pantokratōr* (the reappearance of this divine title at this point in the book can hardly be accidental). Especially striking is the threefold repetition of the word "mouth," underscoring John's view of the uncanny, almost magical quality of speech itself. It is not the hard power of legions and armor that the Christian should fear. Far more dangerous is the soft power of speech, language, and propaganda. From the mouth of Christ, the true witness, proceeds the sharp two-edged sword of the word. From the mouth of Satan and the beasts proceeds nothing but filth and garbage. Besides evoking the plagues of Egypt, the phrase "unclean spirits like frogs" suggests the almost pornographic quality of demonic speech. Frogs are classified among the unclean animals in Lev. 11:9–12. Henry Swete remarks: "Christ expelled unclean spirits, but His enemies send them forth, the False Prophet not less than the Dragon or the Beast" (1908: 207).[7]

In response to the dragon's lies, "the kings of the whole world" (the alliance has already been enlarged beyond the eastern kings) gather to do battle against God and his people at Armageddon.[8] Vast quantities of ink have been spilled trying to determine the spatiotemporal coordinates of this battle, which is mentioned by name only in this passage—reason enough, perhaps, not to overrate its importance. The attempt to locate Armageddon with precision is a fruitless enterprise. To be sure, it is possible to construe the word in Hebrew (John tells us it is a Hebrew name) as Har-mageddon, "Mount of Megiddo," and to find here an allusion to one of the Old Testament's most famous sites. Megiddo was where Barak and Deborah defeated the Canaanites (Judg. 5:19), where Jehu killed Ahaziah (2 Kgs. 9:27), and where the Egyptian armies cut down the good King Josiah (23:30).[9] It was therefore the archetypal battlefield. But the city of Megiddo was located not on a mountain, but on a plain; indeed, control of this plain is what made it strategically important. If John is alluding to Megiddo, it is because he wants to evoke the image of a decisive battle and not because he wants us to locate his story on a map of northern Palestine. Megiddo is where kings meet their judgment, their destiny, their doom. "Har-mageddon" could loosely but creatively be translated as "Mount Doom," with a nod to J. R. R. Tolkien's *The Lord of the Rings*.

We would worry less about the reference to Armageddon if we paid more attention to the verse that immediately precedes it. Right in the middle of the events of the sixth plague, a voice suddenly intrudes: "Behold, I am coming like a thief! Blessed is the one who stays awake, keeping his garments on, that he may not go about naked and be seen exposed!" (16:15). So unexpected is this utterance in context that commentators who assign portions of Revelation to different editors have sought to relocate it to a different point in the book, the most obvious candidate being 3:3.[10]

But such drastic rewriting is unnecessary; the text makes perfect sense as it stands. John has just been talking about "the great day of God the Almighty," in Old Testament terms, the Day of Yhwh. According to Jesus himself this day would come suddenly, like a thief. His saying to this effect became deeply rooted in the memory of the church (Matt. 24:43; cf. 1 Thess. 5:2; 2 Pet. 3:10). The memory of Jesus, however, is never very far from the presence of Jesus. Thus no sooner does John mention the Day of the Lord, than the Lord—in the context

7. Swete also references Zech. 13:2 Septuagint, where Yhwh promises to remove the "false prophets and the unclean spirit."
8. John gives the name as *Armagedōn*. English translations generally render it as Armageddon, no doubt supplying the second *d* to confirm the relation to Megiddo.
9. See also Zech. 12:11, which mysteriously alludes to Megiddo as a place of mourning, in connection with the Day of the Lord.
10. R. H. Charles, *A Critical and Exegetical Commentary on the Revelation of St. John*, International Critical Commentary (Edinburgh: Clark, 1920), 2.49.

of Christian prophecy, this can mean only Jesus—himself speaks. This prophetic irruption, the first since Rev. 13:13, is a reminder that the space and time of the Apocalypse is the space and time of the Spirit. The geography of Armageddon is determined not by the Megiddo plain, but by the body of Christ in its current distress, anguish, and tribulation. The first audience of Revelation is "meant to feel that it is their place where the beasts emerge, their place where the elect are gathered, their place where the final battle is fought. . . . The war is fought in Asia Minor" (Barr 1998: 115–16).

The same will or may be true of present-day hearers of the book, whether in Seoul or Soweto, Boston or Beijing. A certain contextualizing interpretation of the Apocalypse is inevitable, in the sense that the final reading will be textured, local, and fine grained, a discerning of where the battle lines are drawn in one's particular circumstances. The act of interpretation will not be completed until the church, Christ's body, discerns the forms of the reign of death in its midst and allows itself to be led into forms of faithful resistance. The final, apocalyptic Armageddon is preceded by many smaller conflicts, any one of which may be *the* battle for particular communities of disciples.

The apocalyptic scenario depicted here has its roots in prophetic texts like Ezek. 38–39 and Zech. 14, in which God conquers the nations through the seemingly perverse tactic of gathering them—against his own people! In such encounters, Israel wins no glory for itself. Its armies do not go out to fight "Gog of the land of Magog." The whole point of the action—the demonstration of God's glory among the nations of the earth—would be utterly subverted if Israel were to win the battle by its own powers. At best, it is left with the inglorious (and ritually defiling) task of burying the corpses and gathering the cast-off weapons for firewood (Ezek. 38:9–15). If in one sense Israel is central to these stories, being at once the beloved of YHWH and the victim of the nations, in another sense it is but a minor player. The real issue lies between God and the nations. That is why God summons the rulers of the *goyim* for a final showdown at Armageddon. This battle may be seen as the fulfillment of the great messianic prophecy found near the beginning of the book of Psalms: "Why do the nations rage and the peoples plot in vain? The kings of the earth set themselves, and the rulers take counsel together, against the LORD and against his Anointed" (Ps. 2:1–2).

While Armageddon may not be locatable on any ancient or modern map of the Middle East, it is nonetheless important that the battlefield be named, if for none other than storytelling reasons: wars take place in specific times and places. In the Christian imagination, Armageddon is the local habitation and name given to the ultimate, messianic conflict over the future of the earth. We know that the Lamb will emerge victorious in that conflict, because he is already the conqueror. Yet what Jesus experiences as an accomplished fact, the church confronts as its present-day warfare and as its hoped-for, still-to-be-consummated future.

16:17–21 For all this, the expected battle still does not materialize. The armies are still gathering on Mount Doom when the seventh angel pours his bowl out upon the air (16:17). Why the air? Swete points out that air is in some ways the most universal element, the "common air" freely given for sustaining life (1908: 210; cf. Wisdom of Solomon 7:3). This air has been fouled by the *pneumata akatharta*, the "unclean spirits" or "breaths" of dragon, beast, and false prophet (16:13). Paul similarly describes Satan as "the prince of the power of the air" (Eph. 2:2). Although, in an age of global warming, it is tempting to think of the ways in which unbridled consumption has poisoned the physical atmosphere, it might be more apt to think of the poisoning of the air by human thought and speech. In the third millennium's first decade, it has become common to refer to the ceaseless flow of opinion in cyberspace as the "blogosphere" and to note its particular venom. The lack of charity is its own kind of poison. There are spiritual climates as well as meteorological ones. What John depicts here is more than just the ordinary sinful corruption of the human air, but its demonic radicalization at the time of the end.

The pouring out of the seventh bowl is thus a great act of purging and renewal. Once again we hear a voice from the temple, this time declaring *gegonen* ("it is accomplished" or "it is done!")—an echo, perhaps, of Jesus's cry of victory at the cross (John 19:30, although the verb there is *tetelestai*, "it is finished, completed"). There follows an earthquake (also associated with the crucifixion, at least in Matt. 27:51) that signals the coming of the end (Ezek. 38:19),[11] along with the usual fireworks that accompany Revelation's theophanies: lightings, explosions, thunders (*astrapai kai phōnai kai brontai*). God, the one who was and who is, is no longer the coming one. God has powerfully arrived on the scene. God has come.

And because he has done so, there is no longer any time or space for the great act of social imagination known as "Babylon." There can be no coexistence between God and this form of the human city. If Jesus lives, then Babylon cannot help but fall: "The great city was split into three parts, and the cities of the nations fell, and God remembered Babylon the great, to make her drain the cup of the wine of the fury of his wrath" (16:19).

God *remembered* Babylon; more literally, "Babylon the great was remembered before God." The God of the Bible is a God who remembers, not by virtue of his being omnipotent (for then he would not need to remember things at all; he would simply know them), but by virtue of his being the Creator, closer to creatures than they are to themselves, and closest of all to his people.[12] Surely the most obvious scriptural allusion here is to Ps. 137, with its triple evocation of the theme of memory. At the opening of the psalm the exiles sit down by the waters of Babylon and weep as they "remembered Zion." In the middle verses, the psalmist protests against the idea of resigning himself to life in Babylon. He swears: "If I forget you, O Jerusalem, let my right hand forget its skill! Let my

11. On the theme of the "eschatological earthquake," see Bauckham 1993a: 199–209.

12. For a brief but penetrating account of God's presence to and in the world that avoids any easy affirmations of divine suffering, see Herbert McCabe's essay "The Involvement of God," in his *God Matters* (London: Chapman, 1987), 39–51.

tongue stick to the roof of my mouth, if I do not remember you." Finally, in the closing verses the psalmist implores God to "remember . . . against the Edomites the day of Jerusalem," and then prophesies the destruction of the daughter of Babylon. The psalm closes with the infamous blessing spoken on whoever "takes your little ones and dashes them against the rock."

Much modern theology and piety can be reduced to repeating the formula "God loves us" in various forms and tropes. The saying is a true one. It is even biblical. Divorced from any particular context allowing us to identify which God is meant, however, and especially divorced from any language about law and judgment, it is also utterly banal. In some ways it would be far more biblical to say "God remembers us," to affirm that he *has* remembered us and to pray that he *will* remember us, despite our complicity in the city of death. God remembers, he does not forget. He remembers Jerusalem and Babylon alike. He remembers each in the way that is appropriate to it.

As God remembers, so the church is called to remember. The next series of visions (Rev. 17–18) are one long act of remembering Babylon, not only its past and present triumph but also, thanks to prophetic insight, its future doom. Such memory provides the church with resources to inhabit the city faithfully during the time of its exile. It is remarkable how much space Revelation devotes to imagining Babylon.

REVELATION 17

THE GREAT WHORE

She who is at Babylon, who is likewise chosen, sends you greetings.

—1 Peter 5:13

A quick check in an English concordance shows that Israel's scriptures contain no fewer than 280 references to "Babylon," referring either to the empire of that name or to the magnificent city that served as its capital. Babylon plays an astonishingly large role in Israel's historical imagination—first as the threatening foreign power, then as the conqueror carrying the Judean population off into captivity in 587 BC, and ultimately as the place of exile itself. Babylon represented a fundamental threat to Israel's national existence, a great fashioner of chaos whose invading armies seemed to spell the very end of life under the covenant: "How shall we sing the LORD's song in a foreign land?" (Ps. 137:4).

Nevertheless, Israel's history did not come to an end with the Babylonian exile. The conquest of Babylon by Cyrus of Persia, the servant and the "anointed" of God according to Isa. 45:1, made possible a new exodus, a return to the land, and eventually a rebuilding of the temple. Declared beforehand by the prophets, this return from exile led to forms of national existence quite different from the ones that prevailed before the traumas of the sixth century. But the point is that even in Babylon, Israel did not cease to be Israel. This conviction is central to the preaching of Jeremiah, whose life and prophecy were dominated by the Babylonian threat, yet who refused to treat the exile as the unmitigated disaster everyone else assumed it must be. Jeremiah taught that Israel should not simply endure Babylon but inhabit it, planting gardens, taking wives, bearing children, and even praying for the well-being of the alien city: "For in its welfare you will find your welfare" (Jer. 29:7). This prophesy ended up realizing itself historically far beyond what Jeremiah could have envisioned. A vigorous Jewish community would take root in Babylon, persisting into the Second Temple period and beyond. It was in this Diaspora existence that the Babylonian Talmud was born, an accumulation of law and wisdom that nurtured Jewish identity over many centuries in many places, from the Spanish ghetto to the Russian Pale of Settlement to the modern state of Israel.

All of this suggests the power and ambiguity with which the symbol "Babylon" is invested in the Jewish and later Christian imagination. Like Jerusalem, Babylon is a figure of the city, of the human urge to plant, build, trade, protect oneself against the elements and against outside threats, perhaps even fashion works of beauty; the city as an act of making, as culture. From the opening pages of scripture, Babel—"the gate of the god"—is more than just a place on a map. Babel is the first skyscraper, a conscious effort to insure its builders' immortality in the face of death: "Come, let us build ourselves a city and a tower with its top in the heavens, and let us make a name for ourselves, lest we be dispersed over the face of the whole earth" (Gen. 11:4). But while Babel is meant to stave off death, it quickly becomes death's servant. The social project that is the city simply reproduces Cain's violence on a much grander scale. God, then, has little choice but to scatter the peoples and confuse their languages.[1] A reader coming to Revelation directly from Gen. 1–11 would be surprised to learn that the biblical story culminates in the descent of a city.

17:1–6 Revelation 17 opens with one of the angels of the seven bowls inviting John to come and see the judgment of the great prostitute, she who is "seated on many waters." The whore is corrupt, but she is also powerful: her clients include "the kings of the earth" (17:2, 18; cf. 6:15) as well as ordinary citizens of the earthly empire. Both are guilty of "fornication"[2] with her. In a pattern that reminds us of the Lamb's first appearance in Rev. 5, John first hears the angel tell of the prostitute and only then does he see her. This lurid vision is worth quoting from the KJV:

> So he carried me away in the spirit into the wilderness: and I saw a woman sit upon a scarlet-coloured beast, full of names of blasphemy, having seven heads and ten horns. And the woman was arrayed in purple and scarlet colour, and decked with gold and precious stones and pearls, having a golden cup in her hand full of abominations and filthiness of her fornication: And upon her forehead was a name written, "MYSTERY, BABYLON THE GREAT, THE MOTHER OF HARLOTS AND

1. Immediately following the destruction of Babel, God calls Abraham to venture forth from "Ur of the Chaldeans," i.e., of the Babylonians.

2. The Greek verb *porneuō* ("to commit fornication") is cognate with both *porneia* ("fornication, prostitution") and *pornē* ("whore, prostitute"). While ESV's "committed sexual immorality" is not inaccurate, it sacrifices metaphorical resonance for dictionarylike precision. The corruption that John envisions includes sexual sins but goes far beyond them. RSV and NRSV therefore rightly follow KJV: "committed fornication."

ABOMINATIONS OF THE EARTH." And I saw the woman drunken with the blood of the saints, and with the blood of the martyrs of Jesus. (17:3–6 KJV)[3]

Remarkably, this is the first time since 4:2 that John has spoken of the Spirit's transporting him in space to receive a vision. The destination this time is the wilderness, an ambiguous place in Israel's experience, the place of its faithfulness to YHWH (Jer. 2:2), but also the place of foulness and corruption, the place where the demon Azazel dwells (Lev. 16:10). The wilderness is the place where the other woman, the heavenly mother of the Messiah and of the church, took refuge in her flight from the dragon (12:6, 14). Moreover, other clues link the two female figures in Rev. 12 and Rev. 17. The heavenly woman is called a great *sēmeion*, whereas the great whore bears a name that is a *mystērion*, a mystery that evokes John's wonderment. The heavenly woman is robed in the sun, while the whore is arrayed in brilliantly colored clothes and jewels (the same Greek word for "clothed" is used in both cases). Finally there is the link provided by the dragon: the heavenly woman flees the dragon, while the whore rides atop the dragon's offspring the beast, here clearly identified by his heads, horns, and names of blasphemy (cf. 13:1–4).

This is by no means to say that the two women are identical. The woman clothed with the sun is beautiful, while the whore is a "painted lady," vulgar, self-advertising, and more than a little drunk. The woman clothed with the sun is the dragon's victim, the whore in some sense his accomplice. And yet the whore is powerful in her own way. Barr rightly comments that the woman in the present vision is "a figure divided, both attracting John and repelling him, a figure of desire and death: a great prostitute" (1998: 109). Perhaps this helps explain why John "marvel[s] greatly" when he first sees her.[4] What astonishes John is neither the woman alone nor the beast alone, but the conjunction of the two; it is the woman and the beast *together* who constitute the *mystērion*. I suggest that John marvels because he does not expect to see "the" woman—in herself, a supremely positive image, a figure of motherhood and of beauty—in this sort of company. If the whore is on the one hand the dominatrix, "the great city that has dominion over the kings of the earth" (17:19), she is also the victim, hated by the beast and by these same kings (17:16). The whore is literally involved in a love/hate relationship with the beast, a complexity that makes it impossible for us to see her simply as a "bad girl."

William Blake brilliantly captures the dynamics of this scene in his 1809 pen and watercolor sketch *The Whore of Babylon* (British Museum), which shows the beast as having "seven ugly human heads; the plump whore, stripped to the

---

3. Is the word "mystery" itself part of the name, as KJV implies? The Greek simply sets the words "name" and "mystery" in apposition: "On her forehead is written a name, mystery, Babylon the great." "Name of mystery" or "mysterious name" probably captures the meaning.

4. This scene and the visions in Rev. 5 and Rev. 7 are parallel, which are the only times in Revelation when (a) John expresses puzzlement or dismay and (b) his angelic guide offers an explanation for what he is seeing.

waist, rides him side-saddle holding her golden cup out of which fly personified 'abominations and filthiness and fornications.'"[5] Blake insightfully portrays the scene as a mixture of love and death. Thus one of the beast's heads looks back up at the whore, with a leering expression on its face, while another is busy devouring human figures on the earth below. Most striking of all is just how wretched and miserable the whore seems. She is clearly unhappy, trapped along with the beast in a covenant with death. While it would be impossible to call her innocent, it is clear in Blake's portrayal—as in John's own—that she is not just an agent of evil but also its victim. The vision brilliantly depicts the self-consuming, self-destroying power of evil, which lacks the gift of affirmation (both of God and of self) that is built into the fabric of the created order and especially into the life of spiritual beings.

17:7–18 The long discourse by the angel that runs from 17:7 to the end of the chapter is one of the few visions in the Apocalypse that comes supplied with an explanation. While this is one of the most intensely scrutinized passages in the entire book, as an "explanation" it seems remarkably obscure. Third-century commentator Hippolytus wrote: "Tell me, blessed John, apostle and disciple of the Lord, what you saw and heard concerning Babylon"; it is a wish many of John's readers have shared (my translation from Swete 1908: 213). One obvious strategy is to read the angel's discourse as a kind of cipher. Thus the "seven mountains" on which the prostitute sits (17:9) can be seen as a thinly veiled allusion to Rome, a city that was famously situated on seven hills (a commonplace in Roman literature; e.g., Virgil, *Aeneid* 6.782). But the seven heads of the beast are also seven kings; who else can these be except Roman emperors? Moreover, since John says that one of the kings, the sixth, is still reigning, it has seemed an easy matter to count up the emperors to arrive at a firm date for the composition of Revelation.

Yet perhaps it is not so easy after all, because we do not know which emperor John considers to be the first—Julius Caesar or Augustus? Nor do we know whether to include the three emperors who reigned in quick succession in the year 69. Uncertainties like these plague every effort to identify the kings. In fact, most such counting schemes arrive at either Nero or Vespasian, a result at odds with the ancient tradition that says the Apocalypse was written under Domitian. The latter date can be rescued on the supposition that John is backdating his revelation to an earlier time, a practice not unknown among apocalyptic writers.[6] But this seems a rather forced solution to the problem. The most natural interpretation of the king who "is" (17:10) is that he "is" in John's and his hearers' present. Throughout Revelation, the sixth is depicted as the penultimate moment, the time of God's action in *our* history to bring about the new creation.

---

5. Morton D. Paley, *The Apocalyptic Sublime* (New Haven: Yale University Press, 1986), 92, citing Rev. 17:4.
6. Raymond E. Brown, *An Introduction to the New Testament* (New York: Doubleday, 1997), 792.

The problem, perhaps, is not that we lack the key to deciphering the image, but that we insist on treating it as a cipher. If the decoding approach generally shows a lack of imagination, here it defies common sense: John has no need to identify who the current, reigning emperor is. His hearers (like anyone else in the empire) would have been perfectly aware of that. Rather, what he seeks to communicate is how far he and they stand "from the end of the sequence of seven, that is, of the full sequence of emperors of Rome. It tells them there is only one short reign to go before the end of Roman imperial dominance of the world. It tells them, as Revelation frequently does, that the end is near" (Bauckham 1993a: 406–7). This makes a great deal of sense. On this interpretation, it matters very little what the exact sequence of emperors is, since "seven" is simply a construct, indicating the perfect filling out of God's design. God is on the move, hastening history toward its appointed end.

If so, however, then we might want to hold more lightly to the assumption that the term "seven mountains" refers to the city of Rome. Certainly the conventional association of the city with its seven hills is very strong and should not be discounted. But when the mountains in question "are" also kings that "are" also the heads of a monster, we should be cautious about limiting the range of the metaphor to this single, historical referent. Even if the image of the woman on seven hills denotes Rome, what it connotes is something far larger and more foreboding. The decoding approach to the vision takes us only so far.

So we begin afresh. What is important to bear in mind is that everything the angel says is an unpacking of what John has already seen, namely the vision of the woman and the beast. This dual image needs to be clarified. Moreover, the explanation takes the form of a short albeit highly compressed story, whose characters interact with each other in complex and sometimes confusing ways.

17:8 The story begins with the beast, whom the angel describes at great length before turning his attention to the woman: "The beast that you saw was, and is not, and is about to rise from the bottomless pit and go to destruction. And the dwellers on earth whose names have not been written in the book of life from the foundation of the world will marvel to see the beast, because it was and is not and is to come."

This saying about the beast takes the form of an inclusio, bracketed on each side by a formula encountered before. The phrase "was and is not and is to come" is clearly a parodic allusion to the threefold name of God, who is here set in sharp contrast to the beast. God was, the unimaginably eternal Creator; God is, he lives and rules as the *Pantokratōr*; God is to come, he is creation's future, already powerfully unleashed in Jesus's resurrection. God is triune life. But the beast is the embodiment of death, an incarnation of the dragon whose "son" he is; his seven heads and ten horns betray the family resemblance (cf. 12:3). John underscores the point by reminding us that the beast "is not." On the surface this is a puzzling assertion, given that the church lives precisely in the time of the beast. Yet it is understandable if we parse "being" not simply as existence but as that which abides, endures, has a place allotted to it in the new creation.[7] We know that the beast has already been defeated by the Lamb; how, then, can his kingdom possibly endure? Unlike the God who comes and remains, the beast "comes" only as a prelude to his own destruction.

But while the beast is anti-God, he is even more clearly anti-Christ (→13:5–7). What comes more clearly to expression in the present passage is that just as Jesus has a history, consisting in his incarnation, death, resurrection, and ascension, so too the beast has a history, a narrative that unfolds across successive moments. If the beast were merely an idea, he would surely be unable to attract the fascinated adoration of the earth-dwellers (17:8; cf. 13:3). No, the beast is a specific incarnate power, ramified in the form of multiple heads and horns. He lives in a relationship of mutual exploitation with the whore. He entices his followers with the promise that, if only they will bow down and worship him, they too can conquer death. Surely the mastery of death is the ultimate hope underlying all earthly politics, if not de jure and in principle, then at least de facto and under the conditions of the present age. Leviathan conquers by exploiting us at our weakest point: our shared terror in the face of death. But just as the devil is "the one who has the power of death," so Christ is the one who delivers "all those who through fear of death were subject to lifelong slavery" (Heb. 2:14–15).

17:9–11 The verses that follow offer a more detailed accounting of the beast's history. After first summoning us to exercise wisdom, the angel identifies the beast's seven heads with seven mountains on which the woman is seated and also with a series of seven kings. Instead of the standard four-plus-three pattern, the kings are divided into a five-plus-one-plus-one pattern, which has the effect of focusing attention even more strongly on the sixth and seventh items in the sequence. John and his churches (and also we and our churches) are located in the critical sixth moment, the moment of maximum intensity. This is good news under the guise of bad. As terrible as it is to live under the reign of the beast, we know that his defeat is assured. The sixth king is tottering, and even his successor will "remain only a little while" (17:10). The effect of this knowledge is to bring the eschatological fullness of Christ into the midst of history. The Lamb's followers are the conquerors, *right now*. Fleming Rutledge notes that readers of Revelation find themselves "not in the middle of the story but in the middle of the end of the story," citing words often used by Archbishop Desmond Tutu in the time of the anti-apartheid struggle. "I've read the end of the book," Tutu would tell his cheering audiences. "We win!"[8]

As one of the first mercies of the new creation, the beast will be no more. He "goes to destruction" (17:11). This seems straightforward enough. What does it

---

7. Think of the pregnant use of the verb "abide" or "remain" (*menō*) in the Fourth Gospel. Jesus abides, and his followers abide in him (e.g., John 15:1–10). By contrast, evil has no ontological staying power. A similar evanescence is predicated of the seventh king in Rev. 17:10.

8. Fleming Rutledge, *The Battle for Middle-Earth: Tolkien's Divine Design in the Lord of the Rings* (Grand Rapids: Eerdmans, 2004), 232.

mean, however, when in the very same verse the angel says that the beast is an "eighth" and that he "belongs to the seven"? This is a dark riddle—so dark, in fact, that an otherwise sane commentator argues that the whole passage must have been interpolated (Eller 1974: 156–57). This seems unlikely, and in any case our job is to interpret the text as it stands. I would venture the following: the beast is an eighth in the sense that the antichrist is precisely eschatological evil, a tyrant without parallel in the whole prior history of the world. This fits with Daniel's vision of a fourth beast, an empire summing up and exceeding all the empires that have gone before it. No mere succession of kings and emperors can account for this terror. The antichrist in the proper sense emerges only in the end time and may not strictly speaking be identified with this or that historical power. Moreover, there is something supremely fitting in the beast's identity as an eighth. Very early in church history, the number eight became invested with symbolic meaning. Christ's resurrection was seen as the first day of a new creation, an eighth that goes beyond the seven days described in Genesis. This newness is prefigured in the eight human beings aboard the ark (1 Pet. 3:20). Moreover, the beast's number 666 may form a mystical counterpart to 888, the sum of the letters in the Greek name ΙΗΣΟΥΣ (→13:18). Just as Jesus is the *summum bonum* ("the highest good"), so we may say that the beast is the *summum malum* ("the greatest evil"), a bodily recapitulation of all the powers of hell.

Yet he also "belongs to the seven." Commentators often refer this puzzling claim to the first-century rumors concerning a possible return of Nero, leading an army from the east to retake his empire. An eighth king will come to complete the beast's work, and he will be a recurrence of one of the seven kings—surely this must be the tyrant responsible for the great persecution of the 60s, in which so much Christian blood was shed. Perhaps; certainly the tradition that identifies the eighth king with Nero is very old. Just as in our own time, Hitler has come to stand for moral evil beyond all imagining, so Nero may have played a similar role in the mind of the early Christians.

A more careful reading of the passage, however, points in a somewhat different direction. John does not say that the beast is "one of the seven" but simply that he is "from/out of the seven" (*ek tōn hepta estin*); hence ESV's "it belongs to the seven." In other words, the beast displays an essential kinship with the seven kings, the concrete historical powers who rebel against the rule of God. He and they share a common character. Not only are both evil, but both, significantly, are finite: Christianity knows no absolute or ontological evil, no dark strand woven into the fabric of creation itself. The beast lives by and in his heads. These are, we may surmise, something like the rulers of this age of whom Paul speaks, the *archontes* who, lacking God's wisdom, made the mistake of crucifying "the Lord of glory" (1 Cor. 2:7–8). These could be Herod and Pilate, or they could be the Jewish elites in first-century Jerusalem; probably Paul means both. In St.

John's setting, we may imagine similar acts of collusion among imperial, local, and religious authorities.[9]

To say that the beast belongs to the seven, then, is something of a two-edged sword—an appropriate metaphor in our context! On the one hand, in dealing with these powers the church is not simply confronting this or that finite constellation of forces. The activity of the beast may be discerned before the time in the works of his servants. Death is at work in the structures and institutions of human society. The beast's violence is part of the end, but the bloated "defense" budget approved by Congress each year is very historical, tangible, and real. The whore may be an eschatological sign, but there are very real women and children in our world who can eat only by selling their bodies. The beast is at work among the seven kings, who do, and do not, know that they are serving him; such is the nature of sin as self-deception.

But now the other side of the two-edged sword: just to the extent that the beast resembles the seven, he is on the way out the door, he "goes to destruction." The beast has no more ultimate staying power than do the rulers of the present age. His crown is as unsteady as that of any Roman emperor. Like the seventh king in the series, or like all the kings, he will "remain only a little while." The great terror that will appear at the time of the end (and such enormity is truly beyond our imagining) will both recapitulate all the terrors that have gone before it and bring an end to them all, as together they are trampled down by the warring Lamb.

17:12–14 That warfare is the subject of the next part of the angel's discourse, where he explains the meaning of the ten horns. The horns are identified as ten kings, who, although they do not yet rule, are to receive "authority as kings for one hour, together with the beast." To receive authority means that one's authority is derivative. Even by the standards of the beast's kingdom these are not real kings. Rather, John depicts them as being doubly dependent. On the one hand, they are puppets of the beast, handing over to him even such authority as they do have, united with him in a covenant of heart and mind (17:13). On the other hand, the kings are shown standing in a love/hate relationship with the whore. She exercises dominion over them, a subservience they and their master bitterly resent: thus they are said to strip her naked, eat her flesh—a grim parody of the Eucharist?—and burn her alive with fire (17:16, 18). It is a gruesome picture. The kings of the earth are merely slaves of the monster and clients of the whore, pawns in a game they can neither understand nor escape.

In the larger scheme of the Apocalypse, there is a certain dramatic inevitability about this scene. John signals his concern with "the kings of the earth" early in the book: already in the prologue Jesus Christ is said to be "the ruler of the kings on earth" (1:5), while at the opening of the sixth seal the kings head the list of those who cower in fear (6:15). Moreover, these kings have already been identified as the beast's key allies in the coming battle (16:12–16). John reprises this theme

---

9. John even identifies the local synagogue as an agent of Satan (2:9; 3:9).

here, telling us that the confederation "will make war on the Lamb, and the Lamb will conquer them, for he is Lord of lords and King of kings." The entire scene anticipates the climactic confrontation between Christ and the antichrist later in the book (19:11–21).

The very centrality of the kings of the earth throughout Revelation should be enough to discourage any decoding approach to this passage. It is less important to discern *who* these ten kings are than *what* they are. They represent a particular aspect of the earthly system of power: its tendency to spread out and ramify, setting up complex, often unpredictable relationships between centers and peripheries. The beast has seven heads. Any political or economic system has certain centers of power, invested with the resources both for making decisions and for enforcing them. Thus a state is among other things an entity that can police its own borders. But the beast also has ten horns. Not everything can be accomplished directly from the center. Power is distributed toward the periphery—in the Roman Empire, through the army of magistrates, prefects, tax collectors, soldiers, and the like, who would have constituted the everyday face of the empire for most ordinary people. It was a patronage society, of the kind where power and influence are being constantly negotiated less on the basis of what you know than of who you know.[10] If in a certain sense power flows outward from the head to the members, the head is also dependent *on* the members to keep the whole system running.

The ten kings, then, must in some sense be clients of the beast's seven heads and so ultimately of the beast himself. But they seem to be clients of a specifically *military* sort. They are capable of making war. However we are to think of them, whether as allies or mercenary forces[11] or client states, the kings are drawn into the beast's sphere of power and become the local agents of his aggressive ambitions. As the end approaches, John pictures all earthly power as being drawn into a complex system of opposition to the Lamb. Even the antichrist is not so much an individual as an organism, in Bede's language "the body of the ungodly," a kingdom opposed to Christ and his body the church.[12] This point is underscored if we read 17:13–14 as forming a rough chiasm:

10. Fergus Millar, *The Emperor in the Roman World, 31 BC–AD 337* (London: Duckworth, 1977).

11. A few centuries after the seer, the empire would famously incorporate the "barbarian" Germanic tribes into the Roman army.

12. This insight is found in Tyconius, Augustine, and the whole tradition of Latin commentary on the Apocalypse. So Augustine: "It would not, however, be repugnant to the true faith to understand the beast to represent the godless city itself, and the people of the unbelievers, contrasted with the people of faith and the city of God" (*City of God* 20.9, quoted from Bettenson 1984: 91). And Bede: "Antichrist, who is to reign at the end of the age, because of the unity of the body of the ungodly of which he is the head, pertains to the number of the kingdoms of the world" (Bedae Presbyteri, *Expositio Apocalypseos*, Corpus Christianorum: Series Latina 121A, ed. Roger Gryson [Turnhout: Brepols, 2001], 387; English translation from Edward Marshall, *The Explanation of the Apocalypse by Venerable Beda* [Oxford: Parker, 1878], accessed at apocalyptic-theories.com).

A   *These* [*kings*] are of one mind, and they hand over their power and authority to

    B   *the beast*. They will make war on

    B′   *the Lamb*, and the Lamb will conquer them, for he is Lord of lords and King of kings,

A′   *and those with him* are called and chosen and faithful.

"Those with him" are, of course, the saints, a group that John hopes will also include the churches of Asia Minor. Jesus is Lord of lords and King of kings in more than one sense. He triumphs over the kings arrayed against him, yet he also makes his people kings, graciously giving them a share in his royal rule. It is not the faithful themselves who conquer the beast, but the Lamb, although the faithful are said to be "with him." Alone, they would certainly lose this battle. With him, they have the sure promise that they will win it.

17:15–18 Throughout this curious digression, the figure of the whore has been almost forgotten; all the talk has been of the machinery of power. Yet just as Rev. 17 opens with the vision of the scarlet-clad woman, so now it ends with her. The angel explains that the waters where the whore is seated are "peoples and multitudes and nations and languages"—familiar code language for the cosmic scope of redemption in Revelation, although here it is used ambivalently. Insofar as the whore is constituted by many peoples, nations, and languages, she is a "great city" indeed, more cosmopolitan than any city in either the ancient or modern worlds. But insofar as she exploits the peoples of the earth she is an oppressor, drawing on their life to feed her insatiable appetites.

The kings' attitude toward the whore is correspondingly ambivalent, marked by a strange mix of desire, dependence, and resentment. Although they take their pleasure with her, they also despise her and seek to do her harm. The prostitute is quite literally "consumed" by her clients (17:16). By the end of this vision, we get the sense that the beast derives much of his energy from the whore, that it is desire for her that impels his crimes, and that each is the source of the other's corruption.

Who is the whore? John tells us that she is seated on "many waters," a convention for speaking of Babylon-on-the-Euphrates, but which might also be taken as referring to any seagoing power. She has clients who are politically and militarily powerful. She is gaudy and rich. She is drunk with the blood of the martyrs and saints. All the signs point to the whore's being Rome, the murderess responsible for the deaths of the apostles Peter and Paul and more recently for the martyrdom of Antipas of Pergamum. In John's time, there was simply no other "great city" on a par with Rome's scale and ambition. This judgment seems to be confirmed by many voices in the ancient church. No less than St. Augustine called Rome "the second Babylonia, as it were, the Babylonia of the West" (*City of God* 16.17 [cf. 18.2], quoted from Bettenson 1984: 677).

Nevertheless, the Great Whore Babylon is more than just Rome, as the beast is more than just the military power that allowed her to extend her reach across the Mediterranean. Any such simple, empirical identification would be guilty of what William Blake famously called "single vision." It would mean reading an apocalyptic work in a most unapocalyptic way—that is, unimaginatively. Blake's own watercolor of the beast and the whore points to realities of his own time—the beast to be understood as scientific materialism, perhaps, and the whore as the modern spirit of capitalism—even as it gestures toward something more universal.

So it was, too, for Augustine, who identified "the great city" with Rome *and* with the earthly city as such, which is constructed not just of bricks and mortar but of imagination and desire. There is no question but that Babylon is a figure of desire, longing, eros. She is beautiful, yet fallen; powerful, but exploited; strong, but with the kind of strength that seeks to control and dominate—"the great city that has dominion over the kings of the earth." To use Pauline language, we might see the whore as a kind of Adamic figure, a representation of fallen humanity driven by desire gone wrong: "We see then that the two cities were created by two kinds of love: the earthly city was created by self-love reaching the point of contempt for God, the Heavenly City by the love of God. . . . The earthly city glories in itself, the Heavenly City glories in the Lord" (*City of God* 14.28, quoted from Bettenson 1984: 593).

The visions of Revelation often seem to resemble the Russian matryoshka doll, with each figure opening up to disclose yet another, and another, and so on. After John's initial vision of the whore's entanglement with the beast and the kings, he is shown the end of Babylon. The fall of the city is good news for the earth and the cause of much rejoicing in heaven.

REVELATION 18

THE END OF BABYLON

You look at these hundreds of thousands, these millions of people humbly streaming here from all over the face of the earth. People come with a single thought, quietly, relentlessly, mutely thronging into this colossal palace; and you feel that something final has taken place here, that something has come to an end. It is like a Biblical picture, something out of Babylon, a prophecy from the Apocalypse coming to pass before your eyes. You sense that it would require great and everlasting spiritual denial and fortitude in order not to submit . . . not to deify Baal, that is, not to accept the material world as your ideal.

—Fyodor Dostoevsky, *Winter Notes on Summer Impressions*

If it is true, as part of the Christian economy of salvation, that Babylon must die, then Rev. 18 is its funeral dirge. Leaving the beast behind for the moment, John now concentrates exclusively on the prostitute, recounting both what made her "great" and why God considers her continued existence to be intolerable. Interestingly, this chapter marks a strong reemergence of the aural themes noted earlier: we are reminded once again that we are in the midst of a liturgy. This point is underscored when the heavenly worship resumes toward the end of the present vision, stretching into the beginning of Rev. 19.[1]

18:1–2 The vision opens with another angel coming down from heaven, endowed with "great authority" and making the earth bright with his glory. Swete notes that "so recently has he come from the Presence that in passing he flings a broad belt of light across the dark Earth" (1908: 226). This light reminds us of

---

1. The heavenly worship in 19:1–10 forms the real conclusion to the lament over Babylon.

Ezek. 43:2, where the glory of YHWH causes the whole earth to shine as the glory descends upon the temple, but also of the Johannine view of the incarnation, in which the light of the Word shines in the world's darkness with the glory of the Father (John 1:4–5, 9, 14). As so often in Revelation, an angel evokes a particular aspect of Jesus's identity.

But while the angel's appearance may be glorious, his message is one of doom. John renders the fall of Babylon in a rollicking poetic rhythm that really should be experienced in the Greek; here is my free rendering:

> Fallen now, fallen now, Babylon the mighty!
> Now she is become the dwelling of demons,
> a prison for every filthy spirit,
> a prison for every filthy bird,
> a prison for every foul and filthy and despicable beast! (18:2)

This is quintessential prophetic speech, gospel in the form of judgment, the end of an old order as prelude to a coming new world. Allied with the beast, the prostitute had believed herself immune to destruction. Surely she would go on forever: "I sit as a queen, I am no widow, and mourning I shall never see" (18:7). But the alliance with the monster has proved to be a frightful miscalculation on the whore's part. Babylon's real fate is to be a demon-haunted ruin, her mighty towers a nesting place for vultures, her luxury condominiums overrun with rats and other vermin (for this imagery see Isa. 13:21; 34:11). The very designation Babylon "the great" drips with irony: her greatness has not been able to prevent *this*. From the tawdry depiction of "things as they are" in the previous vision, we suddenly and without preparation find ourselves in a situation in which Babylon, unthinkably, is no more. How has all this happened?

18:3 The little word "for" (*hoti*) signals the beginnings of an explanation for Babylon's demise. Babylon is fallen because of the corrupting effect it had on three major sorts of clients: (1) "all nations," who have "drunk the wine of the passion of her sexual immorality [*porneia*]"; (2) "the kings of the earth," who have likewise "fornicated" with her; and (3) "the merchants of the earth," who have "grown rich from the power of her luxurious living." Each group points to a different aspect of the whore's hegemony. The reference to "all nations" indicates that no human community is not implicated to some extent in the system that is Babylon. We might see this as Revelation's peculiar version of the doctrine of original sin, thought of not as an individual inheritance, but as a sort of universal infection of our politics. No nation, not even Israel, is free of the taint of Babylon. All have been drawn into its sphere of influence.

Yet even if the corruption is in some sense universal, John does not assume that all are equally culpable. If all are guilty, the kings are far more so, because as the possessors of power they can enact the fantasies of Babylon in ways that harm whole populations. The same is true of the merchants, who have made themselves fat on the wealth of the city, turning a profit where they might have contributed to the common good. Together these two groups are the *megistanes* ("great ones"; 18:23) encountered earlier at the opening of the sixth seal. It is part of John's genius that rather than simply denouncing these great ones for their crimes, he lets them write their own bill of indictment; thus the laments that follow at 18:9–20.

18:4–8 Before this happens, however, John hears "another voice" (i.e., besides that of the angel) sounding out of heaven, crying, "Come out of her, my people, lest you take part in her sins, lest you share in her plagues." The language echoes that of Jeremiah's great, climactic oracle against the Chaldean Empire (Jer. 51:6, 45). Although the heavenly voice could be understood as saying that the church is to engage in payback, this is not the best way to read the passage. The people of God have just been told to depart out of Babylon, not sitting in proud judgment over it, but simply avoiding the judgment it has incurred—once again, the trope of the church as fleeing for safety into the wilderness (Rev. 12:6, 14, 17). God alone can execute vengeance, visiting "death and mourning and famine" upon Babylon and ultimately consuming it with fire (18:8). The church's only participation in this judgment is to make space for the divine action.

The judgment of God is that Babylon must taste something of the vulnerability and distress that has been the ordinary lot of its victims; we might think of the way the rich man was made to exchange roles with Lazarus in the world to come (Luke 16:19–31). Having lived for so long as the privileged exception, Babylon is now shown what the majority experience of the human race has been under the conditions of the present evil age. And having been shown that, it will be consumed.

18:9–19 The laments of the kings and the merchants now begin, joined by a third group, the shipmasters and seafarers. These *megistanes* ("great ones") function something like the chorus in a Greek tragedy, with each group offering its particular perspective on Babylon's demise.

The first group to speak are the kings, Babylon's lovers, who "weep and wail over her when they see the smoke of her burning" (18:9). The kings were in love with the prostitute, even if they also despised her. If their hatred is partly motivated by her failing them in the end, it is also due to resentment of the power she exercised over them. Yet as they look back, it is their need and desire for the city that comes most clearly to expression. These kings are in fact quite pitiful creatures. Having professed their undying love for Babylon, they now stand apart, watching its torment from a safe distance, as if observing some strange spectacle that had nothing to do with them: "Alas! Alas! You great city, you mighty city, Babylon! For in a single hour your judgment has come" (18:10). That the kings themselves will ultimately be destroyed in the conflagration lends an ironic twist to their words (17:12; cf. 19:19–21). It is much too late in the day for the kings to deny their relation to Babylon. They have been caught *in flagrante delicto* and will inevitably share its doom.

After the kings, we hear the chorus of the merchants. They mourn Babylon's demise for a very practical, self-interested reason: "No one buys their cargo anymore." Babylon's destruction means the loss of a market for their goods. The lament of the merchants is remarkable for the inventory given of the cargo itself, a list that reads like the bill of lading of a prosperous Mediterranean trader in the first century: "Cargo of gold, silver, jewels, pearls, fine linen, purple cloth, silk, scarlet cloth, all kinds of scented wood, all kinds of articles of ivory, all kinds of articles of costly wood, bronze, iron and marble, cinnamon, spice, incense, myrrh, frankincense, wine, oil, fine flour, wheat, cattle and sheep, horses and chariots" (18:12–13).

Why should John go to the trouble of compiling this impressive catalog? We can account for it in part on the basis of Ezekiel's oracle against Tyre, where the prophet likewise lists many of the goods exchanged by that great trading city and its partners (Ezek. 27:12–25). Oliver O'Donovan astutely notes that what draws John's attention to Tyre is its specifically commercial character, quite unlike the Assyrian or Babylonian empires that had gone before it. John too lived under an empire dominated by trade: "Trade is a kind of cultural promiscuity by which one power exploits and drains the resources of many others. John is certainly to be counted among those who have seen mercantile enterprise as a tool of imperialism. The tyranny of the beast in chapter 13 was exercised through the market."[2]

This is an important point. John is acutely aware that the power of death is exercised not simply through the hard power of military force, although such force must surely be reckoned with, but through the soft power of the market and of culture. Human beings do not trade simply in order to stay alive, but to impress others, maintain status, and in general carve out for themselves a certain kind of space in the world. The act of consumption is a mirror for personal identity, reflecting both what we can buy and what we choose to buy. This human trait is not limited to our own economic system of consumer capitalism, although, with our sophisticated techniques of marketing and branding, we have developed it to a high art. Scripture does not demonize trade as such—Solomon's kingdom does a brisk business with, among other places, Tyre—but it views its possibilities with deep suspicion. "You cannot serve God and money" (Luke 16:13). The vision of Babylon in Rev. 18 powerfully depicts the ways in which the cycle of production, trade, and consumption is drawn into the program of the beast. In the present age, trade debases the rich and exploits the poor. In offering this catalog of goods, John is offering his hearers a glimpse of their own world, inviting them to see that it falls under the description "Babylon" and that it rightly incurs God's judgment.

John reserves the most stunning item on his list for the very end: "Cattle and sheep, horses and chariots, and slaves, that is, human souls."[3] While Ezekiel's

2. Oliver O'Donovan and Joan Lockwood O'Donovan, *Bonds of Imperfection: Christian Politics, Past and Present* (Grand Rapids: Eerdmans, 2004), 40.
3. The two terms that conclude John's list are *sōmatōn kai psychas anthrōpōn*, which could also be translated "slaves—and human lives" (NRSV) or "human bodies and souls" (NRSV margin). These translational possibilities do not affect the basic meaning.

oracle against Tyre also speaks of "human souls," the term is buried in a long enumeration of items (Ezek. 27:13). By contrast, John places the human cargo in the emphatic final position. He wants to drive home the point that, in Babylon's system of exchange, humanity itself has been reduced to one more item on a list of things, goods, possessions. This was literally true, of course: slavery was a commonplace in the ancient world. Even Paul seems to have accepted it as a necessary concession to the present order of things, although the bond between slave and slave owner "in Christ" pointed to another, eschatological possibility (as exemplified in the letter to Philemon, for example). But even beyond the specific evil of slavery, Revelation bears witness to an even more fundamental flaw at the heart of Babylon's economy. The list exposes the way in which human beings, made in the image of God, are treated as mere commodities, convertible in principle with other goods. From the merchants' perspective, human souls or lives (the word *psychē* means both) are no different in kind from silk, spices, or sheep, since the value of all these things is determined by the price they can command in the great marketplaces of Ephesus, Smyrna, or Rome itself. Nothing "is" what it is (i.e., as created and established by God). It "is" only insofar as it can be traded for other things or exchanged, even more abstractly, for money. Each thing is worth nothing more nor less than what the market will bear. It is too simple to say that the system thereby objectifies everything it touches, because in some ways it *subjectifies* them: the market is, after all, a marketplace of fantasy and wishes, a field of dreams for those who have the resources to play. Thus the appearance of the highly charged word *epithymia* ("desire, longing, yearning"): "The fruit for which your soul longed [literally, 'the fruit of the longing of your soul'] has gone from you, and all your delicacies and your splendors are lost to you, never to be found again!" (18:14).

The chorus concludes with the lament of the shipmasters and sailors, added, no doubt, to reinforce the Tyre imagery of the aggressive, seafaring power and recalling that the beast himself arose out of the sea (13:1). The note of imperial domination is very strong here. To the shipmasters is assigned the great line "what city was like the great city?" (18:18)—which might stand as a title over the entire chorus. There has been and never will be anything like this city. It is without parallel in human experience. On the merchants' and seafarers' scale of values, its loss is infinitely great.

In Western theology, it was above all St. Augustine who taught us that the human being is essentially constituted by desire (*eros*). Passion in the negative sense (*epithymia*) is nothing else but disordered desire, a longing that fails to acknowledge God as what the heart yearns for: "Our hearts are restless until they rest in thee." At the same time, desire is never simply an individual phenomenon. Far from being simple and self-validating, desire is to be seen as "a social product . . . a complex and multidimensional network of movement that does not simply originate within the individual self but pulls and pushes the self in different directions from both inside and outside the person."[4] What the Apocalypse reveals to us is (a) that not just the human soul, but the human city is constructed by desire—Babylon is a cooperative endeavor—and (b) that this endeavor has become hopelessly corrupted by sin. The city is the glory of humans as political animals—that is God's purpose for it. The city is a whore riding on the back of a pimp, a seven-headed monster who will soon devour the whole world, consuming the whore in the process—that is the eschatological reality on the verge of overtaking John and his hearers. Whatever the city might be in the divine intention, now in these last days it has become violent and exploitative, ugly and deformed, an appropriately haglike consort for its master the beast. God's people have no choice but to "come out of her."

The question once again poses itself, what is the *referent* of such language? Is Babylon what John thought it was in the first century, or does the image expand to encompass other realities that the church has had to struggle with across its history? Even if it could be shown that John believed the empire to be the apocalyptic whore, this would not fix the meaning of the image once for all. The whore is a character from the end of the story whom we encounter in the middle of the story. If the church lives *out of* Christ's victory, it lives *in* the midst of the great city and all it entails. Just what it means to say this cannot be neatly determined in advance, since history (rather inconveniently) has to be lived before it can be narrated. What the Apocalypse does is not to narrate history in advance, but to describe the pattern of suffering, tribulation, and oppression that is intrinsic to the church's historical existence. The church, we might say, is on a pilgrimage through time, in the course of which it encounters Babylon again and again, always in different forms and guises. The Babylon of imperial Rome will be different from the Babylon that Blake imagined in industrial England, which will be different yet again from the Babylon of late modern capitalism, where goods and services are traded electronically and at the speed of light, but where "human souls" are still being traded. The appearance of the figure of Babylon in history is not uniform, nor is every human society or economic system equally deserving of the name. What it means, then, for the church to flee Babylon for the wilderness will also differ in particular concrete situations. Discerning the shape of this pilgrimage is among the chief tasks of theological ethics.

To use simpler and more traditional language, "Babylon" names the world (*ho kosmos*) in the negative New Testament sense. The church cannot avoid living in the world, but it may not itself be "worldly." While the worldly church is a contradiction in terms, this possibility has unfortunately been realized all too often in Christian history. In extreme cases the church may be charged with actually having *become* Babylon, the spotless bride who has traded in her finery for the tawdry dress of the whore. This trope is biblically far more appropriate than the one that

---

4. William T. Cavanaugh, *Being Consumed: Economics and Christian Desire* (Grand Rapids: Eerdmans, 2008), 9.

calls the church or its ministers "antichrist." In the Old Testament, Jerusalem or Daughter Zion can also be castigated as a harlot, and the harlot/bride contrast is implied by Revelation itself. If Israel can be unfaithful to God, so can the church. Theologians who write in this vein can often be quite unsparing:

> God's beloved is the Church, so long as she walks in the footsteps of the Fathers. But now she has become Babylon through her heinousness and infestation by unclean spirits. For God himself she has become an abomination. . . . We are no longer dealing with a bride but with a monster of terrible deformity and ferocity. . . . It is clear that it cannot be said of her in such a state: "Thou art all fair, and there is not a spot in thee."[5]

This is not Luther in one of his more antipapal moments, but rather William of Auvergne, Bishop of Paris, writing in the early thirteenth century. The theme is common among patristic and medieval theologians. We expect the world to be Babylon; that goes with its being the earthly city. But for the church to be so corrupted is an unspeakable evil. It means that the lust for worldly power and influence has replaced fidelity to Christ. Like the whore in our present passage, the church as Babylon consorts freely with "the kings of the earth," in such a way that it is no longer fighting in the Lamb's army; indeed, it has gone over to the enemy. What it means to "come out of Babylon" in such a situation is obviously highly problematic. Suffice to say that, prior to the sixteenth century, the trope was not used to justify separation from the church, but as an impetus to repentance, reform, and renewal. The church is our mother, even when it looks like Babylon. Hans Urs von Balthasar thus reminds us that the church in Christian tradition was often viewed as *casta meretrix* ("chaste harlot"), a people beloved by God despite its manifest faults.[6]

18:20–21 But whether as the earthly city or as the church's complicity in the ways of that city, Babylon is no more. The vision reaches its climax when the mysterious voice once again intervenes, inviting saints, apostles, prophets, and all of heaven to rejoice over the end of Babylon. The pronouncement is then confirmed by a prophetic sign-action, in which an angel takes a great millstone and hurls it into the sea—an image borrowed from Jeremiah's anti-Babylon oracle, where it signifies the watery grave of the city seated by many waters (Jer. 51:63–64). The angel interprets: "So will Babylon the great city be thrown down with violence."

5. Hans Urs von Balthasar, *Explorations in Theology*, vol. 2: *Spouse of the Word* (San Francisco: Ignatius, 1991), 197.
6. Ibid., 193–288. Whether in the Old Testament prophets or in Revelation, the "harlot" language in scripture needs to be taken seriously. This does not necessarily mean that it is to be reproduced. A one-sided emphasis on feminine images for faithless Israel could encourage the notion that the humiliation of Jerusalem/Babylon is a template for the treatment of actual women. At the very least, such negative imagery needs to be balanced by the highly positive feminine images found in Rev. 12 and Rev. 21. The hermeneutical key to all such language is no doubt the example of Jesus; cf. John 8:1–11.

We should not be deceived by the future tense of the verb. Even if Babylon's fall lies in the future from the perspective of the reader/hearer, from God's point of view it has already occurred; but this means that it has occurred in actuality. Babylon the great *is* fallen, fallen; the future is now (Rev. 14:8).

18:22–24 The angel's pronouncement now expands into a kind of elegy, rehearsing the end of the arts and crafts and even the basic forms of human sociality, which had once made up the life of Babylon. The recital is poignant: "the sound of harpists and musicians, of flute players and trumpeters . . . a craftsman of any craft . . . the sound of the mill . . . the light of a lamp . . . and the voice of bridegroom and bride," each followed by the haunting refrain "will be heard/seen in you no more."[7] The once bustling, noisy city is silenced, a point underscored by the threefold repetition of the word *phōnē* ("sound, voice"). Like many passages in the Apocalypse, this one really needs to be read aloud for a full appreciation of its power.

Music, craftsmanship, food, light, marriage—things that make up a habitable world. Babylon's destruction would seem to mark the end of civilized existence, indeed of the city as such. It is tempting to say that the passage invites the hearer to mourn over the loss of Babylon, except that it reaches its climax by offering the reason behind God's judgment. All these things will be "no more": "*For* your merchants were the great ones of the earth, and all nations were deceived by your sorcery. And in her was found the blood of prophets and of saints, and of all who have been slain on earth" (18:23b–24).

The reason that life in Babylon is so attractive, we might say, is because it promises freedom—a word that never appears in Revelation, although it is frequently implied by the mention of its opposite, slavery. The merchants' catalog of goods holds out the promise of freedom from material want. The social and cultural goods named in the elegy hold out the promise of freedom as life in community. Music, food (not just physical nourishment but breaking bread, supping around a common table), the voice of the bridegroom and the bride—all these point to the bonds of accountability, affection, and celebration that make up specifically *human* existence. In this as in many other respects, the Apocalypse recapitulates Genesis, whose early chapters hint at the beginnings of culture in the broadest sense (Gen. 4:21–22; 9:20; 2:22–24). The gifts that God gave to humanity in the beginning, he is now taking back. The world that was made is now being unmade.

All this is so, however, not because God is misanthropic, but precisely because God wishes to bestow on human beings the gift of freedom—negatively, freedom from enslavement to Babylon; positively, freedom for God and for life in the coming city. The fall of Babylon is not an end in itself. In the first allusion to this event in Rev. 14, it appears as a consequence of the eternal gospel proclaimed to "every nation and tribe and language and people" (14:6–8). God is *against*

---

7. The immediate source of the imagery is again Jeremiah, esp. Jer. 25:10; cf. 7:34; 16:9; 33:11.

Babylon, because he is *for* the brothers and sisters of Jesus, the firstfruits of a new creation. It is the Lamb's death and resurrection that lays waste to Babylon. The millstone is cast into the sea, reminding us that Jesus thought such a fate better than giving offense to even one of these little ones (Mark 9:42 and parallels). If Jesus lives, then no city in which such little ones are exploited can stand for long. The power of death withers in the presence of the Lord of life, who was crucified outside—and for—the human city.

Development of this theme requires revisiting the laments in Rev. 18:9–19. Three times John tells us that the great ones stood "far off" (18:10, 15, 17). Their self-distancing from the city may be understood as a final act of betrayal. Even so, the fact remains that they do stand apart. Jacques Ellul shrewdly comments: "The drama that overtakes the city does not overtake them. . . . Then the communion established by the enchantments and sorceries of the city is broken. She no longer possesses men. The latter weep and lament because . . . they are, with her, deprived of that which made them the Great, the Powerful, the Rich. But they themselves, as men, are outside the blow" (1977: 197).

The end of Babylon, then, is an act of divine grace, resulting in God's refusal to let *this* be the definitive embodiment of the human story. If the powerful mourn, heaven rejoices (18:19–20). And even the powerful may discover that the city's fall is good news for them also. We are not told what finally happens to these people, but we have a sense that, despite themselves, they have been spared a fate much worse than the loss of their wealth.

As John's visionary imagination generally has been deeply shaped by the great Old Testament prophets, so his account of Babylon especially reflects Jeremiah. But another, exceedingly minor prophet—Jonah—offers an interesting intratextual commentary on Rev. 18. There are of course significant differences between these two prophets. While Jonah is sent on a mission to the pagan city, John is sent not to the pagans but to Israel (the seven churches). While Jonah flees his calling, John embraces it. Most tellingly, while Jonah's Nineveh is spared on account of the people's repentance, John's Babylon is made to drink the cup of the fury of God's wrath.

All this is true; and yet there are also some curious parallels. Nineveh is described four times in Jonah as "the great city," a phrase not used by other prophets (the exception is Jer. 22:8), but frequently employed in Revelation (11:8; 16:19; 17:18; 18:10, 16, 18, 19, 21).[8] Both books have a monster from the deep (in Jonah's case, a beneficent one), both make reference to the sea and to seafarers, and both refer to the God of heaven who created the sea and the dry land (Jonah 1:9; cf. Rev. 10:6). Slender reeds, surely, and not too much should be built on them. The force of the comparison lies not so much in the parallels as in the contrasting fates of two cities that are called "great." As we saw in Rev. 11, the great city that

---

8. The phrase in the Septuagint of Jonah 1:2; 3:1, 3; 4:11 is the same as in Revelation: *hē polis hē megalē*.

murders the prophets is Jerusalem *and* the cities of the nations. Because Revelation views the city with the bifocal vision of apocalyptic, the mercy of God is displayed under the form of two different cities, one of them doomed, the other descending from heaven. What Jonah shows us—and this is the commentary it offers—is that the city descending is for the sake of the city doomed, or at least for the sake of its inhabitants. The comedy of Jonah helps us see the grace hidden in the vision of Babylon lying in ruins. YHWH says to Jonah, after the latter protests the absurd pardon of the Ninevites: "You pity the plant, for which you did not labor, nor did you make it grow, which came into being in a night and perished in a night. And should not I pity Nineveh, that great city, in which there are more than 120,000 persons who do not know their right hand from their left, and also much cattle?" (Jonah 4:10–11).

PART IV

THE SUPPER
OF THE LAMB

REVELATION 19

THE RIDER ON THE WHITE HORSE

"Listen! The battle trumpet blares from heaven and see how our General marches fully armed, coming amid the clouds to conquer the whole world. Out of the mouth of our King emerges a double-edged sword that cuts down everything in the way. Arising finally from your nap, do you come to the battlefield! Abandon the shade and seek the sun."

She turned back in the book to see what she was reading. It was a letter from a St. Jerome to a Heliodorus, scolding him for having abandoned the desert. . . .

This was the kind of thing he read—something that made no sense for now. Then it came to her, with an unpleasant jolt, that the General with the sword in his mouth, marching to do violence, was Jesus.

—Flannery O'Connor, "Why Do the Heathen Rage?"

19:1a The use of the phrase *meta tauta* (literally, "after these things") signals the start of a fresh set of visions (cf. 18:1). Nevertheless, it is important to see how the vision of the fall of Babylon flows seamlessly into the jubilation that follows. The kings and merchants lament the collapse of Babylon's empire; the people of God celebrate it. The present chapter thus serves as an important psychological transition, marking a return to the key of worship after the prolonged attention to the powers in Rev. 17–18.

19:1b–8 The worship here takes the form of an exuberant "hallelujah" chorus. In a book so replete with liturgy, it is perhaps surprising that we have not heard the psalmist's cry of "hallelujah" ("praise YHWH") until now. It is as if the phrase were being held in reserve for just this moment, where it serves to convey feelings and emotions repressed during the long years of the ascendancy of the powers. It is difficult to sing when you fear the secret police may be coming to get you at any moment. But not only is singing now permitted, it is absolutely necessary. The tyrants have toppled; how can we keep from singing?

There are four "hallelujahs" in this passage. The first points backward, to the destruction of Babylon. God is praised as the one who "has judged the great prostitute who corrupted the earth with her immorality, and has avenged on her the blood of his servants" (19:1b–2).[1] Moreover, not only has Babylon's system been overcome, but it will never again rise to exercise dominion over God's creatures. The finality of God's judgment is voiced in a second "hallelujah" and confirmed by a visible sign: "The smoke from her goes up forever and ever" (19:3).

The third "hallelujah" is spoken by the twenty-four elders and four living creatures, whose reappearance at this point (last mentioned at 14:3) reminds us that we stand in the presence of the throne. A voice speaks from the throne, inviting all God's slaves to praise him (19:4). The accent thus falls on the church's present-day obedience as expressed in its worship.[2] Finally, the fourth "hallelujah" looks to the future. While the victory over Babylon will never be forgotten, creation's song of praise cannot simply be a continual dwelling on the past. God has redeemed his own with a purpose. He wishes to confer an extraordinary dignity and honor on them, an act of self-glorification that is also an act of grace; an act of self-glorification *because* it is grace. The passage concludes with the voice of a great multitude, crying out with a loud voice:

> "Let us rejoice and exult
>   and give [God] the glory,
> for the marriage of the Lamb has come,
>   and his bride has made herself ready;
> it was granted her to clothe herself
>   with fine linen, bright and pure"—
> for the fine linen is the righteous deeds of the saints. (19:7–8)

19:9–10 "The saints" just spoken of, however, are not some anonymous cohort of perfected souls. They are those who have been addressed as God's covenant partners. They are those who have become participants in the paschal reality of Christ's life and death. They are those whose destiny is to be clothed in the fine linen of the bride. In short, "they" are "us"—the worshiping assembly. The point is underscored when John is once more commanded to write: "Write this: Blessed are those who are invited to the marriage supper of the Lamb. And he said to me, 'These are the true words of God.'"

---

1. Or "avenged the blood of his slaves shed by her hand" (Lattimore 1979: 281).
2. As also indicated, perhaps, by the liturgical "amen" spoken at this point (19:4).

We have heard such pneumatic-prophetic asides to the audience before, most notably in the blessing uttered by the Spirit at 14:13. There it was those "who die in the Lord" who are pronounced blessed, while here it is "those who are invited to the marriage supper of the Lamb." Not, we should note, "those who accept the invitation," although we should not doubt that such is implied: to refuse the invitation or to seek admission without being clothed in "fine linen" would be to miss the point of the feast rather badly (Luke 14:15–24; Matt. 22:1–14). God wishes to honor us at the feast; what if we should insult him by not coming or by coming unprepared? Yet while this dark possibility may be lurking in the background, the force of the utterance is pure beatitude, pure gospel: "All those who are invited are blessed," says the Spirit, "and you, who hear me speaking these words, are among the invited." The coda, "these are the true words of God," is at one level a statement about the words themselves, but more profoundly a comment on the one who speaks them—as if to say, "And I who make this promise am utterly reliable, utterly trustworthy; indeed I am truth itself."[3]

The angel bears the words of God, but he is not God. The passage concludes with the first of two episodes (the other is at 22:8) in which John, attempting to worship the angel, is rebuffed by the horrified creature: "You must not do that! I am a fellow servant with you and your brothers who hold to the testimony of Jesus. Worship God" (19:10a). While the first commandment of the Decalogue is evident in many passages in Revelation, this is among the most explicit. The book posits no continuum of divinity, with angels being more divine than human beings but less divine than God himself. Angels are awesome creatures, but we honor them best not by worshiping them but by heeding their message. While the saying "for the testimony of Jesus is the spirit of prophecy" (19:10b) might at first seem a rather odd conclusion to the angel's warning, a little reflection shows that it is completely appropriate in context. What angels and prophets have in common, what makes them "fellow slaves," is their total devotion to the *martyria Iēsou*, the activity of bearing witness to the true witness. What the angel is saying to John, in effect, is: "Rather than you worshiping me, we ought both to be worshiping and serving Jesus in the energy of the Spirit. It is in *this* way that we will obey the first commandment"—a small but decisive confirmation of the trinitarianism of the Apocalypse.

19:11–16 As if on cue, the Spirit comes upon John and permits him to see the opening of heaven. At the beginning of his journeys, John was rapt into heaven as through an open door (4:1). But the present scene is different. Rather than

---

3. We might press this point one step further. While there is certainly the possibility that God's promises will be misperformed by human beings, this does not invalidate the promises themselves. In the case where the church has "become Babylon," for instance, the Spirit's word of blessing may be wrongly heard as a guarantee that God will "back up" whatever way of life we have chosen. In such cases, the blessing may be experienced as a curse. As Paul reminds us, the Eucharist can kill those who despise the poor (1 Cor. 11:30). But this does not change the Eucharist's character as a "true word of God."

the prophet ascending to see the throne, here the Lord himself comes down from heaven. The drama of the moment is captured in a seventeenth century German hymn, frequently sung in Advent, the season of judgment:

> O Savior, rend the heavens wide;
> Come down, come down with mighty stride;
> Unlock the gates, the doors break down;
> Unbar the way to heaven's crown.[4]

It is Jesus whom John now sees, the Savior who tears heaven open and smashes the doors of hell. This is a Christ image different from all that we have seen so far in Revelation. He is neither the Danielic Son of Man from Rev. 1 nor the slain Lamb who dominates the middle chapters of the book. A figure neither of prophecy nor of sacrifice, the rider on the white horse is a type of Christ the King, Jesus in his specifically messianic identity. The seeds of the present vision have, to be sure, been planted earlier. During his time in the heavenly court, John heard the Lion of the tribe of Judah announced, though what he saw was the Lamb. In the vision of the woman clothed with the sun, it was said that her child would one day "rule all the nations with a rod of iron" (12:5), a phrase echoed here (19:15). The child, we might say, has grown up. He is doing what he was born to do, namely to ride forth and conquer all the enemies of God.

None of this is to say that the great vision of Rev. 5 is being reversed, so that the Lamb is now shown in his true colors as the Lion. This might be true if we were to read the image in a flat way, assimilating Christ, for example, to the universal archetype of the warrior-hero. As if to ward off any such misunderstanding, the figure of the rider is accompanied by a rich set of descriptions that serve to anchor the image within Revelation's larger testimony. He rides a white horse, white being the color of victory (3:4–5; 6:2, 11; 7:9–14). His eyes are like a flame of fire (1:14; 2:18). He wields the sharp two-edged sword (1:16; 2:12). Most important of all, however, is the profusion of names in this passage, hearkening back to the letter to Philadelphia with its threefold promised gift: "The name of my God, and the name of the city of my God, . . . and my own new name" (3:12). While the names in Rev. 19 do not align neatly with these three, there is the same hint that Jesus's identity is complex, at once rich, mysterious, and inexhaustible; he may not be named easily. The four names are these:

1. *Faithful and True* (19:11). Jesus Christ is doubly faithful—to God first of all, of course, but also to his human sisters and brothers. He is faithful with the very faithfulness of God himself; that is why he is also called the "Amen" (3:14; cf. 2 Cor. 1:18). Christ demonstrates that fidelity by his refusal to abandon his people to the tyranny of death. "In righteousness

4. *Lutheran Book of Worship* (Minneapolis: Fortress, 1978), 38.

he judges and makes war," not out of any insecurity or craving for power—
what power could he gain that he does he not already have?—but simply
in order to set us free.[5]

2. *A name written that no one knows but himself* (19:12). A limit is set here.
There is a mystery to Christ's being, which is not erased even in our most
intimate union with him. When Jacob wrestled with the manlike being at
the Jabbok, he extracted a blessing from his opponent, but never did find
out his name (Gen. 32:29).[6] Eighth-century Greek commentator Andreas
remarks that while Christ has many names, including "good," "shepherd,"
"incorruptible," and "deathless," yet the "hiddenness of [his] name signifies his incomprehensible being" (my translation from Swete 1908: 251).
Karl Barth says something remarkably similar. Even the phrase "the Word
of God," writes Barth, is to be seen as "a preliminary and veiling concept
for that other and true concept which the Rider on the white horse has of
Himself, which, as it were, consists and is expressed in His very existence."[7]
What both Andreas and Barth are gesturing toward, perhaps, is the mystery
underlying the "I am" sayings in John's Gospel, which reflect Jesus's unity
with "the great I am," YHWH himself. The Orthodox icon of the *Pantokratōr*
is the visual equivalent of this kind of Christology.

3. *The Word of God* (19:13). But Christ has other, more public names, among
which none is higher or more important than "the Word of God." The
only New Testament witnesses that refer to Jesus directly as the Word are
the Johannine writings and the Apocalypse. Intriguingly, these are also the
witnesses that are most insistent in calling him "the Lamb." This important clue suggests that "word" (*logos*) should be unpacked not as abstract
"thought" or "reason" but as a life, *this* life, a progression on a way that
leads from Bethlehem to Golgotha. In the Fourth Gospel, writes John
Behr, the "function of the revealer is so closely bound up with the person
of Jesus, that he is, in fact, the embodiment of the revelation: he is the
Word made flesh. . . . The identification of the crucified one as the Word
of God is continued in the book of Revelation, where it is the rider who
comes on the white horse, 'clad in a robe dipped in blood,' who is called
by the name 'the Word of God.'"[8] But if Jesus is the Word crucified, this
forbids any interpretation of the "rider" image in terms of the standard,
mythic warrior-hero. The blood in which the rider's robe is dipped is not

---

5. An affinity between truth and freedom is stated in John 8:32.

6. In Charles Wesley's hymn "Wrestling Jacob," the final verse assigns a name to the unknown
god: "'Tis Love, 'tis Love, thou diedst for me. . . . Thy nature and thy name is Love." To my mind
this is the kind of midrash that says too much, since the silence of the text is essential to what it is
trying to say. In Revelation, at any rate, there is no hint that the unknown name might be "love."

7. Karl Barth, *Church Dogmatics*, ed. G. W. Bromiley and T. F. Torrance (Edinburgh: Clark,
1957), 2/2.96.

8. John Behr, *The Way to Nicaea* (Crestwood, NY: St. Vladimir's Seminary Press, 2001), 67.

the blood of his enemies. It is *his own* blood—the same blood in which the martyrs have washed their robes and made them, not red, but white (19:14; cf. 7:14). We see no sword flashing in the hand of this warrior. The only weapon he wields is the word of truth, issuing from his mouth (19:15).

4. *King of kings and Lord of lords* (19:16). The final name is the one that seems most appropriate to the context and requires the least explanation. As King of kings and Lord of lords, Jesus cannot help but enter into battle against the rebellious powers of this world. He is *their* King and *their* Lord; the entire Apocalypse narrates the reassertion of his lordship. This designation for Christ has previously been used by the angel of the beast-Babylon vision, explaining how the Lamb will conquer the ten kings (17:14). The present vision seems to be the fulfillment of that prophecy. The heavenly rider goes forth at the head of his armies. The trumpets sound, signaling the attack. We stand on the cusp of the last battle.

19:17–21 Once again, however, Revelation seems to disappoint our need for a neat, tidy narrative in which the good guys win. To be sure, there is no doubt about the outcome of the conflict. The beast and the false prophet are taken prisoner. Both monsters are thrown into the lake of fire, about which more will be said later on (20:10, 14–15). But just as in the episode of the war in heaven in Rev. 12, there is no battle scene in the proper sense. There could be such a scene only if Jesus were one earthly king among others and was forced to fight using their weapons; but from the sequence of names just given, we know that this is not true. Christ is faithful and true, to God, to himself, and to humankind; to employ death's methods would be the great act of unfaithfulness. He is the Word of God and has only to speak that Word—himself!—in order to vanquish his enemy: "One little word shall fell him." He slays his enemies by his perfect testimony to truth, the sharp two-edged sword (19:21). Revelation shows forth this victory under a series of figures, precisely because it is impossible to narrate in the strict sense, unless we were simply to rehearse the Gospels in general and the Passion Narrative in particular.

What is most striking about this episode is not the military imagery it employs, but the literally unsavory metaphor of feasting on flesh. John sees an angel standing in the sun, summoning birds to "eat the flesh of kings, the flesh of captains, the flesh of mighty men, the flesh of horses and their riders, and the flesh of all men, both free and slave, both small and great" (19:18). The language echoes Ezek. 39, where the image of the carrion birds consuming the dead of Magog signifies the cleansing and purifying of the land of Israel, following the time of its desecration by the *goyim*. It thus serves as a sign of God's self-glorifying among the nations (39:12–16, 21). In Revelation, the image conveys a similar sense of the totality of the divine victory. With deep irony, John refers to this event as "the great supper of God," a phrase that is absent from the Ezekiel text. This supper is a dark type of the marriage supper of the Lamb, a feast of death that consumes, rather than a feast of life that feeds and nourishes. Vernard Eller states the point with characteristic bluntness: "You have your choice; either you can go to the Lamb's supper as *guests*, friends of the bride (better, *members* of the bride), or you can go to this other supper as part of the *menu*, food for the vultures" (1974: 177, emphasis original).

Evil corrupts. To be defined by one's loyalty to the beast is be corrupted absolutely, like being feasted on by birds. The vision thus ends on a rather gruesome note. As we approach the end of Revelation, we can see how the light of God (the angel stands "in the sun"; 19:17) shines on the realities of this present age, calling things by their true names, disclosing them for what they truly are. Among ancient authors, this point was especially underscored by Origen, who read this passage in spiritual terms as signifying the triumph of truth over falsehood. Origen thus explains the multiple crowns that Christ wears (19:12) by the multiplicity of the lies he has to overcome: he wears as many crowns as there are powers that have rebelled against him. As for the name that no one knows but himself, Origen writes that "there are some things which are known to the Word alone" and that it is not given to mere mortals to understand (*Commentary on John* 2.4, quoted from ANF 9.327).[9]

Yet for all Origen's insistence on matters of truth and knowledge, his view of Christ and the Christian life is anything but rationalistic. He knows that the Word's faithfulness to the truth was demonstrated in human flesh and blood. What we say about the Word, we must also say about his followers:

> He is clothed with a garment sprinkled with blood, for the Word who was made flesh and therefore died is surrounded with marks of the fact that his blood was poured out upon the earth, when the soldier pierced his side. For of that passion, even should it be our lot some day to come to that highest and supreme contemplation of the Logos, we shall not lose all memory, nor shall we forget the truth that our admission was brought about by his sojourning in our body. This Word of God is followed by the heavenly armies one and all; they follow the Word as their leader, and imitate him in all things. . . . Look also at the white horses of the followers of the Word and at the white and pure linen with which they were clothed. As linen comes out of the earth, may not those linen garments stand for the dialects on the earth in which those voices are clothed which make clear announcements of things? We have dealt at some length with the statements found in the Apocalypse about the Word of God; it is important for us to know clearly about him. (Origen, *Commentary on John* 2.4 in ANF 9.327)

9. Origen, of course, believed the seer and the Evangelist to be the same author, John the Apostle.

REVELATION 20

THE RULE OF THE SAINTS

To see history doxologically meant for John's addressees that their primordial role within the geopolitics of the *Pax Romana* was neither to usurp the throne of Nero or Vespasian, Domitian or Trajan, nor to pastor Caesar prophetically, but to persevere in celebrating the Lamb's lordship.... They were participating in God's rule over the cosmos, whatever else they were or were not allowed by the civil powers to do.

—John Howard Yoder, *The Royal Priesthood*

The term "the millennium" has historically conjured up images of a thousand-year era of bliss, peace, and prosperity, when "the wolf and the lamb shall graze together; the lion shall eat straw like the ox," and human beings will live in harmony with each other and all creation (Isa. 65:25). "For lo, the days are hastening on, by prophet-bards foretold / When ever with the circling years will come the age of gold."[1] Rightly or wrongly, Rev. 20 has been seen as one of the major sources of this idea. The passage has had a decisive role in shaping Western religious imagination, ranking in importance almost with the new Jerusalem itself.

But will there be such a golden age, and will it come on this earth? Not all think so. The passage has thus been a primary site of theological contestation from the earliest days of Christianity onward. In the modern era, the question is often posed whether to embrace premillennialism[2] (the millennium comes only after

1. Edmund H. Sears, "It Came upon the Midnight Clear," original text accessed from www .cyberhymnal.org. This hymn is one of the great popular expressions of the nineteenth-century social gospel. By the late twentieth century, the phrase "the age of gold" had been changed to "the time foretold" in most hymnals, reflecting the chastened hopes of late modernity.
2. Also called "chiliasm," from Greek *chilios* ("a thousand").

Christ's return in glory), postmillennialism (the second coming is the climax of the millennium), or amillennialism (the whole theme should be treated in spiritual or allegorical fashion). The text thus comes burdened with a set of ready-made expectations and categories before we even pick up the page to read. Special care will be needed simply to attend to what lies before us.

20:1–3 John sees an angel descending from heaven, holding a great chain and the key to "the pit" or "the abyss." The angel then proceeds to bind the dragon for a thousand years. This is the dragon himself, rather than his emissaries the beast and the false prophet (who have just been disposed of; cf. 19:20). The use of a full set of names for the dragon—"the ancient serpent," "the devil," and "Satan"—forms an inclusio with 12:9, the passage where this malevolent being is first introduced. If Rev. 12 marks the beginning of the dragon's story—a beginning that already presages his downfall—the present passage marks his end. The abyss is spoken of as "sealed," always a solemn word in the vocabulary of Revelation. The seal will bind the dragon for a thousand years, after which "he must be released for a little while" (20:3).

20:4–6 Now that the dragon's threat has been removed, John's attention is captured by a group of royal figures: "Then I saw thrones, and judgment was given to those who sat upon them, even to the souls of those who had been beheaded on account of the testimony of Jesus and on account of the word of God, and those who did not worship the beast or his image and did not receive a mark on their foreheads and hands. They came to life and reigned with the Messiah for a thousand years" (my translation).

The plural word "thrones" was previously applied only to the twenty-four elders, the heavenly representatives of the people of God (4:4; cf. 11:16). The language in both cases suggests a royal court. Now, however, the occupants of the thrones are the souls of the slaughtered, whose fate has been troubling us ever since the opening of the fifth seal (6:11). Their fate need trouble us no longer. The great reversal has come at last. Those who were judged are now the judges! Those who were tormented on this earth because of their witness to God and the Lamb are those who rule, who determine what counts as justice! A new social and political order has come into existence in which Jesus Christ rules as King—we have seen this coming all along—but in addition, the order is one in which Christ shares his authority with the martyrs, both the named martyrs whose memory is celebrated in the church and countless others whose names are known to God alone. The martyrs rule with Christ, not because they are necessarily more virtuous than others, but because they embody in history the justice of Christ the King, which is the justice of his love. This new state of affairs is more than simply a reward to the martyrs for their subjection to intolerable cruelties on behalf of the gospel, although it is that too. It is a sign that the church's witness throughout history has not been in vain. As the martyrs signified Christ's crucified and risen body by their lives of witness, so their place on the eschatological thrones of judgment signifies the redemption not just of themselves, but of the whole earth. Imagine an occupied country that is liberated from a corrupt, oppressive regime. The justice system is reconstituted from the ground up, with the traitorous lawyers and judges being replaced by patriots, who had languished in prison or in exile throughout the occupation. A truth commission is set up to determine exactly what happened during the years of terror and what justice should be meted out to the collaborators. That, in effect, is what is happening here; except that in this case, the judges are actually those who had been murdered by the dictators. The martyrs return, to determine the fate of those who had served the beast and dragon—and more positively, perhaps, to write the constitution of the city that will be built on Babylon's ashes.

What makes interpretation of the passage so confusing, however, is that the eschatological consummation is divided into a series of discrete stages. The thousand-year binding of Satan provides the opportunity for the thousand-year reign of the saints, an event John refers to as the "first resurrection" (20:4–6). At the end of this period, two further events ensue: the loosing of Satan, leading to a final battle over the "beloved city" and the casting of Satan into the lake of fire (20:7–10), followed by the raising of the rest of the dead and the final judgment before the throne of God (20:11–15).

On John's account of these matters, *that* there will be a thousand-year reign of some sort seems undeniable. But when will it occur? And what role should we assign it within the larger fabric of Christian eschatology? Discussion of these questions in the history of theology has been extraordinarily complex, and I cannot hope to do full justice to the issues involved. In what follows I will focus on four great theologians, each of whom has a different way of reading Rev. 20: Irenaeus and Origen in the early third century, Augustine in the early fifth century, and Jonathan Edwards in the eighteenth-century era of Enlightenment and revival.

Irenaeus is the most notable representative of historic or classic premillennialism, expecting a visible kingdom of Christ to be established at the second coming.[3] There will, Irenaeus believes, be a golden age on earth, a time marked by extraordinary fecundity and material blessing.[4] In a famous passage, he writes of vines bearing ten thousand branches, each branch bearing ten thousand twigs, each twig bearing ten thousand shoots, each shoot bearing ten thousand clusters, each cluster bearing ten thousand grapes. "And when any one of the saints shall

3. This view is to be distinguished from the dispensational premillennialism popularized in the nineteenth century by J. N. Darby, codified in the influential Scofield Reference Bible, and popularized by Timothy LaHaye's *Left Behind* series. For a theologically responsible guide to this tradition, see Craig R. Koester, *Revelation and the End of All Things* (Grand Rapids: Eerdmans, 2001), 19–26.

4. Already in Jewish thought there was speculation concerning a messianic age preceding the end. Thus 2 Esdras (4 Ezra) 7:28–30: "For my son the Messiah shall be revealed with those who are with him, and those who remain shall rejoice four hundred years. After those years my son the Messiah shall die, and all who draw human breath. Then the world shall be turned back to primeval silence for seven days, as it was at the first beginnings, so that no one shall be left" (NRSV). The author immediately goes on to describe the general resurrection and the final judgment.

lay hold of a cluster another shall cry out, 'I am a better cluster, take me; bless the Lord through me'" (*Against Heresies* 5.33.3).[5] While Irenaeus is aware that some will interpret such passages allegorically, he emphatically rejects this option, seeing it as a watering down of the promises of Christ. In support of his views, he cites Jesus's words spoken over the cup at the Last Supper:

> Thus, then, he [Christ] will himself renew the inheritance of the earth, and will reorganize the mystery of the glory of [his] sons; as David says, "He who hath renewed the face of the earth" (Ps. 104:30). He promised to drink of the fruit of the vine with his disciples, thus indicating both these points: the inheritance of the earth in which the new fruit of the vine is drunk, and the resurrection of his disciples in the flesh. For the new flesh which rises again is the same which also received the new cup. And he cannot by any means be understood as drinking of the fruit of the vine when settled down with his [disciples] above in a supercelestial place; nor, again, are they who drink it devoid of flesh, for to drink of that which flows from the vine pertains to flesh, and not spirit. (*Against Heresies* 5.33.1)

Characteristically for Irenaeus, the view begins with an indubitable Christian practice—the sharing of Christ's risen body in the Eucharist—and argues back to its supposition, namely the goodness of the flesh and its rightful place in the new age (e.g., *Against Heresies* 4.18.4). The citation from Ps. 104 is also significant: it is the *earth*, and not just some "supercelestial place," that stands under the promise of God. Irenaeus's millennialism thus goes hand in hand with his fierce opposition to Gnosticism.

Still, not everyone in the ancient church was satisfied with this literal interpretation of the millennium. One of the most prominent antimillennialists was Origen, who finds in the image of the thousand years a figure for deeper, spiritual realities. Central to his argument is the "abyss" mentioned in Rev. 20:1, which Origen sees as being identical not only with the "deep" of the creation story (Gen. 1:2), but also with the abyss from which the demons begged to be spared in Luke's story of the demoniac (Luke 8:31) (*Homilies on Genesis* 1.2).[6] This is the abyss, Origen believes, in which Satan is imprisoned from the beginning of creation onward; his temporary unbinding occurs only at the time of the crucifixion (Kovacs and Rowland 2004: 206). Like other critics of chiliasm, including his Alexandrian pupils Eusebius and Dionysius, Origen finds something rather crass and literal minded in those who hope for an earthly millennium. He is especially hard on those who imagine that in the new world the "natives of other countries" will serve as slaves to the redeemed and that the latter will live off of the wealth of the nations—for Origen, this is a perversion of the promises given in the prophets: "And to speak shortly, according to the manner of things in this life in all similar

---

5. Irenaeus believes he has this saying on dominical authority: he received it from certain "elders," who heard it from John the apostle, who heard it from Jesus.

6. The "abyss" is absent in Mark's and Matthew's versions of this story.

matters, do they desire the fulfillment of all things looked for in the promises, viz., that what now is should exist again. Such are the views of those who, while believing in Christ, understand the divine Scriptures in a sort of Jewish sense, drawing from them nothing worthy of the divine promises" (*On First Principles* 2.11.2, quoted from ANF 4.297).

In the West, the greatest nonmillennial interpreter was St. Augustine. Like his Alexandrian predecessor, Augustine finds the key to the entire passage in the chaining of Satan. Rather than locating this event at the dawn of time, however, he identifies it with the incarnation. In a brilliant intratextual move, he links Satan's imprisonment with the "binding of the strong man" spoken of by Jesus in Mark 3:27 and parallels (interestingly, both Origen and Augustine connect Rev. 20 with texts concerning exorcisms; see Bettenson 1984: 907). But if so, then the reign of the saints commenced with Christ's *first* coming and will conclude only with his coming again in glory; the "thousand years" is simply the time of the church, which means that the "first resurrection" must be interpreted as the new birth that occurs at baptism.

This does not mean, on Augustine's reading, that Satan is not a force to be reckoned with during the time of his imprisonment. He entices and tempts, drawing fallible human beings into his sphere of influence, rather like a Mafia boss who continues to run the family business from behind bars. But by the grace of God, the saints are protected from the full force of his seductive power. Indeed, the plundering of the strong man is not yet finished, for "even now men are being converted to the faith from the unbelief in which the Devil held them in his power, and without doubt they will go on being converted to the end of the age; and this 'strong man' is obviously being bound in the case of every man who is snatched away from him, as part of his property" (*City of God* 20.8, quoted from Bettenson 1984: 912).

There is something undeniably compelling about Augustine's interpretation of the millennium. Who is Jesus Christ, if not the one who has bound the strong man, not in some far-flung future but at the cross? Augustine's great achievement was to effectively demythologize the millennium, making the text available to generations of Christians who lived in anticipation, not of a golden age on earth, but of the joys of heaven. His views shaped the broad tradition of Western Christian eschatology: both Luther and Calvin were Augustinian antichiliasts. At the same time, we should be cautious about applying the label "amillennialism" to the Augustinian tradition. It does not simply conjure away the millennium of Rev. 20, but interprets it in a specific way, historicizing the thousand years to cover the age of the church's witness.

Origen and Augustine, then, provided resources for a spiritual and ecclesial understanding of the reign of the saints. But the chiliast tradition never disappeared entirely. From time to time it has irrupted with fresh vigor, especially in ages marked by social turmoil, interventions of the Spirit, or both. Not only did it enjoy a long, colorful history in the late Middle Ages, it also played a major role in the great sectarian and revival movements of the modern era. And among the revivalists, none was more floridly, hopefully millennial than Jonathan Edwards.[7]

Although Edwards, like Irenaeus before him, interprets the thousand years in a more or less literal way, he adds a distinctive twist: he places the second coming of Christ *after* the time of the saints' rule (hence the name "postmillennialism"). Negatively, the millennium will be marked by the overthrow of the visible kingdom of the antichrist—for a Reformed evangelical like Edwards, this could mean only Roman Catholicism.[8] Positively, the millennium will be a time of extraordinary progress, virtue, and even beauty. Edwards's extravagant picture of the millennium in *The History of the Work of Redemption* rivals that of Irenaeus:

> These will be times of great peace and love. There shall then be universal peace and good understanding among all the nations of the world, instead of such confusion, wars, and bloodshed as has hitherto been from one age to another. . . .
>
> And then shall all the world be united in peace and love in one amiable society; all nations, in all parts, on every side of the globe, shall then be knit together in sweet harmony, all parts of God's church assisting and promoting the knowledge and spiritual good one of another. A communication shall then be upheld between all parts of the world to that end. . . .
>
> A time of excellent order in the church discipline and government [shall] be settled in his church; all the world [shall then be] as one church, one orderly, regular, beautiful society, one body, all the members in beautiful proportion.[9]

It would be tempting to say that the visual counterpart to Edwards's millennium can be found in *The Peaceable Kingdom*, the extraordinary series of paintings by Quaker artist Edward Hicks, depicting Penn's treaty with the Indians as the fulfillment of the peace prophesied in Isa. 65. While this is true to some extent, Hicks's vision is agrarian and pastoral, whereas Edwards's is urban, progressivist, and forward looking. To apply the imagery of the new Jerusalem, Hicks is more interested in the garden that stands in the middle of the city, whereas Edwards is more interested in the city itself.

It is easy to see how Edwards's version of postmillennialism became a kind of charter for the great pan-Protestant movements of revival and reform that have marked American history, from abolition and women's suffrage to the civil rights movement. We might think of postmillennialism as "an eschatology for

7. For some of what follows I am indebted to the account of Edwards in Robert W. Jenson, *America's Theologian: A Recommendation of Jonathan Edwards* (Oxford: Oxford University Press, 1988), 130–35.

8. There is a bit of irony here, because the modern ecumenical movement was born of a combination of the missionary movement and Protestant liberalism, both infused with a certain Edwardsian postmillennialist spirit. I like to think that Edwards would have interpreted Vatican II as part of the "history of the work of redemption."

9. Jonathan Edwards, *A History of the Work of Redemption*, ed. John F. Wilson, Works of Jonathan Edwards 9 (New Haven: Yale University Press, 1989), 482–84.

the social gospel." Its strength lies in its confidence in the power of the Spirit to transform the structures and institutions of society. In a world where God rules and in which Jesus is raised, the way things have always been done is not a good index for predicting the future. "Behold, I am doing a new thing" (Isa. 43:19). Its vulnerability lies in its tendency to blur the distinction between our own time and the millennium and between the millennium and the final kingdom, as if we could succeed in constructing that kingdom by our own efforts. Modern utopianisms can be seen as postmillennialist heresies. Edwards, on the other hand, argued that humankind's progress in the millennium will provide the very means of its apostasy from God.[10] Conditions on earth will get wonderfully, gloriously better before they get worse; but then they will get very bad indeed, in the tumultuous period just prior to the end.

None of these four versions of the millennium can be derived directly from a reading of Rev. 20. All depend in some way or other on combining this passage with other parts of scripture—in the case of Origen and Augustine, gospel stories that bear witness to Christ's overthrow of the demonic kingdom; in the case of Irenaeus, Jesus's words at the Last Supper; in the case of Edwards, perhaps the works of the Spirit narrated in the early chapters of Acts, now marvelously repeated in New England—as read in light of each theologian's peculiar commitments and beliefs. But neither is this to say that these various readings simply float free of Rev. 20. For all their differences, what they have in common is the conviction that Satan is bound, whether at creation, at the cross, or in the consummation, and that this act of binding creates a space where human life may flourish. The dragon is chained in the abyss. Given the large role played by Satan in the Apocalypse, one can scarcely overestimate the importance of this fact. Even if the seer is far more reticent than later tradition about just what the millennium will look like, the text creates an opening that invites an imaginative filling in on the part of the interpreter. If the powers really were removed from the scene, if Christ ruled and the saints ruled with him, what might not be possible for human beings?

Yet even if our passage creates an opening for such speculation, this is not its major function in context. As argued earlier, the most immediate purpose of this vision is to display the vindication of the martyrs. Justice demands not only that the martyrs triumph, but that they "be seen to triumph. Appearances must be

10. Edwards would have wondered to behold globalization and the internet, but he would not have been surprised. There are passages in his writings that seem to predict both the good and evil possibilities inherent in technology: "Of later times, the communication between distant parts of the habitable globe has grown exceedingly . . . but yet there is not such a communication as to make way for a combination of the wicked world. But this communication is daily growing, and without doubt the long continuance of the glorious times wherein there shall be such a union of the whole earth, and wherein all useful arts and the arts of communication shall be carried to the highest perfection—will have wonderfully established a universal communication between all parts of the world of mankind; so that, when the world apostatizes, the way will be open for an universal combination of the wicked world against Christ and his church" (*Miscellanies* 835 in "Works of Jonathan Edwards Online" at http://edwards.yale.edu/archive [accessed February 29, 2008]).

reversed so that appearance now corresponds to truth."[11] St. Irenaeus understood this. Of our four interpreters, it is he, perhaps, who comes closest to discerning the place of the millennium within Revelation's larger story. A purely transtemporal Christian hope would look all too much like Gnosticism, ceding the world of bodies (and the bodies of victims themselves) to the powers of evil. The occupied territory of creation would remain occupied. While we may not be able to imagine what the millennium will be like, *that* there should be something like this visible, public vindication of the oppressed seems entirely fitting. The point is underscored when we recall the role played by the commemoration of the martyrs and other saints within the eucharistic liturgy.

We may say, then, that while Origen and Augustine are right to stress the basis of the millennium in Christ's liberating action, Irenaeus and Edwards are right to see it as pointing to the Spirit's "eucharistic" renewal of created being. Embodiment matters, history matters, time itself matters: how else to explain John's reiteration of the phrase *chilia etē* ("a thousand years") six times within six verses? The millennium is a discrete period of time, beginning with Satan's imprisonment and ending with his release. It is clearly not yet the new creation itself. But it is something like the this-worldly anticipation or foretaste of that creation. It serves as a guarantee that nature and history will precisely not be "left behind," but raised, transformed, transfigured,[12] into the glorious life of the new age. Commenting on Edwards's version of the millennium, Robert Jenson writes: "The light that shines also in fallen history must once triumph within it, if grace, for which history as a whole is the necessary typological occasion, is to predominate in the eternal balance. That in the millennium, 'Nor will that be true, that few shall be saved,' is the inner-historical image of the final triumph, as are the present sufferings and failures of the church the image of what grace overcomes."[13]

20:7–10 Regardless of how we understand the millennium, it is finite. A thousand years intervene between 20:6 and 20:7, although in story time the passage is instantaneous. We are told that Satan will be released from prison so that he can deceive the nations one last time, a mighty host bearing the mysterious names "Gog and Magog," drawn from "the four corners of the earth."[14] Is this a doublet of the battle scene in 19:11–21 or in some sense its continuation? If there is a difference, it consists in the Word of God in the earlier episode waging an offensive campaign against the kings allied with the beast and the whore, while

11. Richard Bauckham and Trevor Hart, *Hope against Hope: Christian Eschatology at the Turn of the Millennium* (Grand Rapids: Eerdmans, 1999), 134; see also Bauckham 1993b: 106–10.

12. The Hegelian term *aufgehoben* (nominal form, *Aufhebung*) might also be used here, so long as one makes clear that evil and death are in no sense a necessary moment in God's relation to the world. Evil is evil. Death is death. Their foul stench resists all clever dialectical maneuvers aimed at normalizing them.

13. Jenson, *America's Theologian*, 135, citing Edwards, *Miscellanies* 1339.

14. The names are borrowed from Ezek. 39, source of the carrion imagery in Rev. 19. They have no particular significance, other than as a suitably barbaric-sounding designation for the enemies of God.

in the present scene it is Satan who attacks: "They marched up over the broad plain of the earth and surrounded the camp of the saints and the beloved city" (20:9). No longer the great city, but the beloved city! Now we see why this scene could take place only after the millennium. The "beloved city" is the human city, reconstituted, no longer as Babylon, but as the earthly counterpart of the new Jerusalem that will descend from heaven. There exists a truly human city, and it is worth defending—an extraordinary outcome, given everything we have seen so far in the book of Revelation.

This also helps to explain what is perhaps the largest question hovering over this scene: why is it necessary for Satan to be unbound at all? If he is locked in the abyss, why not keep him there? The answer, perhaps, is that it is important to demonstrate the solidity and enduring character of what God has done for his people. Satan, we will soon learn, is to be forever consigned to the lake of fire. But even if he were *not* so consigned, he would represent no threat to the city of God, which is also the human city. Under God's protection, the city is absolutely secure:

> God is in the midst of her; she shall not be moved;
>   God will help her when morning dawns.
> The nations rage, the kingdoms totter;
>   he utters his voice, the earth melts.
> The LORD of hosts is with us;
>   the God of Jacob is our fortress. (Ps. 46:5–7)

This great psalm of Zion goes on to state that God "makes wars cease to the end of the earth; he breaks the bow and shatters the spear; he burns the chariots with fire." And that is precisely what happens here. Fire comes down from heaven and consumes the armies of Gog and Magog. The devil is thrown into the same lake of fire where the beast and the false prophet are already burning.

If the millennium is the visible sign of God's "yes" to his creation, then the lake of fire symbolizes the divine "no," his rejection of all that would threaten it. Significantly, the demonic powers are cast into the lake in reverse order of their appearance. The beast and the false prophet were the last to appear on stage (13:1) and are the first to go (19:20). Then comes their master the dragon (20:10), who was introduced as the enemy of the sun-clad woman (12:3). Last of all comes death himself, whom the Son of Man alludes to in the opening lines of the book (1:18), but who is now consigned to an eternity of torment (20:14). The order is suggestive of a hierarchy in the demonic realm, underscoring that even Satan, that ancient serpent, was but a pawn in the hand of death. But now the whole panoply of evil has been disposed of. There are truly no more enemies left to be defeated.

20:11–15 Judgment is not, however, executed simply at a cosmic level. It pertains to each human soul. John now sees the dead, *tous nekrous*, standing before the judgment seat of God. Some interpreters take "the dead" in this scene to refer only to worshipers of the beast, since the Lamb's followers have already been raised to life (Eller 1974: 191). Yet this interpretation seems forced. Surely the martyrs are among those whose names are found in the book of life (20:15). If so, then they, too, must be among those summoned before the throne of judgment. Their thousand-year reign with Christ does not exempt them from this general requirement. "The dead" means, in fact, all the dead. This vast multitude includes not only those who have returned to dust in the usual way, but those who have been swallowed up in the chaos of the sea, indeed all who have been subject to the tyranny of death and hades, that is, every human being who has ever lived. There is no inhabitant of the present age whose life is not overshadowed by the power of death. The all-encompassing character of the judgment is also announced in the inclusion of both "great and small" (20:12), language that hearkens back to the opening of the sixth seal, where we saw millionaires, generals, freemen, and slaves, all cowering together before the wrath of the Lamb. This is one courtroom where the rich and powerful cannot tilt the odds in their favor and where the claims of the poor will not be forgotten. The impartiality of God is among the most deeply seated convictions in all of scripture (Deut. 10:17; cf. Acts 10:34).

It is fitting that, in a book so filled with the imagery of books and scrolls, the final judgment should be conducted literally by "the book(s)." The book is the great instrument of human memory.[15] What is written in a book will not be forgotten, but will leave an imprint, a material trace, that resists the human temptation to forget or to alter the historical record.[16] "Books were opened" (*biblia ēnoichthēsan*), John writes, and "the dead were judged by what was written in the books, according to what they had done" (20:12a, c). There is a wonderful objectivity about all of this. The books of our lives do not lie. It is not we, in the end, who get to narrate our own stories, but God, whose all-seeing eye renders us utterly transparent and vulnerable—or, to alter the metaphor, whose two-edged sword lays us bare, disclosing the truth of the heart (Heb. 4:12). Strange as it may seem, this too is grace: it is important that the end of my story (and of all stories) be marked by a moment of absolute truth-telling, free from the distorting influence of human self-deception and self-interest. There is grace, too, in the conviction that there will be no impunity for the rapist, the murderer, the torturer, or for the secret police who come knocking at the door and cart away the innocent, who mysteriously are

---

15. For the image of the books, see Dan. 7:10. Augustine writes that the last judgment is executed by "a kind of divine power which will ensure that all the actions, good or bad, of every individual will be recalled to mind and presented to the mind's view with miraculous speed, so that each man's knowledge will accuse or excuse his conscience, and thus each and all will be judged simultaneously. This divine power is no doubt called a 'book' because it ensures the recollection of the facts, and those facts are, as we may say, 'read' in the process" (*City of God* 20.14, quoted from Bettenson 1984: 924–25).

16. Of course, human books may be tampered with; thus the dire warning at the very end of Revelation to anyone who would alter the words of the prophecy (22:18–19).

never heard from again. In the last judgment all the "disappeared" will reappear, while those who violated them will be called to account.[17] For "nothing is hidden that will not be made manifest, nor is anything secret that will not be known and come to light" (Luke 8:17).

Grace, then; but a hard grace, a judgment in which our own lives are called as testimony against us. Satan and his false accusations are gone now (cf. Rev. 12:10). There is only the judge and the books that speak the truth. Yet this is not quite accurate, for John tells us that beside *the* books another book stands opened, namely "the book of life" (20:12b). This book was mentioned three times before, once on the lips of Christ himself (3:5) and twice in connection with the slaughtered Lamb (13:8 and, implicitly, 17:8). From the last passage we learn that this book has existed "from the foundation of the world," and from the second we learn that the Lamb himself is integral to God's design for his creation. The world was made through and for Christ (John 1:3; Rom. 11:36; Col. 1:16). And therefore it is he who gets to judge the world (Matt. 25:31–46; Acts 17:31; 2 Cor. 5:10; but cf. Rom. 14:10). While John tells us that the dead are judged by "him who sits on the throne"—in Revelation, always code language for God the Father—the presence of the book of life reminds us that the Father does nothing without the Son; just as, in the judgment scene from Daniel that serves as a model for our passage, the Ancient of Days is joined by a heavenly son of man, to whom is given dominion over "all peoples, nations, and languages" (Dan. 7:13–14). The judgment of God is the judgment of the *triune* God, which means that it is the judgment of the Lamb, the risen crucified. The church confesses this truth each time it says the Nicene Creed: "He will come again in glory to judge the living and the dead, and his kingdom will have no end."

As Christ holds the keys to death and hades, his appearance here immediately leads to these powers giving up "their" dead, after which they are cast into the lake of fire (20:14). The Lord of life triumphs, with the consequence that death is rendered null, impotent, subject to a perpetual state of self-consuming futility, the lake of fire, about which nothing further can be said, unless we employ the metaphor of

---

17. In a notorious passage, philosopher Richard Rorty writes that "when the secret police come, when the torturers violate the innocent, there is nothing to be said to them of the form 'There is something within you which you are betraying. Though you embody the practices of a totalitarian society that will endure forever, there is something beyond those practices which condemns you'"; *Consequences of Pragmatism: Essays, 1972–1980* (Minneapolis: University of Minnesota Press, 1982), xlii. Although Rorty certainly did not believe the innocent should be tortured, as a radical historicist he can back up his views only by an appeal to convention: "This is not how *we* do things in the 'civilized' West." Not only is this rather shaky ground for moral conviction, it has the effect of erecting "our way of life" as an arbitrary standard to which others must adhere, but which is itself immune from criticism. For the Christian, of course, as for the Jew and the Muslim, there *is* that in ourselves that we betray when we do evil. We are violating the law of God, which bears witness to our nature as God's good creatures.

---

death itself: the "second death," John calls it.[18] However we may imagine this, the important thing is that "death shall have no dominion," as Dylan Thomas put it, even if he was not seeking to describe the Christian hope. All that remains in the Apocalypse is the image-laden, metaphorical description of what a city built on life might look like. This is the happy task John undertakes in Rev. 21–22.

It would be an evasion, however, not to say something about the somber note on which the present vision concludes: "And if anyone's name was not found written in the book of life, he was thrown into the lake of fire." For the individual, the second death means death rendered irrevocable and thus permanent, death eternalized, though not in such a way that creaturely existence ceases: the second death is a fate suffered *by* creatures. Whatever one might say about the eschatological theory known as "annihilationism," it does not seem to apply to Revelation.[19]

Who is in this dark, seething lake? Quite simply, anyone whose "name was not found written in the [Lamb's] book of life." If we press this question one step further and ask just who *that* is, we will come up empty. No more than the rest of the New Testament does the Apocalypse encourage us to be predictive about just who is, and who is not, allotted a place in the new creation. The scale and scope of God's work—the overcoming of Satan and the powers; the gathering of a new people out of all tribes, languages, and nations; the establishment of a new *polis*—certainly does not compel us to a narrow view as to its final outcome. To reprise Edwards: "Nor will that be true, that few shall be saved."

What we can say with confidence is that Revelation draws the strongest connection imaginable between the Lamb and life—the book of life, the water of life, the tree of life—and that it sees its hearers' participation in that life as a matter of greatest urgency.[20] Life, the living one, has intruded into their midst, both as compelling power and as tender solicitation. In this regard, we might think of the many blessings we have heard uttered by the life-giving Spirit. "Blessed are those who hear" the words of the prophecy (1:3). "Blessed are the dead who die in the Lord" (14:13). "Blessed are those who are invited to the marriage supper of the Lamb" (19:9). And in our present passage: "Blessed and holy is the one who shares in the first resurrection! Over such the second death has no power, but they will be priests of God and of Christ, and they will reign with him for a thousand years" (20:6).

18. It is not quite clear how to relate John's language in this passage to Paul's affirmations about death being "destroyed" or "swallowed up in victory" (1 Cor. 15:26, 54). Whereas Paul seems to assume the annihilation of death, Revelation suggests rather that it is damned and continues to serve a function in the new eon.

19. George Hunsinger, *Disruptive Grace: Studies in the Theology of Karl Barth* (Grand Rapids: Eerdmans, 2000), 226–49.

20. Along with "Lamb" and "truth," "life" is a term that seems to establish a connection, however tenuous and elusive, between Revelation and the rest of the Johannine literature. *Zōē* and its cognates appear some fifty times in the course of the book.

Christ is life, and to be joined to him—to be a branch of his vine or to sup with him at his table—is to participate in that life. There will indeed be a judgment according to our works, and it will be unsparing: "I know your works!" The books do not lie. But on the other hand, we are not told that places in the heavenly city will be assigned on the basis of what is found in these books. Rather, what is decisive is whether one's name is found written in the Lamb's book of life, the book that is *the* book in an absolute sense. Karl Barth observes that there is no "book of death" corresponding to the "book of life," for this suggests that life and death are two equally balanced possibilities, powers contending with each other in ceaseless conflict. Nor may we import the dualism into the book of life itself, so that we would have to picture it as having two columns marked "saved" and "lost."[21]

The Lamb, slain from the foundation of the world, lives and dies for the life of the world, even the world that is exposed in all its falsehood by the unchanging eye of God. As the Lamb alone is worthy to open the seven-sealed scroll of history, so he alone holds the key to the book of life. It is, after all, *his* book. Rather than inviting us to play guessing games about who is in the book and who is not, the Apocalypse, with its sevenfold blessings uttered by the Spirit, is about the serious business of summoning its hearers to the life that is in the slaughtered Lamb. He speaks blessings, not curses; he absorbs the violence of the violent, he does not seek retribution; his robe is stained with the blood that washes clean our robes and makes them to be garments of victory. He is the very Lord of life. The rhetoric of Revelation is a rhetoric of promise and hope, of participation and daring, of faithfulness and witness; a rhetoric that bids us accept the verdict of the true witness on our lives and to reject every lie proffered by the powers.

"Blessed are those who are invited to the marriage supper of the Lamb." In the vision that follows, we will begin to keep the feast.

---

21. Karl Barth, *Church Dogmatics*, ed. G. W. Bromiley and T. F. Torrance (Edinburgh: Clark, 1957), 2/2.16.

REVELATION 21

THE BRIDE OF THE LAMB

The liturgy is nothing else, but the gathering together of mankind in the house of the Father. It is that marriage feast of the Lamb where all are called, to be reconciled in the Body of the only Son, at the same time with the Father and between themselves. Here all the scattered children are to congregate and to be made at last one in the Bride of the Lamb, the Church.

—Louis Bouyer, *Liturgy and Architecture*

The Apocalypse opens with letters to seven churches in seven cities. Asia Minor of the late first century may be culturally remote from us, but it is, for all that, a relatively familiar and this-worldly setting. We think we can find our feet here. The book then takes us on a wild, Spirit-driven itinerary in which we behold God's throne, see the scroll of history opened, suffer earth's tribulation, meet terrifying monsters, observe with horror the degradation of the human city, and finally see the dead judged and death itself destroyed. Through it all, there have been three constants: (1) the uniqueness and sovereignty of the Creator God of Israel; (2) the victory of the slaughtered Lamb, both in itself and as witnessed in the lives of his followers; and (3) the gathering of a community from all peoples, tribes, nations, and languages, the "kingdom" and "priestly people" alluded to in the book's opening lines (1:6).

21:1–4 Now, as we near the end of the book, we see the convergence of these three themes. The vision in Rev. 21 opens with a great divine act of re-creation. As only God can create, calling suns and stars, water and land into existence at the beginning, so only God can restore, bringing into being a new world in which his will for his creatures is fully realized. Apocalypse recapitulates Genesis.[1] A fresh start is made. The first heaven and the first earth are not said to be destroyed, like death and hades in the previous chapter. John simply says that they "passed away" (*apēlthan*). "The sea was no more," not because the ocean as such is cursed, but because the sea in Israel's imagination represents chaos, darkness, the deep. Now chaos yields to cosmos, disorder to peace, death to life.

God does this. It is not the outcome of any human scientific or technological achievement. The new city comes "down out of heaven from God," a sheer miracle, a gift apocalyptically bestowed at the end of history and not the outcome of history itself. The unmistakable apocalyptic signature here is the word *idou* ("behold"), uttered first by a "loud voice from the throne" (21:3) and repeated by "he who was seated on the throne" (21:5). This unambiguous act of divine speech is the first such we have heard since 1:8. *Idou* invites us not to act but to see, not to perform but to watch in awe, not to take action but to rejoice, welcoming the city's gracious manifestation among us.

This is most emphatically not to say that history is meaningless or that God does not invite human beings to build their cities with as much ingenuity and creativity, but also honor shown to God and justice performed toward the neighbor, as they can muster. There is a place in Christian theology for saying that "grace does not destroy nature, but perfects it" (Thomas Aquinas, *Summa theologiae* 1.1.8 §2). This is as true on the social and political level as it is in individual life. Yet such language has its limits, and the Apocalypse provides us with some sense of what those limits are. The new Jerusalem is not constructed by the inhabitants of the human city (grace as a mere extension or achievement of nature), nor is it imposed *on* the human city as something fundamentally alien and unrelated to its common life (grace replacing nature, or awkwardly imposed on it as a superfluous "upper story"). The city, rather, comes "down out of heaven from God," a new creation, a category that presses our thought to the limit, for how can it be creation if it is new? And how can it be new if it is still creation? In his discussion of the Eucharist, Thomas Aquinas writes that while the substances of the bread and wine are transformed into the body and blood of Christ—thus, "transubstantiation"—this does not mean that these creaturely substances are destroyed in the process. Christ's body and blood replace bread and wine, they do not annihilate them (*Summa theologiae* 3.75.3). They just "become Jesus."[2] God does no violence to the created world in order to be with his people, even if this act of self-bestowal is beyond anything this world has to offer.

1. For a general treatment of Genesis motifs in the New Testament, see Paul S. Minear, *Christians and the New Creation: Genesis Motifs in the New Testament* (Louisville: Westminster John Knox, 1994).
2. Transubstantiation is offered here as an analogy only. I assume the style of interpretation of the doctrine that has become standard in ecumenical dialogues, such as the Anglican-Roman Catholic International Commission.

By analogy, we can say that while the human city in its distorted incarnation as Babylon is overthrown, it is not, as the earthly city, handed over to destruction. Significantly, Babylon is never shown being cast into the lake of fire. Rather, the fire of God's love transforms it into Jerusalem, in a miracle to which the otherwise useful language of nature and grace is simply inadequate. To put it another way, the apocalyptic "behold" speaks the language not simply of grace, but of resurrection. As the risen Jesus stood miraculously among his disciples saying "peace be with you," so Jerusalem, city of peace, descends from heaven, raising up the human city from the ashes of its disgrace, a miraculous transformation that even the Apocalypse can only hint at.

The goal of all this is the establishing of communion: "Behold, the dwelling place [*skēnē*] of God is with man. He will dwell with them [*skēnōsei met' autōn*], and they will be his people, and God himself will be with them as their God" (21:3). The language is drawn from the law (Lev. 26:12) and the prophets (Ezek. 37:27), reminding us that the people of *this* God can only be Israel and not some generic "humanity." If grace does not destroy nature, still less does the new creation annul God's covenant with Abraham! The language bespeaks a covenantal sense of mutuality, God with his people, the people with their God. The long history that reaches from Moses to David to Jeremiah and beyond is not undone. Yet just as in the new creation imagery, John seems to envisage a certain return to the beginning: thus the image of the desert tabernacle, the *skēnē*, the tent of the divine presence. The tape is being rewound, past the historical Jerusalem with its compromised history, past even the settlement of the land, to the time of Israel's wilderness wanderings. It is as though God's new dwelling with Israel will combine the splendor of life in the city with the simplicity of life in the wilderness, when, for Jeremiah anyway, the bride of YHWH was still faithful to her spouse (Jer. 2:1–2).

But *skēnē* is also the language of incarnation. It is the term John the Evangelist uses to speak of the Son of God's "tenting" or "tabernacling" in human flesh (John 1:14). Not, of course, that the heavenly city is identical with Christ's historical sojourn in the flesh. But the city inhabits the space of divine-human communion he has established. The "dwelling of God is with man," first and decisively in Christ himself, then in the church so far as it is joined to his divine-human, life-giving person. I said earlier that the Lamb's victory is the second of three constant themes in Revelation. If this theme seems fairly muted here,[3] it is because that victory has by now been universally acknowledged and no longer requires display in the form of costly witness.[4] The battle is over; it is time for celebrating the fruits of victory.

---

3. An important exception is the verb *gegonan* ("it is done!") in 21:6, which may be taken as an echo of Jesus's cry of victory at the cross (→16:17–21).

4. Indeed, the noun *martyria* is entirely absent from Rev. 21–22, while the verb *martyreō* is used only in Christ's (22:16) and John's (22:18, 20) personal address to the reader at the very end.

21:9–11 The bride, the wife of the Lamb, is announced. The trope of bride and bridegroom runs throughout scripture and can be read at multiple levels. In the simplest sense, they are the individual human couple, whose mutual longing is an aspect of God's good creation:

> By night on my bed I sought him whom my soul loveth. I sought him, but I found him not. I will rise now, and go about the city in the streets, and in the broad ways I will seek him whom my soul loveth. . . . The watchmen that go about the city found me: to whom I said, "Saw ye him whom my soul loveth?" It was but a little that I passed from them, but I found him whom my soul loveth: I held him, and would not let him go. (Song 3:1–4 KJV)

It is surely no accident that in this, among the most haunting and sensual passages in all of scripture, the woman should conduct her search through the streets of "the city." What city could this possibly be but Jerusalem? Jewish and Christian tradition have always found in the lovers of the Song of Songs a figure of YHWH's marriage to Israel or of Christ's love for the church. The frustrated longing on both sides of this relationship may be understood as the energy that propels the whole biblical narrative. God loves his people, but is rebuffed and rejected; the people long for God, but foolishly lose their way in the streets of the great city, where they fall victim to violent and abusive thugs.

But now, the woman and her lover find each other at last. "Then came one of the seven angels who had the seven bowls full of the seven last plagues and spoke to me, saying, 'Come, I will show you the Bride, the wife of the Lamb'" (Rev. 21:9). It may seem strange that an angel of wrath should lead John to his vision of the bride, but it is also dramatically appropriate, helping to resolve a tension. The anger of God is not a perfection internal to his being, like his love or his holiness. It is that love and holiness as expressed in judgment on fallen creatures. The judgment is past, the victory has been achieved, and so the angel of the bowls can be released for a more pleasing and natural form of service: leading the seer on a tour of the heavenly city.

Across human cultures, the central focus of attention at a wedding is generally the bride rather than the bridegroom. We can give anthropological reasons for this: concern for the bride's virginity on the part of the husband, her family's desire to show off their wealth and the dowry she brings to the marriage, or simply the universal human response to feminine beauty. Interestingly, analogies to all three factors can be found here. The sign of the bride's purity is her being clothed in "fine linen," which is "the righteous deeds of the saints" (19:8; cf. the male virgins in 14:4). The description of the city that follows is not least of all concerned to show off its wealth, which, unlike the riches of Babylon, has not been gained by exploitation. And the city is, of course, beautiful, "having the glory of God, its radiance like a most rare jewel, like a jasper, clear as crystal" (21:11).

21:12–14 The city has a great, high wall. This in itself is interesting. The city is not infinitely extended in all directions, but a defined, habitable space. The new Jerusalem will be blessedly free from suburban sprawl: its inhabitants will not need cars to get around! But while the city is bounded, it is also open, having twelve gates, with three gates each facing north, south, east, and west. On the gates are inscribed "the names of the twelve tribes of the sons of Israel" (21:12). This is the culmination of imagery encountered throughout the book. The city of God is cosmic, universal, the pinnacle of creation—thus the four marks of the compass—while at the same time entry *into* the city is along the particular road that Israel traveled with God. "And the wall of the city had twelve foundations, and on them were the twelve names of the twelve apostles of the Lamb" (21:14). Paul likewise speaks of the church being built up "on the foundation of the apostles and prophets, Christ Jesus himself being the cornerstone" (Eph. 2:20). The apostolic character of the *ekklēsia* is no mere accident. It is the perpetual reminder that it is Jesus Christ we are called to build on, not some "other gospel," and that this gospel is identical with what has been handed down from the apostles. What is true of the church in history is true of the city of God in eternity.

21:15–21 As John himself once measured the temple, symbolizing the holiness of God's people set apart from the world (11:1–2), so now his guiding angel measures the city with a rod of gold. It turns out to be a cube, each side equaling 12,000 stadia (about 1,500 miles). The cubical shape is a sign of the city's perfection, its inherent harmony and order, not only in architectural but in political and economic terms: "A city that is bound firmly together," enjoying peace within its borders (Ps. 122:3, 7). We should perhaps picture a translucent golden cube (Rev. 21:11, 18), with the city's towers and dwellings arranged in a kind of latticelike structure inside; like many of the visions in Revelation, we cannot help but try to imagine it, and we cannot imagine it. Many commentators point out that the wall, measuring 144 cubits (roughly 215 feet), is absurdly small relative to the size of the city itself. It cannot possibly be a defensive wall. In any case, there are no more enemies left to repel. As the description in 21:19–21 makes clear, the wall—besides defining the boundary of the city against the world outside—is essentially ornamental in character. The jewels are part of the finery with which the bride greets her husband. Unlike the whore, whose "gold and jewels and pearls" derived from the booty plundered by the kings and merchants (17:4; cf. 18:16), the bride's adornment is a gift that comes to her from God.[5]

21:22–23 The vision reaches its surprising climax in John's report of something he does *not* see, namely, a temple. The city has no need of a temple, "for its temple is the Lord God the Almighty and the Lamb." Their radiance is such that

---

5. For Old Testament references to bridal jewelry, see Song 1:10; Isa. 61:10. Ezekiel describes how YHWH stripped unfaithful Israel of its jewels, which it had treated as idols (16:17, 39; 23:26). Finally, there is a possible echo here of the twelve precious stones that adorned the breastplate of the high priest in Exod. 28:17–20.

even the illumination provided by sun and stars is superfluous. Special sacraments are no longer necessary, because in the new eon "all truth will be openly and perfectly revealed" (Aquinas, *Summa theologiae* 3.61.4 §1). The life of the city will not point to God, it will be *in* God. But John's remark that "[the city's] lamp is the Lamb" permits us to say something St. Thomas does not: in the age to come, the vision of God will be mediated through the risen, glorified flesh of Jesus. The heavenly city is not the end of the church, for the church is simply God's people. It is, however, the end of religion, the demarcation of sacred space from profane space and liturgical time from ordinary time, for the purpose of making present the absent god.

21:24–27 But perhaps the most unexpected thing of all in the new Jerusalem comes in the lines that follow: "By [the city's] light will the nations walk, and the kings of the earth will bring their glory into it, and its gates will never be shut by day—and there will be no night there. They will bring into it the glory and the honor of the nations."

How did these kings get here? Are these the same kings who consorted with Babylon and participated in the beast's warfare against the Lamb? While the kings in the present passage do not seem to be inhabitants of the city, they are evidently welcome in it. This scene, in fact, represents the eschatological fulfillment of Christ's identity as "the ruler of kings on earth" (1:5). The Messiah rules not only over his people Israel, but over the *goyim*. Christ's exercise of power radically differs from that of the earthly city, as Bernd Wannenwetsch comments: "Rome/Babylon's wealth was extorted from all the world, in the New City the kings of the earth are said to bring their glory into it—of their own free will."[6]

John's report that the gates of the city are never shut also tells us something important (21:25). The kings come and go. The nations pour in with their treasures, enriching the city; must we not also assume that they are enriched by it? It is not that commerce has disappeared, but only the unjust commerce of the old eon, which gorged some while starving others. Moreover, the openness of the city's gates to the guest, the stranger, and the pilgrim—perhaps even to the idly curious and the sightseer!—suggests that this is the very opposite of a closed society. We define our human spaces by the goods they hold in, but also by the threats they help to exclude. But the new Jerusalem rests securely in the generosity and the peace of God. It is fundamentally unthreatened. This extends to the city, while clearly established at the very center of the earth, not (unlike Babylon) feeling the need to take over the earth. There is, we are surprised to discover, an "outside" to Jerusalem, a land beyond, in which Christ reigns, in a different way but with no less authority than in Zion. Wannenwetsch notes that while there may be people living outside the gates (21:27), there is no suggestion that these have been forcibly

6. Bernd Wannenwetsch, "Representing the Absent in the City," in *God, Truth, and Witness: Engaging Stanley Hauerwas* (Grand Rapids: Brazos, 2005), 179.

excluded. Rather, they have chosen this lot for themselves. They simply recognize their "essential non-fit with the city."[7]

That "nothing unclean will ever enter it, nor anyone who does what is detestable or false," should come as no surprise to anyone. This is after all the holy city; the practices and attitudes of Babylon will not be tolerated here. But the holiness of God goes hand in hand with the mercy and patience of God. Although this vision is not quite finished—it extends through 22:5, so that I conclude the discussion of it in the next chapter—I pause here to note the remarkable picture of a city at peace with itself and its neighbors, receiving gifts (not tribute) from kings and shining with the radiant splendor of God and the Lamb.

7. Ibid., 176. The entire preceding paragraph is much indebted to Wannenwetsch's insightful reading.

REVELATION 22

COME, LORD JESUS!

Belief in the resurrection is not the solution to the problem of death. God's "beyond" is not the beyond of our cognitive faculties. . . . God is beyond in the midst of life. The church stands, not at the boundaries where human powers give out, but in the midst of the village.

—Dietrich Bonhoeffer, *Letters and Papers from Prison*

22:1–5 The account of the new Jerusalem continues from Rev. 21. Having been shown the external appointments of the city, its boundaries, gates, and foundation walls, John is offered a glimpse of what lies at the very heart of the city—what makes it a place of life: "Then the angel showed me the river of the water of life, bright as crystal, flowing from the throne of God and of the Lamb through the middle of the street of the city; also, on either side of the river, the tree of life with its twelve kinds of fruit, yielding its fruit each month. The leaves of the tree were for the healing of the nations" (22:1–2).[1]

As is true throughout the world, but especially in the arid Middle East, a city without an adequate water supply would be useless. The river John sees has its antecedents in the water that flowed out of the temple in Ezekiel's vision of a restored Jerusalem (Ezek. 47:1–12) and ultimately in the river that watered the garden of Eden (Gen. 2:9–10). In both of these passages, the water serves for irrigation. Moreover, both of these passages have a particular focus on trees: in the

1. The syntax in 22:1–2 is ambiguous. Another possibility is to place a full stop after "of the Lamb" and to read 22:2 continuously, as in NRSV margin: "In the middle of the street of the city, and on either side of the river, is the tree life."

case of Genesis, the mysterious tree of the knowledge of good and evil, and the
even more mysterious tree of life; in the case of Ezekiel, a grove of trees bearing
fruit every month and whose leaves shall be "for healing."

In both the Genesis and the Ezekiel passages, the water is, first of all and *ad
litteram*, simply water: God provides for his creatures this most fundamental
necessity of life. But already in these passages, there is a hint that water is more
than simply water, as indeed the trees are more than just trees. Both the garden
in Genesis and the city in Ezekiel are places where God and humanity dwell
together in harmony, communion, *life*, a life that goes beyond (though it also
affirms) the biological existence of the creature. The economy will be marked
not by scarcity but by abundance, and the food and water will not only sustain,
they will give joy:

> There is a river whose streams make glad the city of God,
>   the holy habitation of the Most High. (Ps. 46:4)

> Jesus said to her, "Everyone who drinks of this water will be thirsty again, but
> whoever drinks of the water that I will give him will never be thirsty forever. The
> water that I will give him will become in him a spring of water welling up to eternal
> life." (John 4:13–14; cf. 6:35)

The passage thus marks the climax of the "Apocalypse as Genesis" motif, which
I have noted several times. But this is no return to Eden. The leaves of the trees
growing on each side of the river are, John notes, specifically "for the healing of
the nations," a slight but crucial modification of Ezekiel, who had said simply that
the leaves are "for healing." We stand on the far side of history, with its war and
violence, its cruelty and oppression, its typical connivance between political power
(the kings of the earth) and corrupt, disordered desire (Babylon). All of that is
connoted by "the nations." But now the nations are redeemed in a double way:
(1) by the gathering of a people out of all nations, tribes, and languages to be the
inhabitants of the heavenly city, the bride of the Lamb; and (2) by a mysterious
healing of *the nations themselves*, symbolized by the grove of trees growing on either
side of the river. If the riding forth of the word of God was about truth-telling
and if the vision of the millennium was about justice, then the present vision is
to a great extent about *therapeia*, the healing of the human city from every hurt
inflicted by the powers.[2]

There is no trace in this passage of any opposition between humanity and
nature, the city and the garden. The "built" world and the "natural" world are
mutually reinforcing. Writing in the idiom of the nineteenth century, F. J. A. Hort
describes the heavenly city as "the elaborated and thickly aggregated home of man

---

2. It is not the least part of Tolkien's genius to recognize that victory over evil does not automati-
cally bring healing in its wake. The latter takes both time and care. The concluding chapters of *The
Return of the King* make this point in multiple ways. King Aragorn is a type of the king-as-healer.

after a process of civilisation, set down in the midst of the enclosure of the fresh world of nature, from which his ideal history takes its first start."[3] Given the city's miraculous descent from heaven, the word "process" in this definition might be questioned. Otherwise it neatly summarizes the city's twofold character, both as Jerusalem restored and as Eden renewed.

The water of life, John tells us, flows "from the throne of God and of the Lamb." An ancient tradition sees the river as the Holy Spirit; indeed, the verb for "flowing" in 22:1 is *ekporeuomenon*, the same word used in the Nicene-Constantinopolitan Creed to denote the Spirit's procession "from the Father." The image in Revelation might seem to be a proof-text for the Western teaching that the Son, too, is a cosource for the Spirit—"from the Father *filioque*," meaning "and the Son."[4] This argument will probably seem persuasive just to the extent that one is already inclined to view the economy of salvation as a clue to the inner life of the Trinity. Revelation's own concern is less with establishing inner-trinitarian relations than with affirming the Spirit's central role in the ecology of the new age; and here he certainly is a joint gift of the Father and the Son. Together, they irrigate the city with the one who is himself "the Lord and giver of life."

While the new creation is not a romantic return to Eden, it does reverse the catastrophe that began to be unleashed there; thus John's comment: "No longer will there be anything accursed, but the throne of God and of the Lamb will be in it, and his servants will worship him. They will see his face, and his name will be on their foreheads" (22:3–4). The cursing of the ground that began in Eden is now undone (Gen. 3:17). Instead of the mark of Cain, the city's inhabitants will bear the name of Christ, in fulfillment of the promise made to the church at Philadelphia (Rev. 3:12). Indeed, setting the vision of the new Jerusalem side by side with the promises made to the conquerors is an instructive exercise. In some cases the correspondence between promise and fulfillment is exact, in other cases less so:

		promise	fulfillment
Ephesus	tree of life	2:7	22:2, 14, 19
Smyrna	crown of life, protection from second death	2:10–11	21:6–8; 22:5
Pergamum	manna, white stone, new name (eucharistic language)	2:17	22:4
Thyatira	authority over the nations, the morning star	2:26–28	20:4; 22:16

3. Fenton J. A. Hort, *The Apocalypse of St. John I–III: The Greek Text, with Introduction, Commentary, and Additional Notes* (London: Macmillan, 1908), 24 (punctuation added).

4. Interestingly, ancient Greek commentator Andreas remarks that the Spirit proceeds "from the one who is God and Father, and through the Lamb" (my translation from Swete 1908: 298). The formula "through the Son" is often proposed as a way beyond the *filioque* controversy, but has never met with wide acceptance on the Orthodox side. For a creative ecumenical proposal by a Western theologian, see Thomas G. Weinandy, *The Father's Spirit of Sonship: Reconceiving the Trinity* (Edinburgh: Clark, 1995).

		promise	fulfillment
Sardis	white garments, name in book of life	3:5	[19:14]; 21:27
Philadelphia	pillar in the temple, three names	3:12	21:22; 22:4
Laodicea	eating with Christ, sitting on the throne	3:20–21	[19:9]; 22:5

The beginnings and ends of lists are often of disproportionate significance. The tree of life, promised to the victors at Ephesus, is among the most prominent features of the new Jerusalem. This is the same tree as in Genesis, and its leaves are for healing. But what tree heals the nations, if not *the* tree that was erected outside Jerusalem of old? The ancient commentators saw here an obvious figure for the cross (Cyprian, *Treatises* 2.22; Bede, *Explanatio Apocalypsis* 22.2).[5] But perhaps it is even more appropriate to think of the tree as identical with Christ himself. This typological link is made in a lovely folk hymn from eighteenth-century New England:

> The tree of life my soul hath seen, laden with fruit and always green.
> The trees of nature fruitless be compared with Christ the apple tree.
> I'm weary with my former toil, here I will sit and rest a while.
> Under the shadow will I be of Jesus Christ the apple tree.
> This fruit doth make my soul to thrive. It keeps my dying faith alive;
> Which makes my soul in haste to be Jesus Christ the apple tree.[6]

It is appropriate that this idea should be expressed in the form of a hymn. From the heavenly worship onward, Revelation has depicted the life of the blessed in essentially musical terms, as an ecstatic being-caught-up in the voices of angels and cherubim around the throne. Whatever else we may want to say about the city, it will surely be a place of song. Bede writes concerning the tree of life: "If the fruit is taken to be the reward of a blessed immortality, the leaves are rightly understood to be a perpetual song, in that it is for health to those who sing in their now blissful lot. For there is the true healing of the nations, full redemption, everlasting bliss" (*Explanatio Apocalypsis* 22.2).

If the assembly in Ephesus is promised the tree of life, a figure of nurture and of healing, the assembly in Laodicea is offered the promise of rule with Christ: "The one who conquers, I will grant him to sit with me on my throne" (3:21). This messianic theme of God's rule over the nations is massively present throughout John's vision of the city. Yet this promise made to the Laodiceans, a people strangely both arrogant and lukewarm, must be read in light of the verse that immediately precedes it: "Behold, I stand at the door and knock. If anyone hears my voice and

---

5. The understanding of the cross as "tree," so rich in typological possibilities, was already being made within the New Testament; cf. Gal. 3:13; Acts 5:30; 1 Pet. 2:24.

6. *Common Praise* (Toronto: Anglican Book Centre, 1998), 488.

opens the door, I will come in to him and eat with him, and he with me" (3:20). The Eucharist, too, is a theme that dominates the book's later sequences, from the invitation to the Lamb's marriage supper, to the solemn fencing of the table against outsiders, to the liturgical cries of "come!" and "amen!" in the closing lines (19:9; 22:15, 17, 20).[7]

If we read Revelation's eucharistic language apart from its messianism, the temptation will be to see the Eucharist as a privatized meal, disconnected from Christ's claim of rule over the nations—the ultimate in consumerist "fast food." The church thus understood will see no need to wash its robes in the blood of the Lamb. But if we read the messianism apart from the Eucharist, the temptation will be to view the church in instrumental terms, as a community that has little to offer the nations beyond its own, all-too-human goals and ideals. The church is more than just a religious advocacy group or an NGO. The church is the earthly community that drinks from the springs of living waters and that has the very tree of life planted in its midst. What the church finally has to offer the nations is God's promise of life and communion. That life and that communion are present in the church's supper, an anticipation of the great supper of the Lamb on the last day.

22:8–9 With these references to the church, we begin the move out of the realm of prophetic ecstasy, back into the present-day world of the hearers. In fact, 22:5 marks the last of John's visions. The spell is broken, as the language dissolves into a series of interjections, outbursts, and liturgical cries by a variety of speakers, including the angel, Jesus, and John himself, whose (nonecstatic) "ego" returns at this point: "I, John, am the one who heard and saw these things." The moment John returns to self-awareness, he commits the fundamental error of trying to worship "his" angel, who immediately forbids this action, repeating the words he used in the similar episode recounted at 19:10. John is a prophet, not a religious hero. He is using his own fallibility as a summons to the churches to obey the first commandment—as if to say, "It is perilously easy to exchange the worship of God for a lesser being. If I made this mistake with an angel, don't you make it where the beast is concerned!"

22:6–16 But if John's ego begins to reemerge at this point, the closing lines are, somewhat paradoxically, also rich in first-person discourse on the part of Jesus. The voices blur and blend as throughout Revelation, but as the end approaches it is the voice of Jesus that comes through most clearly. The first example occurs at 22:7, where the angel's discourse unexpectedly gives way to this announcement:

7. Barr 1998: 172–73 helpfully points out the striking parallels between Rev. 22 and the picture of the Eucharist offered in the *Didache*, a document of uncertain date that may reflect traditions as old as the second century. Specifically, both Rev. 22 and the *Didache* (a) allude to Jesus's descent from David, (b) draw a sharp distinction between those worthy to participate and outsiders, (c) refer to these outsiders as "dogs," (d) offer spiritual food and drink to the hearer, and (e) include the responses "Lord Jesus come!" and "Amen!"

"And behold, I am coming soon. Blessed is the one who keeps the words of the prophecy of this book."

The saying echoes 1:3, which likewise asserted that those who hear and keep the prophecy will be blessed. The phrase "I am coming soon" (cf. 1:7; 3:11) underscores that the situation is urgent—so urgent, indeed, that the warning is immediately repeated: "Behold, I am coming soon, bringing my recompense with me, to repay everyone for what he has done. I am the Alpha and the Omega, the first and the last, the beginning and the end" (22:12–13).

This is the last of the "Alpha and Omega" sayings in Revelation and the only one that incorporates all three of the relevant formulas. The cumulative process by which God's identity as Alpha and Omega—which, as we have seen, is very likely a cipher for the name YHWH (→1:8)—has been transferred to Christ is complete. The hearers know that when they are worshiping Jesus they are worshiping the Creator and that no worship of the Creator does not involve devotion to the Lamb slaughtered "from the foundation of the world." Just as there is nothing before Christ, so there is nothing beyond him. "Before Abraham was, I am" (John 8:58).

As the lector read the Apocalypse aloud before the assembly, the voice of Jesus has been heard in many particular expressions and in the work as a whole. Yet it is only at the very end that he openly identifies himself: "I, Jesus, have sent my angel to testify to you about these things for the churches. I am the root and the descendant of David, the bright morning star" (Rev. 22:16). *Epi tais ekklēsiais* ("for the churches"): we end where we began—with the church, whether the implied audience of the first-century churches of Asia or the real audience of some community in the present that is drawn into the *apokalypsis Iēsou Christou*.

One of the more disorienting features of Revelation is the way it scrambles our sense of time. It is not that past, present, and future do not matter, dissolving into a timeless "eternal now." It is rather that our usual ways of reckoning these things has to yield before the one who is and who was and who is to come, the God who holds time itself in his hand and disposes of it as he will. The time of Revelation is the time of the Eucharist, which means that in important ways it is like the time of the Passover. God freed Israel from Egypt, an event in history; but that event is not simply past, it is the living reality of Jewish existence, as a family gathers around the table each year for the Seder meal; and it points to the day when every Pharaoh, Haman, and Hitler will have been defeated, and all that is left is celebration. Memory and hope converge and release energies and expectations of an appropriately this-worldly sort: "Next year in Jerusalem!"

This is something like the spirit in which we should approach the question of time in Revelation. If we ask ourselves "when will these things happen?"—this is of course *the* question for commentators in the decoding tradition—we arrive at the disconcerting answer that, in a certain sense, they already have. Barr makes the point in the bluntest terms possible: "There is nothing described in Revelation that Christians do not believe has already happened in the death and resurrection of Jesus" (1998: 174). The slaughtered Lamb has conquered, and is acclaimed in heaven—and in the assemblies of Asia Minor! He is opening the seals of history even as we watch. The woman clothed with the sun gave birth to the child of destiny, who grew up to defeat the dragon and his angels. The ancient dragon fought back by sending the beast, chief among the powers that determine the character of life in this world; his seat is in Babylon, the great empire that fattens itself on the world's wealth and enslaves kings; call it Rome, for now. Yet which of these powers was not subdued at the cross, so that—terrifying as they remain in certain ways—they are in a very real sense living on borrowed time, belonging to the old eon that is passing away. The "hallelujah" choruses in Revelation would be impossible, apart from the conviction that the cosmos is determined by what might be called life in the aorist tense: "The kingdom of the world *has become* the kingdom of our Lord and of his Christ, and he shall reign forever and ever" (11:15).

To say less than this would not be Christian, for it would suggest that there is something deficient in the Lamb's victory. The worship of Jesus in the early church makes both a high Christology and a high doctrine of the work of Christ inevitable, indeed each implies the other. A Christ who is given the same honor as the Creator—how could his victory be less than complete and world encompassing? A Christ who has redeemed his people and liberated the enslaved earth itself—how could this be less than the eternal Son of God? Here it can truly be affirmed that *lex orandi lex credendi*, "the law of worship is the law of belief."

On the other hand, it would also not be Christian if this were the only thing we said. The gospel forbids any collapsing of the present or future into the past. Already Paul confronted this heresy among the Corinthians, who believed that their own resurrection had already occurred, and it has been a perpetual temptation ever since. While Desmond Tutu was certainly right to say that he had read to the end of the book and determined that "We win!" he was saying this in the midst of the struggle against apartheid in the 1970s and 1980s. History is not over, even if we know who is worthy to open history's scroll. It is the knowledge that the Lamb holds this scroll securely in his hand that enables the church to live confidently in the face of powers it cannot defeat, but also does not have to defeat. The church is not—to invoke the hoary but still useful World War II metaphor—the Allied forces invading across the Channel. It is more like the resistance, holding out, bearing witness, entering without reserve into a life where God is worshiped and not the powers. Like the historical resistance, the Lamb's resistance army is an odd and imperfect group of warriors, whose motives for joining up are perhaps better not examined in detail. Although the question of what motivates a person to request baptism or to undertake a new seriousness about the Christian life is always interesting, it is much less important than what the new Christian undertakes to do: negatively, to renounce Satan and all his works; positively, to embrace Christ, to "follow the Lamb wherever he goes" (14:4).

The first coming of Christ does not make his final coming redundant, nor does it erase the life of God's people stretched out between these two events. As Jews do not simply remember the Passover, but are themselves present with Moses and Miriam at the Red Sea, so Christians do not just look back on the apocalypsing of Jesus Christ, but are caught up in it, in a life that Revelation describes as that of the conquerors. The tribulation of the Lamb's followers is their entrance into his victory.

22:17 Worship is the place where the church's confidence in Christ's defeat of the powers merges most clearly with longing for his coming again. The entire Apocalypse may be heard as the voice of Jesus. Now in the closing lines, the church's own voice is heard, together with that of the Spirit: "The Spirit and the Bride say, 'Come!' And let the one who hears say, 'Come!' And let the one who is thirsty come; let the one who desires take the water of life without price!" (Rev. 22:17; cf. Isa. 55:1).[8]

The cry of "come!" is threefold. The first utterance is that of the bride, anticipatorily embodied in the worshiping assembly, crying out in expectation of the bridegroom's coming. The terrors and beauties disclosed in John's visions serve only to heighten longing for the arrival of that day. The second utterance is that of the individual worshiper, who is invited to speak with the bride, and indeed *as* the bride. No one who has heard the Apocalypse and is willing to "keep the words of the prophecy" should be excluded from the feast. To invert Bonhoeffer's famous saying, we could say that while grace is not cheap it is free—as free as the waters of life, which flow from the throne of God and the Lamb to anyone who is thirsty. This third member in the triad does not bid the listener to *say* "come!" but simply to come, to slake one's thirst at the waters that cannot be bought. Revelation is a book that draws many sorts of boundaries: between the church and the world, between the holy and the unholy, between the life appropriate to God's people and the life of Babylon. The urgent call to holiness of life is reiterated in these closing verses (22:11, 14–15). Yet like the gates of the city, the doors of the church are or should be fundamentally open. All are invited not to "come as they are," but to come *as the bride*. John would have been bemused at the notion that seriousness about witness and seriousness about Christian holiness are somehow in competition. In fact, they demand each other.

22:10 In contrast to the prophet Daniel, who was enjoined to seal the contents of his vision until the time of the end (Dan. 12:4), John is explicitly commanded *not* to "seal up the words of the prophecy of this book." The difference has to do with the location of each prophet relative to the end. For the historical Daniel, the overthrow of the final beast was an event that lay far in the future. For John, on the other hand, "the time is near" (Rev. 22:10; cf. 1:3). His situation more resembles that of the sage in the second century BC who compiled the stories of Daniel and

---

8. Exclamation points added to the ESV rendering of this verse.

who believed the final beast to be emerging in his own day, although the shifting calculations at the end of the work bespeak his uncertainty on this point.

The end did not come as prophesied for Daniel, nor did the final consummation arrive for John the seer by any human method of reckoning. This is an interesting problem, yet it is such only for those who see the Apocalypse primarily as a problem rather than as an act of witness. Indeed, the various theories of interpretation that have grown up around the book (preterist, futurist, church-historical, etc.) can be seen as a series of well-intentioned efforts to deal with the problem of the nonarrival of the end. Read charitably, they can be seen as different ways of relating the book to events in the ongoing history of church and world, a history that, no matter what the theory, remains under the sway and dominion of Christ the Lamb. Yet they still miss the point.

To hear the Apocalypse as it is meant to be heard—in the context of worship and as a prophetic word spoken to the *ekklēsia*—is to hear it not as a problem to be solved but as an authoritative testimony to and by Jesus Christ. When John speaks, Christ speaks. The visions are *his* self-apocalypsing to his people; thus the crucial role of the letters to the churches at the beginning, which anchor the testimony in the life of the churches of Asia Minor, and by analogy in the life of the churches today. That the scroll is not to be sealed up, but left unsealed, indicates that the message does not concern some future generation but this one. The book of Daniel slyly makes this point in its own way, for while Daniel binds up the scroll, it now lies open for us to read. What else can this mean but that we are the very community for which the prophecy was intended, Israel at the end?

To say that we are the community of the end times does not, to be sure, absolve us of the burdens of history. An apocalyptic-messianic faith like Judaism or Christianity cannot flee history, not only because this is impossible, but because messianism inevitably has the life of the nations in view. There is no Messiah apart from either his people or the nations he rules as king. Even the summons to flee Babylon (18:4) is not a summons to flee the human city as such; rather it highlights that *in* the human city fidelity to God is impossible. The question is not whether the church is in history, but how it is there. The church lives in history restless, dissatisfied, filled with longing for the final apocalypse of the one who has graciously come to dwell among us in the flesh. The reason Christianity is "beyond tragedy," as Reinhold Niebuhr put it, is that while the church suffers tribulation and has its martyrs, it knows that the death of the martyrs is their participation in the blood of the Lamb; the same holds true for those who suffer with Christ in less dramatic ways.[9] The Lamb's victory, his life poured out in excess and flowing like a river through the city of God, means that there is more of comedy than of tragedy in this story. The church lives in Babylon with a kind of sovereign freedom, knowing that Babylon does not get to dictate what constitutes ultimate victory, defeat, and truth. The Lamb's followers conquer not

9. Reinhold Niebuhr, *Beyond Tragedy: Essays on the Christian Interpretation of History* (1937; repr., New York: Scribner, 1965).

by defeating the beast on his own terms (cf. 13:7), but by enduring faithfully to the end on God's terms.

22:18 The Apocalypse exhibits no false modesty about itself. What we have heard over these twenty-two chapters are not John's opinions, but a faithful report of what he received from the angel, from Christ, and ultimately from God (cf. the reappearance of the "chain of revelation" language at 22:16; cf. 1:1–3). It is crucial that the churches encounter the *apokalypsis Iēsou Christou* in its unvarnished form; thus the rather dire warning issued to anyone who would alter "the words of the prophecy of this book" (22:18–19). At the very least, the churches should be given the opportunity to respond to the prophecy as John has received it. Just as hearing and keeping the prophecy brings blessing (1:3; 22:7), so tampering with it carries enormous risks, insofar as it might prevent others from receiving the blessing.

There is, perhaps, a larger point to be made concerning the inseparability of form and content in holy scripture. Christianity is not an idea that can be easily separated from the concrete forms of speech employed by the apostles and prophets or even from their at times rather odd psychology (think of Ezekiel, for instance). However strange the Bible may seem to us at times, it renders God's speech in the odd, peculiar language of human beings, the Word embedded in the words, by analogy to the eternal Word made flesh. This—plus the sheer fecundity and mystery of the word of God—is why the church's activity of commenting on scripture is never ending. Each reading of the Apocalypse sends us back to the beginning, to hear once more what John wrote from the island called Patmos to the seven churches of Asia.

22:20 Just a few lines earlier, we were told that it was "I, John, . . . who heard and saw these things" (22:8). But now: "He who testifies to these things says, 'Surely I am coming soon'" (22:20). Jesus alone is the true witness, John is a witness only in a secondary sense. The visions we have seen and heard are guaranteed by the full authority of Christ. At the same time, that he chooses to speak through his prophet is only a temporary measure. He is *coming soon*. The verb "to come" (*erchomai*) is densely present in these closing lines, reminiscent of its frequent occurrence in the letters to the churches. It expresses Christ's affirmation of his own coming (22:7, 12, 20a) and the church's longing for his appearance (22:17a, 17b, 20b), as well as the believer's coming forward to receive the gifts (22:17c). The Apocalypse closes, then, with a complex event of coming on the part of Christ *and* the church *and* the individual worshiper. "And at the time for the banquet he sent his servant to say to those who had been invited, 'Come, for everything is now ready'" (Luke 14:17).[10]

The assembly affirms Christ's promise and extends an invitation of its own: "Amen. Come, Lord Jesus!" (Rev. 22:20).

---

10. The words "come, for all is now ready" are used for the bidding at Communion in some Reformed liturgies.

The bridegroom and bride greet their guests at the wedding feast. These words fulfill the promise made to the church in Laodicea and so implicitly to all the churches: "Behold, I stand at the door and knock. If anyone hears my voice and opens the door, I will come in to him and eat with him, and he with me" (3:20).

22:21 Following this rapturous exchange, the actual final words might seem something of an anticlimax: "The grace of the Lord Jesus be with all. Amen." This is the formal ending of the Apocalypse as a letter, forming a bracket with John's bestowal of "grace and peace" to his readers at 1:4. The textual history of this verse is extremely complex.[11] One of the variant forms, "the grace of the Lord Jesus be with all the saints," is reflected in both the RSV and NRSV. Since John frequently employs the term "the saints" to refer to the body of the faithful, this variant is certainly appropriate. And yet (textual criticism aside) there is perhaps a deeper logic at work in the ESV's "with all." This "all" may refer to every member of the *ekklēsia* gathered to hear the letter. Or it may mean "all the churches" (2:23). Or it may mean simply "all" in an unrestricted sense, in line with the cosmic, universal use of the word *pas* throughout Revelation, denoting the cosmic scope of God's action in Jesus Christ. "Every creature" gathers around the throne to sing God's praise (5:13). The eternal gospel is preached to "every nation" (14:6). The strange message of the Apocalypse bears witness to God's concern for all that he has made, and so John concludes by wishing the grace of our Lord Jesus Christ on "all." Just as there is no qualification for drinking the living water, other than the fact of being thirsty, so there is no potential hearer who is not embraced in this "all."

"Behold, I am making all things new" (21:5). In the apocalypsing of Jesus Christ, the God of Israel is at work to draw all creatures into the life of the new eon. Although Revelation has many images that gesture toward that truly unimaginable life, none is more powerful than that of singing. If, in the present age, it is only the 144,000 sealed who are permitted to learn the new song sung by the living creatures and elders, John assures us that these are but the firstfruits of a much larger chorus (14:4). The new city will be permeated by song, with voices both beautiful and strange joined together in a surprising, universal harmony. While this is something we truly cannot know until we get there, perhaps we can imagine something like the old shape-note hymn cited at the beginning of this commentary:

> To God and to the Lamb I will sing, I will sing,
> To God and to the Lamb I will sing.
> To God and to the Lamb, who is the great I am,
> While millions join the theme, I will sing, I will sing,
> While millions join the theme, I will sing.

11. Bruce M. Metzger, *A Textual Commentary on the Greek New Testament*, 2nd ed. (London: United Bible Societies, 1994), 690–91.

And when from death I'm free, I'll sing on, I'll sing on,
And when from death I'm free, I'll sing on.
And when from death I'm free, I'll sing his love for me,
And through eternity I'll sing on, I'll sing on,
And when from death I'm free, I'll sing on.[12]

All this, of course, is in the realm of the "not yet." But in the worship of the suffering, yearning church, the "not yet" comes into the present, infusing the assembly with power and life and hope.[13] "The Spirit and the Bride say, Come! . . . Amen. Come, Lord Jesus!"

---

12. *Common Praise* (Toronto: Anglican Book Centre, 1998), 400.
13. "It is in worship that one fights the dragon and its minions and where the final victory is won: worship God" (Barr 1998: 148).

BIBLIOGRAPHY

Aune, David E. 1997. *Revelation 1–5*. Word Biblical Commentary 52. Dallas: Word.

Barr, David. 1998. *Tales of the End: A Narrative Commentary on the Book of Revelation*. Santa Rosa, CA: Polebridge.

Bauckham, Richard. 1993a. *The Climax of Prophecy: Studies on the Book of Revelation*. Edinburgh: Clark.

———. 1993b. *The Theology of the Book of Revelation*. Cambridge: Cambridge University Press.

Bettenson, Henry, trans. 1984. *Augustine: Concerning the City of God against the Pagans*. New York: Penguin.

Boring, M. Eugene. 1989. *Revelation*. Interpretation. Louisville: Westminster John Knox.

Caird, G. B. 1984. *A Commentary on the Revelation of St. John the Divine*. London: Black.

Eller, Vernard. 1974. *The Most Revealing Book of the Bible: Making Sense out of Revelation*. Grand Rapids: Eerdmans.

Ellul, Jacques. 1977. *Apocalypse: The Book of Revelation*. Translated by George W. Schreiner. New York: Seabury.

Kovacs, Judith, and Christopher Rowland. 2004. *Revelation: The Apocalypse of Jesus Christ*. Blackwell Bible Commentaries. Malden, MA: Blackwell.

Lattimore, Richmond. 1979. *The Four Gospels and the Revelation*. New York: Farrar, Straus, Giroux.

Minear, Paul S. 1968. *I Saw a New Earth: An Introduction to the Visions of the Apocalypse*. Washington: Corpus.

Swete, Henry Barclay. 1908. *The Apocalypse of St. John: The Greek Text with Introduction, Notes, and Indices*. 3rd edition. London: Macmillan.

SUBJECT INDEX

SCRIPTURE INDEX

James

3:9 187
5:17 136n1

Jeremiah

2:1–2 239
2:2 195
4:31 150
7:34 211n7
10:1–11 126
11:19 88n7
13:27 121
15:2 164
15:16 132
16:9 211n7
22:8 212
25:10 211n7
29:7 194
31:15 85
33:11 211n7
51:6 206
51:7 175n4
51:33 177
51:45 206
51:63–64 210

Job

9:8 128
26:6 123n9
28:22 123n9
31:12 123n9

Joel

1–2 122
2 25
2:30–31 147
3:13 177–78

1 John

2:18 162
2:22 162
4:3 162

2 John

7 162

John

1:3 234
1:4–5 205
1:9 205

1:14 185, 205, 239
1:29 88
1:36 88
1:51 25n8, 39–40
2:21 135
2:25 58
3:16 125
4:13–14 245
4:35 177
4:48 147–48
6:16–21 128
6:35 245
8:1–11 210n6
8:32 140n5, 221n5
8:44 154n15
8:58 249
11:35 85
12:24 152
12:28–29 129
15:1–10 198n7
16:21 150, 152
16:33 125
19:17 179
19:20 179
19:30 90
19:39 191
20:11 85
21 88n7

Jonah

1:2 212n8
1:9 212
3:1 212n8
3:3 212n8
4:10–11 213
4:11 212n8

Joshua

13:22 62
24:9 62

Jude

6 153
9 118
11 62

Judges

5:19 189

1 Kings

16:29–34 64
17–18 136

18:40 138
22:19 75

2 Kings

6:16 158
9:27 189
23:30 189

Leviticus

3 102
4 102
8 102
9 102
11:9–12 188
16:10 195
17:14 102
26:12 239

Luke

1:19 118
1:26 118
1:35 46
3:17 177
3:22 46
4:13 154n14
4:25 136
5:8 51
6:20–22 61
6:24–26 121
8:17 234
8:31 227
9:22 74
10:1 137
10:2 177
11:37–54 121
12:49–50 119
14:15–24 219
14:17 253
16:13 207
20:15 179n7
21:23–24 135
23:29–30 106

2 Maccabees

6:1–11 160

Mark

1:22 138
2:20 136n2
3:22 159
3:27 228